WALTER CRANE

WALTER CRANE

ISOBEL SPENCER

Macmillan Publishing Co., Inc.
New York

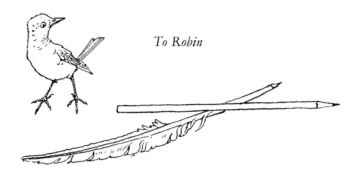

To Robin

The tailpieces come from
Household Stories from the Collection of the Brothers Grimm
translated by Lucy Crane and illustrated by Walter Crane.
The drawings on these pages are from *Baby's Own Aesop*.
Endpapers are a detail from *Iris and Kingfisher* filling design.

Macmillan Publishing Co., Inc.,
866 Third Avenue, New York, N.Y. 10022

First published in the U.K. by Studio Vista, a division
of Cassell and Collier Macmillan Publishers Ltd.

Library of Congress Catalog Card Number: 75–18567

Designed by Sally Muir

First American Edition 1975

Printed in Great Britain

Contents

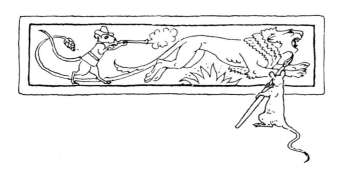

Acknowledgements

The main holdings of letters and original designs by Walter Crane are in America: in the Caroline Miller Parker Collection in the Houghton Library, Harvard University; and the Catherine Tinker Patterson Collection in the Beinecke Rare Book and Manuscript Library, Yale University. I am very grateful to the Advisory Council of the Paul Mellon Centre for Studies in British Art whose generous grant made it possible to carry out the necessary research in these places. I should like to thank the staff of the Houghton Library and Miss Marjorie M. Wynne of the Beinecke Library for all their help and cooperation. Mrs Catherine Frangiamore of the Cooper-Hewitt Museum of Design, New York, has been a most generous advisor concerning Crane and American arts and crafts. I also wish to thank Boston Museum of Fine Arts, Boston Public Library, Robert Blackwell, Phillip H. Curtis of the Newark Museum, William Donovan of Chicago Public Library, Mrs W. B. Floyd, Mrs Marjorie Freytag of the Munson-Williams-Proctor Institute, the Library of Congress, the National Gallery of Canada, New York Public Library, Mrs Andrea Rawle of the Metropolitan Museum of Art, Ruth Schoneman of the Art Institute, Chicago and Salve Regina College.

In Great Britain I have received help and encouragement from the artist's grandson, Anthony Crane. Liverpool City Libraries have two fine collections of miscellaneous printed material by Crane, and I am indebted to Mr J. D. Rogers, librarian of the Hornby Library, for the care and patience with which he has dealt with many queries and requests. Dr Stefan Muthesius generously put the un-published manuscript of his book *Das Englische Vorbild* at my disposal. His colleague at East Anglia University School of Fine Art, John House, is a Crane enthusiast of much longer standing than myself, and kindly allowed me to consult his collection. For details concerning Crane's educational activity I am indebted to Dr Stuart Macdonald. Of libraries consulted I should like to thank the staff of the British Museum, the Victoria and Albert Museum and the University of Birmingham, the John Johnson Collection in the Department of Printed Books at the Bodleian Library Oxford, Nuffield College Oxford, and particularly Cambridge University Library, St Andrews University Library and the National Library of Scotland, where most of my research has been carried out.

Many others have assisted in a variety of ways. These include R. Benton of Chester Public Library; George Breeze of the Department of Art at the City Museum and Art Gallery, Birmingham; Dr Lorne Campbell; Anthony Cross; Richard Dumbreck, Headmaster of Boarzell; The Convent of the Holy Child Jesus, Combe Bank; Stephen Croad; the Fabian Society; Norah Gillow of the William Morris Art Gallery, Walthamstow; Robert Hogg of Carlisle Museum and Art Gallery; Bill Hardie of Dundee Art Gallery; the late Andrew McLaren Young, Roger Billcliffe, Robert Gibbs and Margaret Macdonald of Glasgow University Fine Art Department; John Gorman; Elizabeth Johnson and Charles

Hajdamah of the City of Manchester Art Galleries; J. P. Howgago of the Guildhall Art Gallery, London; H. Jefferson Barnes and Robin Rennie of Glasgow School of Art; Ruari McLean; Professor Charles Mitchell; Christopher Monkhouse; Anthony d'Offay; A. F. Meredith; Andrew McIntosh Patrick; David Peace, Master of the Art-Workers' Guild; the late Miss Margaret Pilkington; John Rabbets of Manchester Polytechnic; J. M. Roberts; The Most Reverend C. R. Schroeder of the Cathedral Church of the Good Shepherd, Rookwood Road, London; Charles and Rory Spence; Mrs Valerie Mendes, Lionel Lambourne and the staff of the Print Room of the Victoria and Albert Museum; the City of Liverpool Walker Art Gallery; Bruce Tattersall of the Wedgwood Museum, Barlaston; Mrs Joan Allgrove and Christopher Allan of the Whitworth Art Gallery, Manchester; Worth Abbey; and the Fabian Society.

For responses to enquiries about Crane's reception on the Continent and collections of his work there, I should like to thank Peter Anker of the Vestlandske Kunstindustrimuseum, Bergen; Dr Hanna Dornik-Eger of the Austrian Museum of Decorative Art, Vienna; Dr Hans Ebert of the Staatliche Museen, Berlin; Frau Magdalene Haberstock; Dr Henning Bock of the Dahlem Museum, Berlin; M. Ph. Roberts-Jones, Martin Wittek and A. Rouzet of the Bibliothèque Royale de Belgique, Brussels; Dr Hans Klaiber of the Wurtembergisches Landesmuseum, Stuttgart; Dr Kurt Löcher and Frau Dr Bernd Rau of the Staatsgalerie, Stuttgart; Leipzig Museum of Decorative Art; Erik Lassen of Copenhagen Museum of Decorative Art; Inger-Marie Lie and Aase Bay Sjövold of the Oslo Museum of Applied Art; Dr Klaus Popitz of the Kunstbibliothek, Berlin; Dr Eleonore Reichert of Hamburg Art Gallery; Dr Reinheckel of the Museum of Decorative Art, Dresden; Dr Hella Robels of the Wallraf-Richartz-Museum, Cologne; Anna Westholm of the National Museum, Stockholm; Dr Annemarie Winther of Bremen Art Gallery; Dr Werner Zimmermann of the Staatliche Kunsthalle, Karlsruhe.

Without the excellent typing of Mrs Penny Crowe, and the timely help on one occasion of Mrs Marcia Gordon, the final phases of this work might have been much more difficult. At this stage too I could never have managed without the willing assistance of Mr Peter Adamson, of the Photographic Unit, University of St Andrews, who photographed many of the illustrations. For warm hospitality in London I must also thank Lisa Pontecorvo. To the many other friends and relatives who have patiently borne with me and Walter Crane over these last three years I should like to take the opportunity here of expressing my gratitude. Above all, however, I owe most to my husband who was initially largely responsible for turning my art historical interests towards the nineteenth century and thus towards Crane himself. His advice, encouragement and criticism have been invaluable sustaining and stimulating factors throughout.

Introduction

In a lecture about his paternal grandfather given at Yale University on 3 October 1956 Anthony Crane rightly observed[1] that no book apart from Gertrude Massé's bibliography of first editions had been written about Walter Crane since his death in 1915. The need for such a book has become increasingly obvious in the last few years, as Crane has often been given all too brief notices in the many recent publications of Victorian art and design. This study is meant to provide a comprehensive picture of his wide-ranging artistic activity, its ideological basis and his work for education and Socialism. A detailed account of his private life I leave to the surviving members of his family who are naturally much better equipped to speak on such matters. Meanwhile Crane's own *Reminiscences*, published by Methuen in 1907, give valuable and often amusing insight into his life and times. Of the two major studies published while he was alive that by Otto von Schleinitz in the Knackfuss Künstler-Monographien series issued in 1902 was just, objective, and copiously illustrated for its reasonable price. Crane was unfortunately unable to judge its merits as he could not read German. The English speaking public had to rely on the account of the young Hungarian critic, Paul G. Konody whose *The Art of Walter Crane* came out at the same time. He praised Crane as the 'Academician of the Nursery' but was sceptical about his aims for socialism and critical of his fine, as opposed to his decorative art. When this lavish book was published by George Bell and Sons with a cover, end-papers and a title page by the artist, Crane insisted on having a slip inserted disclaiming having given any sanction to the text.

It is very much the image of Crane as 'Academician of the Nursery' that survives today when his name is linked with Kate Greenaway and Randolph Caldecott whose children's picture books did so much to brighten up the Victorian nursery. With the printer Edmund Evans's help, Crane had been busy transforming the style and quality of toy books for over ten years before Greenaway and Caldecott became famous for theirs. He had hardly finished his first series for Routledge in 1875 than he turned his attention to other branches of decorative art, to ceramic design, wallpapers, textiles, stained glass, mosaic and gesso relief. His indefatigable activity as an art worker inevitably invites comparison with William Morris, who was his senior by eleven years. He was a major inspiration to Crane – not just through practical example but through his ideals, being primarily responsible for his conversion to socialism. But Crane was by no means a mere follower of Morris. Even Konody acknowledged that there were two 'isolated high peaks' among the 'minor summits' of the many artists contributing to the English Revival in the last decades of the nineteenth century. He meant Morris and Crane. Morris was a figurehead and great general propagandist for the socialist movement. Crane's contribution was of a less charismatic personal nature than Morris's but was equally important. He was the artist of socialism. His designs were published in

8

left-wing papers on the eve of workers' rallies. They were sold separately to be pinned up in homes, factories, and meeting places, and they were stitched in the brilliant silks of trades-union banners. While Morris, who died in 1896, was a mythical figure to many – especially to people abroad – Crane's prolific output and his presence, for he travelled more widely than Morris, made him the most familiar exponent of English decorative art during the vital decade of the 1890s when Europe made constant reference to English art and ideas. America, in its turn, was somewhat shocked at its encounter with the 'anarchist' aesthete but Crane's example nevertheless helped further their arts and crafts movement.

Crane was small in stature and quite a shy man but he had immense drive stimulated at first by the sheer necessity of earning a livelihood and later by his powerful conviction of his role as artist and handicraftsman in a reforming society. His gaiety and sense of humour were perhaps less to be seen on official and formal occasions than in the company of close friends or at home with his wife and children. He loved children and quite lost his habitual reserve when with them. His own romantic childlike fancy was entirely in tune with theirs and the spontaneity of this response may be gauged from the pages of the hitherto unpublished picture books reproduced in this volume. These were designed in place of bed-time stories for his own children, Beatrice, Lionel and Lancelot. Family life with the Cranes seems to have been often not unlike that described in the nursery books. Walter Crane was passionately fond of animals and his Kensington house at various times contained quite a menagerie, including a jerboa, golden pheasant, alligator, marmoset, an owl, rabbits, guinea pigs and the inevitable cats and dogs. He was often to be seen at work with a squirrel perched on his shoulder. Anthony Crane remembers his father Lionel describing how Walter took a delight during parties in letting loose a little mongoose which would dart for cover under the nearest long skirt then climb up the owner's leg causing consternation among the company. Crane loved dancing and dressing-up. He took immense pleasure in devising outfits for the new year parties held at Holland Street which were a major event in London's artistic social calendar.

Mary Frances Crane was most ambitious for her husband and set her heart on his becoming a Royal Academician, something that never came near approaching a reality. Although he was to make it his crusade that artist and handicraftsmen were equals, Crane's life was devoted to proving that he was capable of being both a master of the fine and the decorative arts, despite the fact that he excelled in one while remaining only fairly competent in the other. His paintings by no means lack interest. They provide valuable insight into his own philosophy and into Victorian attitudes in general. In many ways however, they reflect Crane's poetry, being full of earnest purpose and concern for the fate of mankind, yet lacking that fluency of expression which came to him so naturally when he picked up a pen to draw. Although he was always concerned about content Crane was a natural decorator with an unerring sense of colour, line and formal arrangement. He developed the transformation of Victorian narrative illustration begun by the Pre-Raphaelites to a level where the expressive qualities of the purely artistic values of line colour and form become independent of their literary source. The French writer J. K. Huysmans declared that the pages of the toy books were more finely conceived and complete works of art than many of the elaborately framed paintings he saw each year at the Paris Salon. Not surprisingly these also met with approval from the Belgian symbolists. Till the end of his very active life Crane remained keenly interested in contemporary art. Impressionism had struck him as somewhat superficial in its preoccupation with fleeting effects but he approved of Post Impressionism because of its formal qualities and its more profound symbolic intentions. 'His mind' William Rothenstein remarked in a charming description expressive of the affection Crane aroused in many of his friends 'perhaps like his house, was too full to be kept dusted and tidy; but he had unusually broad sympathies, and while he followed in the footsteps of Morris and Burne-Jones, he was free from prejudice – his spirit kept open house.'[2]

Crane's belief that an artist should have a noble mission in life and his untiring efforts to convey this through his art are a tribute to the Victorian conscience. But it is his continuing youthfulness, the 'spirit that kept open house', and his talent for succeeding on a popular level which readily appeals to the modern imagination. He is an outstanding figure not so much for any single facet of his art but as a many sided genius whose adventurous attempts to master art, science and philosophy are a remarkable tribute to the optimism of his age.

Childhood

There was a tradition in Walter Crane's family that they were descended from Sir Francis Crane, 'Yeoman Arras Worker and Arras Taylor' to King Charles I at the Mortlake tapestry workshops, and Walter's father used the coat of arms that belonged to Sir Francis. (Walter did not, and was to devise his own rebus of a bird flanked by initials.[1]) Although Sir Francis and his family were East Anglian, Walter's father, Thomas Crane (1808–59), came from the branch of the family that lived in Chester, where borough archives record it as far back as the sixteenth century, associated with craftsmen and tradesmen, and later the professions. Thomas had attended the Royal Academy Schools and enjoyed a considerable local reputation as a portrait painter. He began his Academy training in 1824, winning a gold medal for drawing from the antique in the following year, after which he returned to Chester to begin a career as a painter of portrait miniatures. A little self-portrait reproduced in his son's *Reminiscences* gives some idea of Thomas Crane's delicate, sensitive style and explains why it soon attracted the attention of a number of distinguished patrons. He was a versatile artist and in addition to larger portraits in water colour and oils and silhouettes he painted landscape, figure and animal subjects and was a contributor and active committee member of the Liverpool Academy. He was interested in architectural drawing and lithography. His lithographs date from the late 1820s and the 1830s and were printed at a press shared with his brothers, William, John and Philip in the back garden of the Newgate Street house. Thomas also illustrated books such as R. E. Warburton's *Cheshire Hunting Songs*, which bears the imprint 'Lithog. by T. and W. Crane Chester'. This volume was published in 1834 and includes a portrait frontispiece and more boisterous graphic examples of his art. This humorous aspect of Thomas Crane's work may also be seen in *The History of Mr Pig and Miss Crane* composed by Lady Delaware of Vale Royale, for the Tarvin Bazaar in 1836 and lithographed by the Crane Press. The page depicting Mr Pig eyeing elegantly-attired Miss Crane is a delightful foretaste of Walter's own animal fantasies.

The Crane family went to live at 12 Maryland Street in Mount Pleasant, Liverpool in 1835. Three of their five children were born there, Lucy in 1841, Thomas in 1843, and Walter on the 15 August 1845, but Thomas Crane's worsening consumptive condition forced them to move to Torquay three months after Walter's birth. Here another daughter, Mary Emma (1847), and a son, Arthur (1848), were born. Walter was too small to remember much about the first two houses they lived in but his memories of 'Laureston Villa' at Upton, then a village inland from Torquay, he later described as 'almost Pre-Raphaelite'. In 1854 they moved back again back to a larger house in Torquay, No. 3 Park Place. These seem to have been the summertime days of a happy childhood in unspoilt rural England. Marie Crane Kearsley was an energetic and sensible woman, devoted

Thomas Crane *Mr Pig and Miss Crane* lithographed by T. and W. Crane of Chester, late 1830s. This drawing by Walter Crane's father provides a sprightly foretaste of his own animal fantasies. Reproduced from Walter Crane's *Reminiscences*.

to her family. She, like her husband, came from Chester where her father was a prosperous maltster. Few real hints of hardship appear in Walter's account of his early years and theirs was a comfortable middle-class home where visitors were welcome and the parents occasionally managed to get away on an excursion, as in 1851 when they went to see the Great Exhibition in London. In the fine Devon air Thomas Crane's health improved. At Upton he had formed a sketching club with several friends. They did not enjoy great affluence for it was difficult to build up a portrait clientèle and Walter's father had often to make trips to Lancashire and Cheshire to fulfil commissions where he had first made his reputation.

Walter's earliest education was at a nursery school run by the Misses Nicholson. Their brother was an amateur photographer who sometimes used the little Cranes as subjects for his black box, which delighted them despite the strain of posing for the long exposures. The first resident governess to come to Park Place was unpopular and her teaching seems to have epitomised Victorian education at its least imaginative, full of tedious learning by rote. She introduced them to Latin but the children lived in constant anticipation of the moment when they would be free to go off and play in the fields or on the beach. Her successor, Miss Clarke, was a family friend and a much more sympathetic character although even she, who taught them French, could make no linguist out of Walter.

Walter's unofficial schooling in his father's studio and browsing through copies of the *Illustrated London News* and the *Art Journal* provided more stimulating material. He seems to have been equipped with a pencil from a tender age and to have been fascinated by pictures of all kinds. Among his father's books Nash's *Mansions* was a great favourite and so also were the antediluvian beasts and birds in the various parts of Goldsmith's *Animated Nature* published by Charles Knight. Though he could not, like William Morris, claim to have read Walter Scott's novels at the age of four, he soon grew to love these tales of adventure and romance and to admire Liversedge's *Works* which illustrated both Scott and Shakespeare. The general sabre-rattling of the Crimea encouraged a small boy's interest in warfare and, shortly after the outbreak of war, he drew a battle of

Turks and Russians on his slate – a scene considered worthy of preservation by means of Mr Nicholson's photographic plate.

His talent for drawing, at any rate for decorating, became evident as early as his sixth year when Walter made several portraits using sketches of hands taken from his father's studio and combining them with his own variations on the theme of head and torso dressed in fancy flowered and tartan waistcoats. Thomas Crane encouraged him to jot down impressions and guided his son generally in acquiring a versatile and fluent technical style and choice of subject matter.

For a few long months beginning probably in the Autumn of 1856 Tom and Walter attended Page's School on the Teignmouth Road. Crane Minor (as Walter was known there) disliked this intensely, especially the brutality of the Headmaster, who used the cane too much. His later description of handsome portions of roast beef at lunchtime indicates an un-Squeers-like liberality which suggests that Page's establishment was not without compensating features. Nevertheless it was a nightmare to him and he became acutely nervous. Mental arithmetic was anathema and any calculating ability he had possessed Walter considered 'from that time hopelessly deranged'. He became so nervous in fact that he had to stay away from school. The doctor diagnosed 'congestion of the brain'.

Meanwhile, his father's health was much better. Under these propitious circumstances it was decided to move back to London, where there were better prospects for commissions and it was hoped that he might have more work accepted at the Royal Academy. He went ahead to arrange lodgings and in the Spring of 1857 the furniture and effects of Park Place were sold and the house given up.

London in the 1850s continued its expansion. More and more fields were classed as desirable building land for the inevitable rows of brick and stucco terrace houses and semi-detached villas. Opposite the furnished house at No. 2 Alfred Villas in Starch Green, Shepherd's Bush, where the Cranes settled in May 1857, was a brickfield. Here young Walter could watch the manufacture of those very materials which symbolized the march of progress. Green places still abounded in the vicinity: there were pleasant walks westward by Stamford Brook to Turnham Green, Beck Common[2] and Acton, which was set apart from the sprawling metropolis; or he could explore southwards down Paddenswick Road and the New Shaftesbury Road, still flanked by orchards, to Hammersmith. Their house in Alfred Villas was a typical early Victorian semi-detached with painted cement facade, a small front and long narrow back garden, and 'Mr Ruskin's abomination', an Ionic portico displaying characteristic Victorian bourgeois aspirations to elegance. The heart of London town itself seemed far off and the omnibus ride to Oxford Street quite an expedition where the noise of traffic on cobbled streets must have been alarming to people fresh from the country. After a month or so the family moved nearer Hammersmith to Shaftesbury Terrace, a row of new houses at the end of Shaftesbury Road. From here Walter soon found the subjects he liked best in the cattle and horses grazing on Beck Common.

The boys' schooling had yet to be settled. Lucy was already in a London boarding school run by a family friend whose own son was at Christ's Hospital School. Attempts were made to have Tom and Walter accepted here, where they would not have had to pay fees, but these failed and the matter of formal education was dropped. Walter was secretly delighted. His sketching trips went on uninterrupted except for occasional visits to town. His father continued to supervise his artistic efforts and in the summer of 1857 he painted his first study in oils, the head of a black and white greyhound. He was also put to painting still-life groups

Study of setter drawn at Ireland's Farm, 1858, pencil. 7¾ × 9¾ in. (19.8 × 24.4 cm). By courtesy of Liverpool City Libraries.

but animals remained his favourite subjects. On one occasion Robert Rawlinson, a well-known member of the Society of Art who had commissioned a portrait sketch from Walter's father, lent the young artist a study by Richard Ansdell of 'Donkeys on a Common'. Walter's copy of this was so successful that it was put in a picture shop at Knightsbridge where it sold for ten shillings.

In 1858 the family again moved house to Lambton Terrace 'on the outskirts of Westbournia'. The immediate surroundings were newly built up but, as before, Walter sought out the countryside. Where Notting Hill Station now stands there was a small farmhouse and farther out there was more good sketching ground at Wormwood Scrubbs and Old Oak Common. He made friends with a farming couple called Ireland who allowed him to roam freely and draw what he liked.

Journeys to town included visits to the sights of London as well as to museums and galleries. Apart from his father's own work Walter's knowledge of painting was gleaned from reproductions. The reality of a picture like B. R. Haydon's 'Marcus Curtius Leaping into the Gulf', which he saw in the upstairs picture gallery of the Pantheon, Oxford Street, staggered him by its heroic scale. At the National Gallery, which was shared by the Old Masters and the Royal Academy and also showed the R.A. annual exhibitions, he saw his first Landseers and works by other popular animal painters like Ansdell and J. F. Herring. He also had his first glimpse of the Pre-Raphaelites at the Academy of 1857, where J. F. Millais' 'Sir Isumbras at the Ford' impressed him most with its prominently-featured horse. He remembered his father's amusement at Frederick Sandys' 'Nightmare' cartoon, which was exhibited at the time in Colnaghi's window, with Ruskin in

14

place of the knight, D. G. Rossetti and W. Holman Hunt as the children and the charger as a braying ass. Thomas Crane often took his children to the 'Brompton Boilers' which then housed South Kensington Museum's collection of decorative art and painting. The newly acquired Sheepshanks collection boasted some fine Landseers, though its chief interest for Walter's father lay in Mulready's work. Paintings apart, young Walter Crane remained fascinated by prints. The collection at South Kensington included examples by Dürer, Burgmair and the contemporary German graphic artist, Rethel, as well as a comprehensive survey of English wood engraving of the late eighteenth and the nineteenth century. There he made a close study of the products of printmaking workshops like the one to which he would very shortly be apprenticed.

Before leaving Torquay Walter had tried his hand at illustration and as a parting present gave some of his school friends drawings of Sir Walter Scott's tales and ballads.[3] This practice continued after the removal to London and in 1858 several pen and ink designs to Cowper's *Task*, Scott's Ballads, Blomfield's *Farmer's Boy* and a coloured set of 18 pages for *The Lady of Shalott* (see p. 33) were shown to John Ruskin through the agency of a friend, Mr Wooldridge. Ruskin commented encouragingly on the colour of the Tennyson set.

With the exception of one page, which has no illustration, each of these has a picture and one or two verses framed in a floral border. This format follows a pattern established in the elaborate chromolithographed 'illuminated' gift books designed by Owen Jones in the 1840s. Young Walter's borders are less luxurious and his style probably reflects the trend of more recent publications in which the original ideas of the previous decade were popularized. A certain ineptitude is seen in his figure drawing which generally follows the style of John Gilbert and Daniel Maclise. Nevertheless his borders with their sensitive studies of willow, barley, corn, poppies and convolvulus add to the evocative quality of the scenes themselves and reveal careful study from nature as do the scenes of the river and twilit fields, harvesters reaping and tying stooks of corn. These subjects also appear in medieval calendar pictures, a common source for the illuminated gift books.[4] His water colour technique of little brushstrokes suggesting leaves and rippling water is very delicate. The border flowers are set against backgrounds of solid colour whose tints are picked up or contrasted in the scenes and decorated initials which head each verse. When asked for his opinion the wood engraver, William James Linton, was so impressed by the overall concept of design found in these Tennyson pages that he agreed to take the young draughtsman on as apprentice without the usual premium.

Apprenticeship

With his indenture of apprenticeship signed and sealed in January 1859 Walter Crane found himself at thirteen years of age entering one of the best engraving workshops in England. His task was to learn the craft of a draughtsman on wood, a skill then necessary for anyone seeking a career in book illustration. On his arrival at Linton's office, up on the third floor of No. 33 Essex Street, Walter found a row of engravers, or 'woodpeckers' as they were nicknamed, seated before a long green baize-covered bench by the windows. For night work there was a round table with a circle of clear glass globes filled with water which magnified the gas light cast on the engraving blocks. Linton employed about six engravers and a similar number of engraving apprentices, each of whom had to study five or six years to master his intricate craft. Many were deaf and dumb, and Walter was fascinated at the speed of their sign-language conversations and impressed by the way in which Linton's partner, Harvey Orrin Smith, could communicate with them.

Orrin Smith took charge of the new recruit on his first day and set him to transfer one of his own sketches to a small block of boxwood prepared, as was the custom, with a thin solution of zinc-white powder and water rubbed until quite dry across the smooth surface.[1] The design was traced on the block and then drawn with a hard pencil to get the lines as clear and precise as possible for the engraver. Accustomed as he was to quick sketching with something more sympathetic than the 4H pencil, Walter's enthusiastic efforts resulted in the first day's exercise looking 'as shiny as a black-leaded grate'. In the days that followed he continued to make little drawings on off-cuts of boxwood on which the engraving apprentices would practise their part of the process. He quickly felt at home in the office and soon struck up a friendship with Linton's son, Willie, who kept the books. At dinner time they played hide-and-seek in the Temple nearby, or sauntered down to the river to watch the barges and 'penny steamers'. They worked government hours, from 10 am to 4 pm weekdays and a half day Saturday and each day Walter walked in from Shaftesbury Terrace right across central London and back again in the evening.

His master was in his forty-eighth year when Walter met him and he made a striking impression on the young apprentice. He was an eccentric radical who combined an engraving career with a variety of political, literary and poetic activities. Later when Crane became a socialist he readily acknowledged the influence of Linton's radical thinking. This is how he described him.

W. J. Linton was in appearance small of stature, but a very remarkable look-ing man. His fair hair, rather fine and thin, fell in actual locks to his shoulders, and he wore a long flowing beard and moustache, then beginning to be tinged with grey. A keen, impulsive-looking, highly sensitive face with kindly blue eyes looked out from under the unusually broad brim of a black 'wideawake'. He wore turned down collars when the rest of the world mostly turned them up – a loose continental-looking necktie, black velvet waistcoat, and a long-waisted coat of a very peculiar cut . . . trousers of an antique pattern belonging to the 'forties' rather tight at the knees and falling over Wellington boots with small slits at the sides. He had abundance of energy and moved with a quick, rapid step, coming into the office with a sort of breezy rush, bringing with him always a stimulating sense of vitality. He spoke rapidly in a light-toned voice, frequently punctuated with a curious dry, obstructed sort of laugh. Altogether a kindly, generous, impulsive, and enthusiastic nature, a true socialist at heart, with an ardent love of liberty and with much of the revolutionary feeling of '48 about him.[2]

Linton had seen more of the foreign events of the revolutionary '48 than most Englishmen, having accompanied Dobson Collet and Guiseppe Mazzini to Paris conveying an address 'To the Brave French Nation from the Working Men of London' to the Provisional Government. They arrived within a week of the revolt which had replaced the monarchy with a republic, and were in time to see the funeral procession of those fallen in the Three Days. Afterwards, Linton continued to keep the English informed about continental liberal movements in his magazine *The Cause of The People*.[3] This was not his first republican publication nor was it to be his last.[3]

At the outset, however, Crane was probably more acutely aware of Linton's skill as an engraver whose freedom of touch upon the boxwood was 'astonishing'. At this time engravers ranked as artisans rather than artists, and were regarded in much the same light as the jobbing printers with whom they worked, but a master engraver like Linton enjoyed a more privileged place and was on familiar terms with those at the centre of the art and publishing worlds. Among those whom he knew well were the black-and-white artists Kenny Meadows, William Harvey, John Leech, the painters William Bell Scott and Edward Duncan; and the *Punch* personalities Douglas Jerrold and W. M. Thackeray. Shortly after Linton became a joint proprietor of the firm Smith and Linton in the autumn of 1842, it was handling most of the engraving for the *Illustrated London News* which then commanded a large circulation. Numerous illustrated journals and magazines were to follow its example and the mid-Victorian age saw a great increase in the number of wood-engravers to meet this growing demand. Fine engraving was also required for lavishly illustrated gift books.

It was a thoughtful decision on Walter's father's part to guide his son into this artistic, busy and business-like world at a time when black-and-white work was on the threshold of the 1860s, and assumed an artistic importance of its own. In this development the names of well-known painters, like Millais and Frederic Leighton, and black-and-white artists, like John Tenniel, Charles Keene and George du Maurier, were inextricably linked with those who engraved their work, the chief amongst whom were Linton, Swain and the brothers Dalziel.[4] In Linton's shop young Crane worked alongside craftsmen who maintained the finest standards of English wood-engraving, a tradition established in the late eighteenth century by the Newcastle-on-Tyne engraver Thomas Bewick (1753–1828) whose work, together with that of his famous pupils, had raised the craft to a high level.[5] Instead of the crude effects of the cuts in so many chapbooks of the time, Bewick's engraving ensured more precise control over line and a wider range of light and shade; effects depending upon a series of innovations including the use of the endgrain of hard boxwood and, in place of the knife, a sensitive tool, a 'graver', normally in use for metal engraving. In a simple printed woodcut the gouged-out lines register as white and the untouched surface as black. Bewick's famous 'white line' technique required an interpretation of the artist's idea rather than a line for line copy. Faithful line for line copies of artists' designs, known as 'facsimile' or 'black line' work, were scorned by Bewick's followers as mechanical, although this was the method used by earlier engravers including sixteenth century German masters, and most nineteenth century engraving shops used both techniques. Bewick took pride in being an artist and also drew his own designs on the wood. Many of his successors did the same, including Linton who was a good draughtsman.

When Walter Crane came to Essex Street, practical changes in the interests of speed and efficiency were being made. Linton employed a 'tint' and a 'facsimile' man to do easier mechanical work. Large prints for the press were often prepared using more than one piece of boxwood (the average size for these blocks was about four inches square) and to increase the speed necessary in press work, the squares were often cut into even smaller pieces which were specially jointed so that they fitted together again for printing. In this way several hands cut the picture simultaneously: the master taking difficult areas like faces, the less expert members of the workshop doing facsimile work and doubtless also 'a good deal of meaningless scribble and cross hatching'[6] to equate this with vague shadow and tint areas indicated by a wash tone in the drawing instead of by line. Walter Crane's task was to draw on the block rather than cut it and this particular division of labour was a shop practice established a good deal earlier. Bewick had rightly emphasized the merit of an engraver who was his own draughtsman, but the combination of talent and skill required in this was a luxury which could be dispensed with, especially as black-and-white work grew more and more commercial. When the second edition of Jackson's *Treatise on Wood Engraving* was issued in 1861 thirty-one artists were listed as professional draughtsmen on wood, including Charles Bewick, Owen Jones, Noel Humphreys, Charles Keene, M. J. Lawless, T. Macquoid, 'Phiz' among many other familiar names.[7] These were the ranks young Crane was to join when he completed his three years as an apprentice draughtsman.

In July 1859, a few months after beginning his apprenticeship, Walter's father died. His health had worsened in London. Hopes centered on Academy success and more commissions had not materialized. This was a sad loss. Marie Crane's anxieties on her husband's death must have been greatly increased by the knowledge that her children were not provided for, and all, except Lucy perhaps, were yet too young to fend for themselves. Her brother, Edward Kearsley, came to their aid and the family moved to live with him at a new address, Westbourne Park Villas. For Walter this bereavement meant that he had lost not only his father, but a wise and sympathetic artistic supervisor.

Changes also overtook Linton at this time. Financial pressures, which were always ready to descend on him, forced him back to the old premises occupied by the firm in earlier days at 85 Hatton Garden, much less salubrious quarters than Essex Street with its delightful view of Fountain Court. Some of Walter's drawings of engraving office subjects date from this time and reveal an increasing command of brush and pencil. Apart from the Hatton Garden house-top cats the only wild-life interest afforded by the new offices was a pair of peacocks, who strutted along the parapets and provided an exotic, perhaps also rather prophetic, contrast to the dingy environment.

The carefree days of sketching cows were over but Linton encouraged him to

View from the Hatton Garden workshop.
MS. p. 54.

Wood engraver at work 1860.
MS. p. 48.

Wood engravers Globe, &
'pork pie' hat of the period 1861.

Volunteer uniform. (London Irish)
MS p. 55.

D. G. Rossetti *Sir Galahad*, wood engraving, from the Moxon *Tennyson*, first published in 1857.

develop his skill in animal drawing and helped him acquire a student season ticket to the Zoological Gardens. On these visits, which began in the summer of 1859 and continued during the three years of his apprenticeship, and well into the 1860s, Crane accumulated sheaves of animal sketches which were to be invaluable for his later work as an illustrator. As his pupil's skill increased, Linton would ask Walter to redraw parts rubbed out in the course of engraving, and sometimes also to improve the faulty animal drawing of others. An example of his own animal drawing was printed by Linton in a pamphlet advertising a new engraving process called Kerography.

This invention which was an early attempt to adapt the engraving of metal plates for 'on-surface' printing, aroused some interest at the time, notably within the Pre-Raphaelite circle.[8] William Michael and Dante Gabriel Rossetti asked Linton to use the Kerographic process to prepare plates for Alexander Gilchrist's *Life of William Blake* (1863). The engraver was already well known to the Pre-Raphaelites, having cut blocks of their designs for the Moxon edition of *Tennyson* (1857),[9] a book remarkable as the earliest significant contribution made by Millais, Rossetti and Holman Hunt to wood engraving. Young Walter's own *Lady of Shalott* drawings are quite unlike those in the Moxon *Tennyson* and he only became familiar with the book during his apprenticeship, when the Pre-Raphaelite cuts particularly impressed him. Their influence, however, is not apparent in what survives of the work done under Linton's supervision.

Apart from zoo studies many of his tasks were routine and dull, such as the seemingly endless ranks of brass bedstead designs for Heal's catalogues, demanding maximum precision and no imagination. He also helped prepare medical drawings for illustration and lecture demonstrations and there was a constant demand for speedily executed material for newspapers and journals. One of these was *The Ladies Treasury*, for which Linton cut a monthly fashion plate, and the twopenny monthly, *Entertaining Things*, for which he designed a wrapper and provided various other cuts. Among these are some of Crane's earliest published designs, including one of the African explorer P. B. Du Chaillu's encounter with a gorilla,

M Chaillu and the gorilla, wood engraving, published in *Entertaining Things*, May 1861. By courtesy of the Trustees of the National Library of Scotland.

The Lord Mayor's Show – Scene in Fleet Street, wood engraving, reproduced in *The Illustrated News of the World*, 16 November 1861.

which shows him already equipped with remarkable facility in rendering exotic beasts, though he was still rather less at ease when it came to his own species.

After his first year's apprenticeship, Walter was paid ten shillings a week and towards the end of the final year was sometimes sent out as a press artist. Often in his lunch hour he walked through to Fleet Street to see the latest *Punch* cartoons in the office window, and he was familiar with the work of its Old Guard: Harvey, Thackeray, John Gilbert, Kenny Meadows, John Leech, 'Phiz', and a more recent recruit, John Tenniel who had joined the staff when 'Dicky' Doyle resigned in 1850. Among several illustrated papers rather belatedly following the lead of *The Illustrated London News* was *The Illustrated News of the World*, for which Walter worked briefly at this time. One of his first jobs was to cover a trial, but he was so embarrassed at sketching in public that it was not a success. Two sketchbooks surviving from this year show him studying everyday subjects, practising for his new role as an artist of modern life with many drawings of people in contemporary dress. Several relate to other designs for the paper. His work here is not signed and dates from October 1861 to February 1862, just after his apprenticeship officially ended. Crane considered his best effort to be 'The Lord Mayor's Show – Scene in Fleet Street', which appeared on 16 November 1861. The lively subject is handled with the kind of enthusiasm 'Phiz' brought to illustration although Crane's line is broader and a 'tint' man has obviously been used to cut the darker areas. Some of the clown-like profiles are reminiscent of Linton's own style in less meticulous productions like his children's book, *The History of a Quartern*

Page from a sketchbook of 1861, pen drawing, $5\frac{1}{8} \times 3\frac{3}{4}$ in. (13 × 9.5 cm). Collection the Houghton Library, Harvard University.

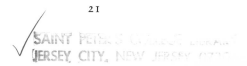

Loaf, published in 1860. *The Illustrated News of the World* generally shows the apprentice draughtsman working in a vigorous style, but one showing less attempt at refinement than the rather stiff, tight drawing of 'M. Chaillu and the Gorilla' which, as a black and white illustration for a journal, probably demanded more time and attention than was usually devoted to press work.

During his last year with Linton, Walter's uncle married and the family took lodgings at No. 45 Argyle Square, Kings Cross, a central situation nearer the Hatton Garden office and also one which was to be convenient for the next few years when Crane worked as a freelance draughtsman. In January 1862 he was given his indenture of apprenticeship with a note by Orrin Smith confirming the successful conclusion of their three years' association: 'Returned with thanks and full expression of satisfaction at Walter Crane's thorough good conduct, his readiness, his industry and his ability.'[10]

Black-and-white Illustration:
The Sixties

Walter Crane's first step in seeking work was to take his small portfolio around the various publishers to whom he had introductions. At this date he looked quite serious and professional for his age, still cleanshaven and with a high, broad forehead and well-shaped features. He obviously dressed with some care and a striped cravat hints at his smart but 'artistic' turn-out of later years. He was small and lightly built.

The first month or so yielded only meagre contracts from publishers of religious tracts, in particular the firm of Wertheim, Macintosh and Hunt which issued twopenny pamphlets with homilies by the Rev. Philip Bennet Power.[1] The cover of *The Eye Doctor* shows Crane trying to put humour into work which was certainly more challenging than bedsteads but not very rewarding either financially or artistically. He experienced the usual vicissitudes besetting the draughtsman

Below left
Photograph of Walter Crane aged sixteen, 1861.

Below
Cover for *The Eye Doctor*, 1862, wood engraving. By courtesy of Cambridge University Library.

whose careful efforts are hacked about by an inexpert engraver, in this case a
certain W. D. Willis. The latter also cut five landscape vignettes which Crane
adapted from sketches by the Rev. Henry Stern for his *Wandering among the
Falashas in Abyssinia* published by the same firm in 1860. Linton and Orrin Smith
also helped him with commissions such as A. J. Symington's *Pen and Pencil
Sketches of Faroe and Iceland* for which Crane tidied up the author's 'rather vague'
originals in transferring them to boxwood to be cut by Linton.[2] He was given
more of this type of hack draughtsmanship in a project preparing designs for an
encyclopaedia. This, however, yielded the unexpected reward of research in the
British Museum Reading Room which soon became a favourite retreat.

So far the work completed in 1862 was of a fairly anonymous kind, but the
young illustrator's prospects changed with a major commission to provide
drawings for *The New Forest: Its History and Its Scenery*, by John R. de Capel Wise.
He owed this partly to Linton (who was to engrave the blocks) and partly to Mr
Wooldridge of Smith and Elder. *The New Forest* was an elegant gift book, a small
quarto with eighty-three engravings and a fine gilt-cloth binding by John
Leighton. Crane's illustrations are not framed but, as was more usual at that date,
in vignettes. In format it resembles Wise's *Shakespeare, his Birthplace and Neighbourhood*, also published by Smith and Elder (1861) with cuts designed and engraved
by Linton, but these are surpassed by Crane in *The New Forest* which, with its
impressive binding, is a much more attractive book. The commission entailed
sketching on the spot under the author's supervision and at the end of May 1862,
Crane had set off with Wise for Hampshire. John Wise was about ten years
Crane's senior. He had been educated at Oxford, and was a cousin of the historian
and biographer of Carlyle, J. Anthony Froude. Wise introduced his young friend
to the work of J. S. Mill and Herbert Spencer and encouraged him to widen his
views about philosophy. Throughout June and early July they were busy at work
in the New Forest. Among the best of Crane's drawings are those heading each
chapter. His style is naturalistic but not over-meticulous, with an impressionistic
handling of leaves and branches quite close to the pretty and acceptable work of
Birket Foster. In the vignettes he was able to demonstrate all he had learned from
Linton about how they should 'vanish gracefully into white margin at the edges'.[3]
The young artist had every reason to be pleased with the reception given to
The New Forest among Christmas publications of 1862.[4]

24

In *The Cornhill* it was described by George Henry Lewes as 'a work of erudition as well as a work of art'. He added that it might surprise the reader to learn 'that these exquisitely characteristic bits of foliage and forest life are the productions of a youth of seventeen', for whom he prophesied a bright future. Although Crane was a little annoyed at this reference to his youthfulness, he can have had few mixed feelings at the handsome fee of £100 – vastly different to the meagre instalments received from impecunious publishers of moral tracts (one of whom

In Kensington Gardens, 1862, pen and ink drawing with gouache, 7 7/16 × 4 11/16 in. (18.8 × 11.9 cm). Collection John House, England.

Picnic scene at a race course, 1861, pen and pencil drawing, 3⅜ × 5¼ in. (8.7 × 13.5 cm). Collection the Houghton Library, Harvard University.

had insisted on a 5 per cent discount for paying cash on a £1 bill). In the early autumn of this year he heard of the acceptance of his first submission to the Royal Academy, a water colour called 'The Lady of Shalott'. His future certainly looked promising.

As an illustrator, *The New Forest* had restricted him to landscape, but Crane must have cherished ambitions of joining the ranks of the most progressive black-and-white artists of the day whose work added allure and interest to many new and flourishing journals. Their draughtsmanship was distinguished by a monumental figure style. Many of these were associated with *Once a Week*, which appeared in July 1859. It was the first serious literary magazine to place equal emphasis on illustration. Among the younger artists were Millias, Charles Keene, Fred Walker, M. J. Lawless, Frederick Sandys, G. J. Pinwell, George du Maurier, and A. B. Houghton, and, appearing less frequently, T. Morton, Edward Poynter, Frederick J. Shields, J. W. North, J. D. Watson, and Holman Hunt. F. Leighton, Simeon Solomon and Arthur Hughes worked in a similar style but for different periodicals which also went in for high-quality engravings.[5] Of these the most significant were *The Cornhill* and *Good Words*, first published in 1860. In February of the next year, *London Society* was issued, followed by *The Churchman's Family Magazine* (1863), *The Shilling Magazine* (1865), *Cassell's Magazine* (new series, 1865), *The Month* (1864), *The Argosy* (1866), *The Quiver* (illustrated from 1866), *The Churchman's Shilling Magazine* (1867), *Good Words for the Young* (1868), *The People's Magazine* (1867) and others.

Crane made his debut as a sixties artist in *London Society* whose first number had opened with an essay on the delights of a stroll in Hyde Park, a somewhat trivial theme compared with the literary aims of *Once a Week* or the moral intentions of *Good Words*; but matched by pictorial treatment of elegant and fashionable London. The young draughtsman had assessed his market well when he showed James Hogg, the editor, a drawing of 'Fashionable Promenades in Kensington Gardens'. It was just the kind of subject *London Society* liked. Hogg paid him £2 and commissioned more. Crane's introduction to Hogg doubtless came from Linton, who engraved a few designs for the first volume of the magazine as well as those by Crane himself. High society already fascinated Crane, although the modern life represented here is very different to that for *The Illustrated News of the World*. A study by Crane of a 'Picnic Scene at a Race Course', dated 1861, now in

26

the Houghton Library, shows his early interest in more fashionable press work of the kind to be seen in *The Illustrated London News* as well as in contemporary English painting. In this case an obvious parallel would be the picnic scene in Frith's *Derby Day*. The well-heeled world of William Frith was an obvious source for *London Society* artists, as well as Crane, though in comparison, with the latter's photographic realism, Crane's work has too much of the flimsy elegance of the fashion-plate. His expressionless figures with their tiny nerveless hands are remarkably reminiscent of Linton's for the *Ladies Own Treasury*. They are vapid and have none of the humour which enlivens Du Maurier's cartoons of fashionable society and are entirely lacking in the panoramic virtuosity with which Constantin Guys handled modern life subjects for the *London Illustrated News*. But Crane's sense of fun is already to be found in his animal drawing for 'Dickens's Dogs; or the Landseer of Fiction' published in *London Society*, July 1863.[6]

Meanwhile, rather more earnest subject matter had encouraged him to try to develop a stronger figure style. This may be seen in *Stories of Old: Bible Narratives for Young Children* by Caroline Hadley, published by Smith and Elder in two volumes at Christmas 1862. Not all fourteen drawings are equally good but the best, like 'Samson and the Lion', show him incorporating firm outline with clearly defined and quite constructive hatching and cross hatching. Here he was responding to Charles Keene's impressive illustrations to 'A Good Fight' published in Volume I of *Once a Week*, which were characterised by a comparatively simple and agressive style, very appropriate to the subject.

Samson and the Lion, 1862, wood engraving from *Stories of Old*.

This development of a medievalizing technique expressive of the technical limitations of wood engraving is consistent with a general interest in the Middle Ages encouraged by the German Nazarene and the English Pre-Raphaelite championship of the primitives. As a child, Crane was fascinated by early German wood engravings especially Dürer's 'Great Horse', 'Melencolia' and 'Knight, Death and the Devil', which were reproduced in his father's copies of the Art *Journal*. At the time of the Great Exhibition, recent German art as well as medieval art was being freshly appraised.[7] This interest was to encourage draughtsmen and engravers to work in a less complicated manner, and stop emulating the fine-textured effects of metal engraving which characterized much good wood engraving of the previous decade.

William Harvey's design to E. W. Lane's translation of *The Thousand and One Nights*, issued by Chas. Knight between 1828 and 1840, and a book Crane knew well, enlisted the energies of about forty engravers including Landells, Jackson, Thompson and Linton. Some of the younger generation continued to be influenced

The Castle of Mont Orgeuil, wood engraving, reproduced in *Once A Week*, 19 December 1863.

by this style, for instance, Dicky Doyle whose hirsute elfin fantasy frontispiece to John Ruskin's *King of the Golden River* (1851) is described with a scratchy line and nervous handling. Although this development was only made possible by Bewick's refinement of engraving techniques, it involved extraordinary demands of time and skill on the part of the engraver and cannot have been wholly welcome, especially when an expanding market forced engravers to work quickly. The two styles of cutting continued side by side for a time, and, for instance, while Rossetti preferred the sensitive interpretation given to his drawings for Moxon's illustrated edition of Tennyson when they were cut by Linton to the severe lines cut by Dalziel, nevertheless, his few black-and-white designs published in the 1860s make use of a thicker outline and stronger simple contrasts. In this he follows general development of work of the decade in which Swain and Dalziel, after Linton went to America in 1866,[8] were to assume primary importance as engravers.

The Pre-Raphaelite example set by the Moxon *Tennyson* designs was important for the impact of their detailed and realistic interpretations of events. Millais was to continue as a very prolific black-and-white artist during the 1860s, and Hunt was also fairly active in this field. Rossetti produced very little, but each of his designs was to be enormously influential. Young Crane, who had saved pocket money to buy the Moxon *Tennyson,* found 'the three Rossetti woodcuts therein . . . entirely fascinating and practically inexhaustible'.[9]

Crane's line and hatching in *Stories of Old* is looser and bolder than Rossetti's in the Moxon volume but closer to his black-and-white work of the sixties including the designs to Christina Rossetti's *Goblin Market* (1862), which he had seen in preparation in Linton's workshop, and to work by *Once a Week* artists, Lawless, du Maurier, and Millais, and the most frankly Germanic of all, Sandys, who between 1861 and 1862 developed an intricate Düreresque style. Crane had greatly admired Sandys' 'Legend of the Portent' design when he saw it being engraved by Linton but he chose a less affectedly primitive technique for the Bible pictures of 1862.[10]

By the end of 1863, Crane had his first drawing accepted by *Once a Week*, an illustration to the 'Castle of Mont Orgueil' (Volume IX, Dec. 19). Its bold figures, strong outline and chiaroscuro reveal a true affinity with other *Once a Week* artists. This design, and one for 'Treasure Trove', published in *Good Words* late in 1863 (p. 795) are most obviously influenced by Frederic Leighton, whose illustrations for George Eliot's *Romola* were serialized in *The Cornhill* (Volume VI, July 1862, to Volume VIII, August 1863). Many of Leighton's drawings were cut by Linton and although his artistic development was different to that of the original Pre-Raphaelites, Leighton, who studied in Europe, shared their sympathy for Nazarene art. He, in fact, became part of a nineteenth century graphic tradition of Bible illustration which the Nazarenes established, and which was perhaps best known in England from Schnorr von Carolsfeld's *Bible in Pictures* published in England in 1860. Crane himself later remarked how much he admired Schnorr's Bible designs among other wood engraving products of 'the powerful German imagination'. It would have been quite natural for him to have referred to the *Bible in Pictures* before preparing his own *Bible Narratives*. A fine unfinished study for 'Balaam', dated 1866, suggests that he may have contemplated contributing to a later Bible project. Perhaps he even had his eye on Dalziel's well publicized *Bible Gallery.*

Geraldine Massé's bibliography is particularly inadequate with regard to the 1860s; partly because Crane himself made little attempt to list all he had done at that time in the *Reminiscences,* and also because he frequently worked anonymously and his name does not always appear in booksellers' lists. Most of his work for Smith and Elder is included. In 1862 he designed a title-page for Wilkie Collins's novel *After Dark* and illustrations for another volume by Caroline Hadley, *Children's Sayings, or Early Life at Home*, which do him more credit than the six designs cut by Willis for *Stories of Memel for the Young* by Mrs Agnes de Havilland, published in 1863. This was the year Walter Crane met Edmund Evans, the young engraver and printer who had become increasingly involved in developing colour techniques. He was often to use Crane's designs and at this stage also cut some of his black-and-white work including five illustrations for *The Moors and the Fens* by F. C. Trafford (1863) and four for *Poor Match* by Holm Lee (1863).

In 1865 Smith, Elder and Co. issued *Transformation or the Romance of Monte Beni* by Nathaniel Hawthorne with five illustrations drawn by Crane and cut by Linton. Among these is a pictorial title-page which shows greater concern for structure and balance in its design than the reedy landscape and more old-fashioned rustic character of that for *The Moors and the Fens*. The Italian setting of the story may have reminded Crane of the *Romola* drawings; and two of his illustrations here suggest Leighton compositions although there is less of the latter's stream-lined authority and weight than in Crane's figure work of 1863. Between August 1864 and June 1865 he collaborated with Linton on a drawing for each issue of *The Month*, and in 1865 produced an elegant frontispiece and title-page to *Broken to Harness* by Edmund Yates. He also drew two sets of illustrations, for *Sandford and Merton* by Thomas Day and for that collection of improving tales so popular in the Victorian nursery, *Evenings at Home* by Dr Aiken and Mrs Barbauld.[11] Crane's style here is more consistently assured than the varied quality of that of 1862 and 1863. He moved from the severity of his better drawings of that time to more complex arrangements with an accompanying loss of dramatic authority – possibly a natural result of working for children who enjoy anecdote and detail.

Crane's life around 1865 began to take on the familiar pattern of work for children's books for which he is best known. Publishing for the nursery was as much a booming industry as that for parlour and library and for a while he contributed to one of the new journals for boys, Routledge's *Every Boy's Magazine*, beginning with a coloured frontispiece and title-page, printed by Evans who produced most of the colour plates which were often star features of the monthly issues. He also cut black and white designs by Crane to Henry Wood's serial 'Orville College', which ran throughout 1868.[12]

In February 1866, Walter Crane had spent a few days on holiday in Paris with his brother Thomas, who was then a clerk in the General Post Office. They visited the Louvre and the sights, attended theatres and generally enjoyed Parisian café life, from where no doubt there were opportunities to make some of the little sketches of fashionable ladies and men in military costume which survive in a sketchbook of the trip. From these, he prepared a humorous drawing, memorable because it was the only one he ever had accepted by *Punch*. 'Great Show of Chignons', appeared on 21 July 1866. Crane never came near to one of the coveted seats at *Punch's* weekly meetings, although he did work for its cheaper rival, *Fun*.[12] This illustration for *Punch* is among his earliest works signed with a bird mono-gram and not by an initial and surname, or initials, as is usual up to this date. The use of monograms was common practice among the Pre-Raphaelites and black-and-white artists, and it is perhaps surprising that he did not devise one earlier. The Egyptian-looking device on the cartoon alternates with an initial encased within the letter 'C' in the later 1860s until he finally decided on the well-known monogram incorporating a bird and a 'W' divided into two 'V's within the 'C'.

Beset by beasts at Bassen-Thwaite,
8 August 1870, pen and ink,
$4\frac{7}{16} \times 7$ in. (11.2 × 17.7 cm) from
a Hazelford sketchbook.
Collection the Houghton Library,
Harvard University.

Nothing conveys Crane's likeable character better than the informal sketches which he would make when he was away from home. The earliest of these date from the later 1860s when he spent his summers at Hazelford Hall near Hathersage in Derbyshire.[13] He had first visited the Peak District with Wise in the summer of 1863, when his friend was planning to do for this area what he had so successfully accomplished for the New Forest. Through Wise, Crane had made many friends in the neighbourhood and he continued to widen his circle of acquaintances over the next seven years when he visited Derbyshire. He was often joined by his own brothers, sisters and friends, including Harry Ellis Wooldridge (1845–1917), who was the son of Mr Wooldridge of Smith and Elder and then a student at the Royal Academy. Crane's drawings of the delights and hazards of sketching in the open, the trials and triumphs of hill-walking and curious local characters and customs are full of merry wit. He dwells with appreciative attention on the evening meal, which was served early in this unsophisticated spot to leave time to linger over bottles of excellent port. Among the earliest Hazelford sketches is one dated 25 June 1865, showing his spacious room at the Hall (where he had taken lodgings) with its view of trees and moors. These holidays seem to have extended right across the summer months, often from July to September, but different members of the family would come and go, though Walter himself was quite a permanent steadily working fixture. A letter written by Tom to Lucy on 17 August 1865, describes him as too busy finishing drawings for Evans to go out very much. From art and nature the holiday-makers often turned to music under Wooldridge's direction, for he was a gifted musician and musicologist. In a series called 'Our Entertainments' he is shown leading the company as choristers, in a whistling quartet, a Morris dance to pipe music, and a brass band. Inevitably, Walter Crane's slight figure is contrasted with the thickset Wooldridge frame, and the dapper moustache he now wore with the other's magnificent French-style beard. In a delightful sequence, 'Bradshaw on the Brain, or the Mainline Maniac', Crane makes fun of his friend's obsession with detail and train timetables. For a while, in place of letters home, those at Hazelford (with Walter as Editor) compiled *Walter's Weekly*, 'a journal of public, private, particular and general

31

information for family reading', which ran to nine issues from July to September
1868. In reply came *The Argyle Advertiser and Bloomsbury Budget*, 'a weekly review
of Literature, Art and Fashionable Society'. Four issues of this survive and it was
mainly the work of Lucy. *The Argyle Advertiser* of 29 August contained the
'fashionable intelligence' of a presentation of a private address card from a Mrs
Andrews and the significance of this becomes clearer in Hazelford sketches of
two summers later where Walter is accompanied in his sketching exploits and
hill-walking by a young lady of distinctly fashionable appearance and great
heavily-lashed eyes. This was Mrs Andrews's daughter, Mary Frances, whom he
was to marry in the autumn of 1871.

*And from ye halle forthe rode ye
three*, from a Hazelford
sketchbook of 1867, pen and ink,
5 × 4 in. (12.8 × 10.3 cm). Crane
as the lady of the castle bids farewell
to his brothers Tom and Arthur,
and his friend Ellis Wooldridge.
Collection the Houghton Library,
Harvard University.

Willows whiten, aspens quiver,
Little breezes dusk and shiver
Thro' the wave that runs forever
By the island in the river
        Flowing down to Camelot.

From 1865 onwards Crane was occupied with colour work for Evans, but he continued with black and white commissions. For *Wait for the End* by Mark Lemon, published in 1866, he provided a frontispiece and title-page. It is not clear who cut the blocks in this case but he was still very much at the mercy of whoever gave him work as can be seen from a letter, written by Orrin Smith in 1867, in which the engraver criticizes his drawing:

My Dear Walter,

    This is very nice but not at all what I wanted . . . it is charming but it is not effective. Your treatment of the Church itself is most expensive to us, you being so long here must know that . . . (it) involves an awful lot of toil for the engraver . . . The man on left hand will look like a black beetle when engraved. Please give yr. figures greater definition, I would rather pay more for the drawing as I can save it on the engraving and make a better block . . . I'll send for it at noon tomorrow.

Yrs

H.O.S.[14]

The first of a series of twelve illustrations to 'Anne Hereford' by Mrs Henry Wood appeared in *The Argosy* on 1 December 1867. From dates on preliminary sketches for these now in the Houghton Library, it seems to have been Crane's custom to prepare the drawings as they were required, rather than all at once. They were not always cut by the same engraver. The original *Argosy* consisted of a set of four half-yearly volumes issued in 1866 and 1867, and Crane helped launch the new monthly series begun in December 1867 by designing a wrapper with a rather prosaic argonaut in a boat. Another *Argosy* drawing by Crane, to a poem called 'Margaret' by Lucy Crane (2 March 1868), shows him to be in greater sympathy with a romantic medieval theme than with the contemporary life style of Anne Hereford. This preference is amusingly illustrated in a drawing and a mock ballad composed at Hazelford in the summer of that year. The illustrations to the story of Tuflongo appeared in *The People's Magazine* in March 1868 and were cut by Orrin Smith.[15] These and others in this volume are described with the economy of line the engraver wanted. Linton had returned to America in 1867 with the intention of settling there, and left his son Willie as his agent and book-keeper in the firm managed by Orrin Smith. Walter's elder brother, Thomas, also joined the business and this renewal of the family connection may explain why much of Walter's work in the later 1860s was cut by Linton's partner. In August 1868 the first of his illustrations to 'Esther: a Story of Cologne' appeared in *The People's Magazine*. The whole series was engraved by Orrin Smith. Enthusiasm for its medieval subject inspired Crane here to produce some of his most vigorous work to date. Crane makes use of enclosed and compartmented interiors as Rossetti, and more recently, Burne-Jones had done, following Quattrocento and Early Netherlandish examples. The gentle intimacy of the little preparatory sketch at Harvard for 'The Steward's Suit Rejected' is quite Rossettian in feeling although this is lost in the larger printed version of the subject. The other Crane designs engraved by Orrin Smith in this magazine are in a simpler style than the 'Esther of Cologne' drawings, more schematized and flat, and closer to the outline designs of his colour work of the period. This was the natural outcome of Crane's interest in developing an economical wood engraving style – an interest stemming from his love of early woodcuts, from technical reasons such as those given by the engraver, Orrin Smith, and from Crane's own experiences in designing for colour printing. The confidence and clarity of this style is to be seen in a design

cut by Linton illustrating 'A Lonely Life' by G. Stanley Arnold, one of three drawings of 1868 for *The Churchman's Shilling Magazine*.[16]

Around this time Crane was introduced to John Hamer, who was then acting as literary adviser and art director to the publishing firm of Cassell, Petter and Galpin. This contact led to several commissions containing some of his best black-and-white work to date as well as a book with fine colour plates, *The Merrie Heart* not published until 1871. *Huan and Anthy: or the Magic of Kindness* by the Mayhew brothers and *King Gab and his Story Bag* by W. Marshall, who used the pseudonym Heraclitus Grey were issued in 1869. Each has eight designs. *Stories of the Olden Time* arranged by M. Jones and *Labour Stands on Golden Feet* by H. Zschokke appeared in 1870, each with two designs. Among the best of the exotic crowded scenes of the anti-slavery fairy-tale *Huan and Anthy* is the relatively simple scene of the 'Martyrdom of Huan and Anthy' in which the face of the Spirit of Kindness, her wings and crumpled drapery, strongly suggest the influence of Burne-Jones's *Earthly Paradise* drawings, some of which had been engraved by Morris. Proofs of these had been circulated privately among their friends but it is not certain that Crane saw them as early as 1869, though he might have had the opportunity to do so in the studio of Simeon Solomon whom he knew several years before meeting Burne-Jones around 1871. Of the two books of 1869, however, *King Gab*

No more pills or any other medicine,
1865, engraved and printed in
colour by Edmund Evans. One of
a set of page proofs for the toy
book *The History of Jenny Wren* in
the collection of Liverpool City
Libraries.

Right
Colour proof of a cover for
Sensational Novels, c. 1875, printed
by Edmund Evans. By courtesy of
Liverpool City Libraries.

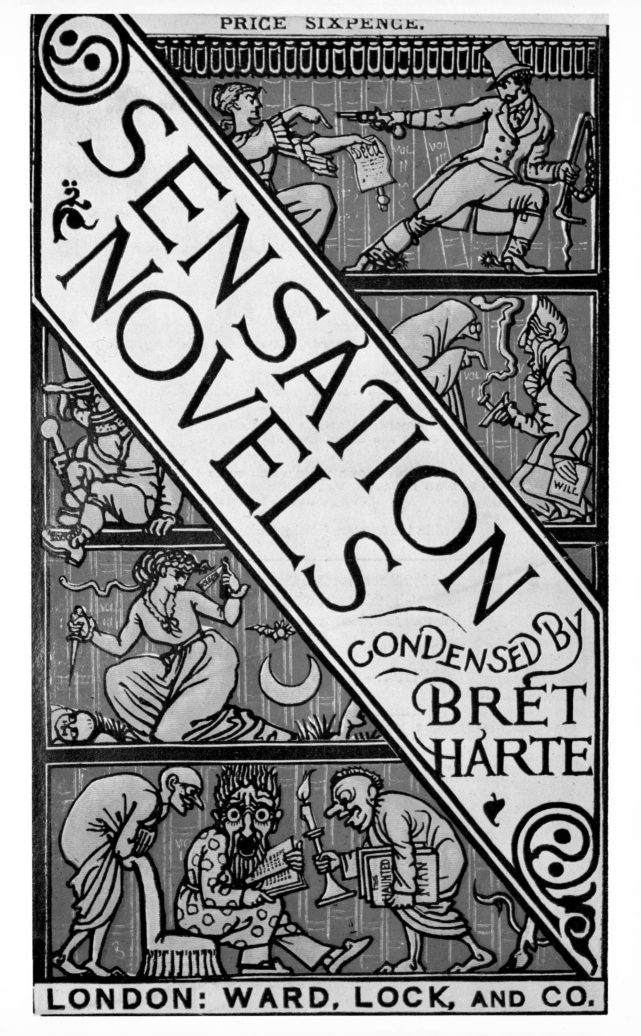

PRICE SIXPENCE.

SENSATION NOVELS

CONDENSED BY BRÉT HARTE

LONDON: WARD, LOCK, AND CO.

is much the better one and it is significant in concluding this chapter on engraving in the 1860s that this volume was advertized as having 'Illustrations after Albert Durer'. Crane found inspiration in these splendid tales for flights of Gothic fancy, which lend a new vitality to his now confident draughtsmanship.

Colour Work for Edmund Evans: Yellow Backs and Toy Books 1863-75

Walter Crane's reputation as a children's book illustrator is founded on colour work for sixpenny and shilling picture books printed by Edmund Evans and published by Routledge between 1865 and 1875.

His first colour works, however, were designs for 'mustard plasters', or yellow backs – cheap editions put out by many publishers to meet the growing demands of an expanding literate class and bored railway travellers. These were bound between straw boards usually clad in yellow glazed paper with a picture printed on the front.[1] Among the many other artists employed by Evans to design these covers were Birket Foster, John Gilbert, 'Phiz', G. Cruickshank, Harrison Weir, Kenny Meadows, J. Absolon, W. S. Coleman, Charles Keene and Charles H. Bennet. Although Evans printed colour for more expensive books, the prosperity of his firm depended on work for the yellow back market which he had already been in for about ten years and in which he had the largest share of any London colour printer. The name 'yellow back' derived from the use of a yellow enamelled paper introduced by Evans after he had received complaints from the trade about how easily paler paper covers were soiled.

On his now frequent visits to Evans' offices in Raquet Court, Walter Crane had his first opportunity to learn the intricacies of wood block colour printing, one of the most exciting aspects of the expanding book market. The increase in wealth and education in the early Victorian period had encouraged all kinds of experiments in printing techniques, chiefly in the area of reproducing decoration and illustration. It was only in the 1830s that colour became a viable proposition in the commercial and competitive world of book production and not until the 1850s that printed colour became relatively common in books when several firms produced it at reasonable cost. Most of these, like Evans, relied on wood engraving but there were other techniques, notably lithography, which allied with photography were to completely supersede wood block colour printing by the end of the century. Evans himself had begun his experiments in the 1850s. He used oil-based inks and wood blocks, abandoning a previous method developed by George Baxter which used a precision key printed from metal. By the early 1860s his firm was in competition with others working variations on Baxter's patent.

It is difficult to form an estimate of Crane's earliest work for Evans, most of which must have been anonymous. Full ranges of yellow backs are not easy to check as most libraries bought more expensive editions. But among the Evans colour proofs in the Constance Meade collection in the Bodleian Library is a cover by Crane for *The Moors and the Fens*, published by Smith and Elder in 1863 and printed in red and blue with a black key on off-white paper. The adaptation of this design for a two shilling 'yellow back' edition may have been done a while after the original five shilling volume was issued, possibly to help boost flagging sales of stock. But the design certainly dates from the first year of Crane's collaboration

Overleaf
Centre page of *The Sleeping Beauty in the Wood*, 1876, printed in colour by Edmund Evans. By courtesy of the Victoria and Albert Museum.

But said, that in the future years the Princess young should die,
By pricking of a spindle-point—ah, woeful prophecy!
But now, a kind young Fairy, who had waited to the last, [are past;
Stepped forth, and said, "No, she shall sleep till a hundred years
"And then she shall be wakened by a King's son—truth I tell—
"And he will take her for his wife, and all will yet be well."

In vain in all her father's
In vain in all the country
For in a lonely turret hig
There lives an ancient w
The Princess found her o
Alas! the spindle pricked

pinning-wheel's forbid
ndles sharp are hid ;
winding stair,   [care
still turns her wheel with
and tried to learn to spin ;
the charm had entered in !

And down she falls in death-like sleep : they lay her on her bed,
And all around her sink to rest—a palace of the dead !
A hundred years pass—still they sleep, and all around the place
A wood of thorns has risen up—no path a man can trace.
At last, a King's son, in the hunt, asked how long it had stood,
And what old towers were those he saw above the ancient wood.

with the printer. Evans, although quick to appreciate the gifts of the young illustrator, saw his limitations – 'he did all sorts of things . . . he was a genius. The only subjects I found he could not draw were figure subjects of everyday life, such subjects as appear in *London Society* . . . .'[2] Much of Crane's earliest yellow back work for Evans almost certainly involved scenes of everyday life for they

Cover for *The Moors and the Fens*, *c*. 1863, engraved and printed in red, blue and black by Edmund Evans. From the Constance Meade Collection, the Bodleian Library Oxford.

were the stuff of so many popular novels. Crane's growing preference for imaginative subjects and his skilful and sympathetic animal drawing were better suited to the illustration of children's books, where there was less insistence on a realistic interpretation of the text and more scope for invention. Evans was to take advantage of this when he soon extended his colour printing to the field of inexpensive children's books. Nevertheless, he continued to print Crane's designs for pictorial covers throughout the decade and later. The earliest yellow back by Crane, which the writer has traced, is an 1869 edition of Sheridan Le Fanu's *Guy Deverell* published for Chapman and Hall's Select Library of Fiction. The drawing itself has little to distinguish it but the red crossed with blue on the bright ground gives the two shilling volume all the gaudy glory associated with its species.

Many of these covers were black-and-white drawings adapted for colour by the printer. This is true of those by Crane for *The Moors and the Fens* and *Nursery Songs* both of which also appear in black-and-white.[3] Thus, in his earliest work for Evans, Crane was less involved in colour design than might have been expected. He was invariably required to produce drawings which looked equally well in black and white and was given little scope to develop a style specifically suited to three-colour printing.

As a child, Walter Crane's most vivid memories of books were of the pictures in Nash's *Mansions* and Goldsmith's works on natural history, and then of Scott and Shakespeare. He and his brothers and sisters had been subjected to the predictable but dull moral diet of tales published by the Religious Tract Society – little books which were often without illustration, occasionally having one or two black and white cuts but seldom any colour. When he grew more familiar with book printing and publishing in London he appreciated the changing attitudes towards books for the young and of the potential in this expanding business which had already been explored by a few enterprising individuals.

In the early nineteenth century, William Darton was among the few publishers working for a children's market, a tradition started in the previous century by John Newbery and continued by his successor John Harris. One of Harris's most successful publications had been *The Butterfly's Ball and Grasshopper's Feast* (1807), a fantasy rhyme by William Roscoe of Liverpool and illustrated by Mulready, but such flights of fancy were rare at this time when ideas on bringing up children were still dominated in England by the rational and moral influence of Locke and Rousseau. It was not until 1840 that Henry Cole (1808–82), the future Director of South Kensington Museum, looked around for suitable reading for his own young family, and finding little to please him in either the content or the appearance of children's books, devized The Home Treasury, a series of books issued between 1841 and 1849 under the pseudonym of Felix Summerly. Sometimes Cole's desire to educate inhibited a more obvious appeal to the simple tastes of the young, but his re-introduction of fairy tales was a happy reversal of previous policy and a symptom of the reviving ascendancy of the imagination.[4] This was reinforced in 1846 with the publication of two different, but equally delightful, imaginative *tours de force*, an English translation of Hans Andersen's *Tales* and Lear's first *Book of Nonsense*, which in turn had their effect on Lewis Carroll's *Alice Adventures* published some twenty years later. Meanwhile, adventure stories for boys written by Captain Marryat appeared soon to be followed by those of W. H. G. Kingston and R. M. Ballantyne. Crane became well known for his illustrations to books by Mrs Molesworth, one of three women authors, including Mrs Ewing and Mrs Hodgson Burnet, outstanding for their contribution later in the century to literature for children catering especially for different categories of age and sex.

At the youngest end of the children's market come the picture books. These

The cover of Routledge's sixpenny
toy book *Sing A Song of Sixpence*,
1866, printed in colour by
Edmund Evans. By courtesy of
the Victoria and Albert Museum.

:THIS LITTLE PIG:

:WENT TO MARKET:

This little pig went to market, 1869, printed in colour by Edmund Evans. By courtesy of the Victoria and Albert Museum.

large slim volumes for which Crane produced his first designs in 1865 were issued by many firms in this decade. Their rapid increase and eventual proliferation depended on the growing demand for books for the young as well as technical advances which facilitated production and kept the cost within the reach of most middle-class pockets. Leaning heavily as they did on fantasy and folk lore for their story-line, Victorian picture books mark the complete rout of the rationalists. Here, fairy tales which had been relegated to chap books where they were published in crudely printed and often drastically abbreviated form, finally re-emerged like butterflies from a chrysallis.[5]

Apart from some ABCs, other primers, and stories written by Crane himself and his sister Lucy, the choice of subjects for the books printed by Evans between 1865 and 1875 reflects this revival. Among the collections of stories first compiled in France in the late seventeenth century, Crane illustrated those written by Charles Perrault: *Cinderella, Little Red Riding Hood, Blue Beard, Puss in Boots* and *The Sleeping Beauty. The Yellow Dwarf, The Hind in the Wood* and *The Three Bears* were all written by Countess d'Aulnoy.[6] *A Gaping Wide-Mouth Waddling Frog, One, Two, Buckle My Shoe, The Fairy Ship* and *This Little Pig* were traditional English rhymes as were also the cumulative tales, *The House that Jack Built, Cock Robin* and *The Story of Jenny Wren.*[7] Translated from the French in the seventeenth century, the medieval romance of *Valentine and Orson* had long been familiar in Britain. *Ali Baba* and *Aladdin* came from the oriental compendium, the *Arabian Nights*, already popular in the West. *Goody Two Shoes* and *My Mother* were more recent inventions whose sentiments ensured their place in the nursery throughout the nineteenth century.[8]

The pioneer publisher of inexpensive picture books was Dean and Son, a firm which, in the 1840s, began to cater for a cheaper market than it had done before. They were among the earliest children's publishers to use chromolithography, though many of their products continued to be hand coloured even into the 1860s, by which time they also used Bewick's oil-colour process. The firm was ingenious in devising books intended, not for reading, but for colouring with moveable parts and dolls to dress. They were protected from 'Tommy Tearem' by being printed on linen but, in spite of their 'indestructability' they still had to fight for survival in a toy-box; and it is difficult to be specific about what was published in the decade before the picture book boom of the 1860s. An advertisement of 1858 described a new octavo sixpenny called 'Mama Lovechild's Series' 'each page embellished with large coloured pictures and cover in colours' which 'makes above 200 different sorts of Dean and Son's justly celebrated coloured sixpenny children's Toy-books, all of the same size'. This gives some idea of the quantity already issued. At Christmas, the same year, the first thirteen of a large folio-sized sixpenny series 'with coloured pictures and very little reading' was announced.[9] There followed the appearance of an increasing number of coloured children's book series, from a variety of publishers, catering for all levels of the market. Competition was extremely keen and by Christmas 1865 the boom was well under way.

'The books for babies current . . . – about 1865 to 1870 – of the cheaper sort called toy books were not very inspiring. These were generally careless and unimaginative woodcuts, very casually coloured by hand, dabs of pink and emerald green being laid across faces and frocks with a somewhat reckless aim. There was practically no choice between such as these and cheap German highly coloured lithographs.'[10]

This is how Crane later assessed the range of inexpensive nursery books available when he began to design them. He minimizes the efforts of good printers, other than Evans, such as Vizetelly and Vincent Brooks, who were working variations on Baxter's patent, and the reference to cheap coloured lithographs probably alludes to the firm of Kronheim which, by that date, was run by Oskar Frauenknecht whose standards were not as high as those of the firm's founder. Crane's comments on bright colour are critical of a generally held belief among publishers that the brighter the book the better suited to the taste of children. However, his earliest toy books are as brash as many of their companions in different series, and it was only gradually with Evans's help that this was modified, although Crane rarely made use of the very gentle colour harmonies printed by Evans for Kate Greenaway.

Walter Crane's earliest toy books reveal his skill as an animal draughtsman. The characters in the first, *The History of Jenny Wren* (see p. 36), are drawn with a naturalist's attention to detail and yet are treated in a sympathetic and comical way guaranteed to make an immediate appeal to children. This was one of three titles

The House that Jack Built, 1865, engraved and printed in colour by Edmund Evans. By courtesy of Liverpool City Libraries.

illustrated by Crane for a New Shilling Series issued by Ward Lock and Tyler at Christmas 1865.[11] All were printed by Evans. *Jenny Wren* was prepared with a black key and backgrounds, a practice quite common in picture book printing at the time, and three colours, red, brown and green. The gold overprinting of the backgrounds in the surviving examples may have been added to relieve what originally must have been a very sombre colour scheme. Crane's designs are well balanced but the amount of stippling and hatching on the key block shows how unfamiliar he was with the effects of colour printing. The other two books were printed in five colours and a black key, *The House That Jack Built* having bright blue backgrounds with pictures printed in ochre, red, green and brown. The result is quite crude and, as with *Jenny Wren*, confused by too much texture drawing on the key block. Crane remedied this fault by the time he came to design the *Comical Cat* with its clear outline and minimal furry texturing. This picture toy has cheerful red backgrounds. A design such as that of the 'Fox and Cock' in *The House That Jack Built* shows the young artist following a fairly traditional line of animal drawing and in this respect he is every bit as accomplished as well established animal draughtsmen like J. B. Zwecker and T. W. Wood. Other pages are more remarkable for a new wit and vitality and Crane may well have been influenced by Grandville's amusing interpretations published in *Scènes de la vie privée et publique des animaux* of 1842. *The Comical Cat* has a surprising gay abandon and her large scale and anthropomorphic role are oddly disconcerting. She is, nevertheless, a more sympathetic companion for children than the sinister inhabitants of Katzland illustrated by Baxter's former pupil, Harrison Weir, for *The Cat's Tea Party*, one of Routledge's New Shilling Series of Toy Books printed by Vincent Brooks, which also came out at Christmas 1865.[12]

49

Crane and Evans worked for Warne as well as Ward Lock at this time. In 1864, Crane had designed two frontispieces which were printed in colour for Warne's 32mo series, for books by S. Warner, *Maggie's Christmas* and *Gertrude and Lily, or Good Resolutions*. In the following year he drew more colour designs, this time for a new series of sixpenny alphabets in oblong octavo.[13] These were followed in 1866 by work for a new Aunt Friendly series in imperial 16mo at threepence each. This series included twelve titles and Crane was responsible for the six designs to *Cock Robin's Death and Burial*, two pages of which are signed with his monogram. Thus in his first two years of working for children's books he completed at least two sets of designs to the Cock Robin story.

The firm of Routledge soon took over the publication of Crane's designs for children and by 1875 this totalled twenty-nine picture books in the sixpenny toy range and eight at one shilling. The dating of these presents certain difficulties, but it is fairly clear that their publication followed the pattern described in Appendix B. For a good many years the firm of Routledge, Warne and Routledge had published Sixpenny Toys in their Aunt Mavor series[14] and this continued under George Routledge and Sons, but the Aunt Mavor title was gradually dropped. Many of the original books of this series continued in print and in later lists are included on the back of Sixpenny Toys. Crane's first Routledge contributions, *The Railroad* and *The Farmyard Alphabets*, are numbered 37 and 40. This numbering is consistent with Crane's Toy Books, which is a help in confirming sequences and dating. Gaps between numbers signify books designed by others. The only point at which numbering runs consecutively for more than four titles (his maximum annual output in the original Sixpenny Series) is for the twelve numbers of the new Sixpenny Series of Walter Crane's Toy Books beginning in 1873 (Nos 103–113) and it may be concluded from this that these were the only Sixpenny Toys issued over these years. The sequence is interrupted before *The Sleeping Beauty* at No. 116 after Crane disputed the terms of his contract and when Routledge realized they must once again call on other designers.

All this work was carried out with Evans's collaboration. The success of these books owed more to him than just good colour printing because he consulted Crane about the original choice of subject, advised on page layouts and then, finally, carried the transaction through with the publishers. An idea of how he acted as the younger man's artistic agent may be had from a letter written by Evans probably before Christmas 1867 when *Multiplication Table* was published:

My dear Sir,

   I cannot get Routledges to look at the book or anything for which you make sketches, they say they will not 'till after Christmas. However, I am so short of work for some of my engravers I will venture on one of them. I think the Grammar the safest as a companion to Multiplication Table. So kindly let me have two or three of these as soon as done.

In haste,

Yours faithfully . . .[15]

As a financial proposition these picture books seem to have been something of a liability to the publishers who always maintained they had to print large editions, at least ten thousand, in order merely to cover cost and show minimum profit. The designer was given one payment for his drawings, usually a small sum. Crane received £12 for *Chattering Jack*.[16] At this early stage the procedure still involved drawing the final design on the blocks. It was not until Evans began to transfer it from paper to block using photography that he was able to keep the original drawings. Having pulled a proof off the key, Evans handed it back to be coloured before preparing the colour blocks. He printed in shades mixed from the same powdered pigment as that used by the artist for the coloured proof. Evans may have begun to work for this picture book market in the same capacity as for yellow backs: that is, printing covers only. Routledge's Aunt Mavor Sixpennies were originally hand-painted and continued to be so up to the time when Evans assisted with their printing. A hand coloured example, *The Three Bears,* which was No. 17 in the series, was re-issued around 1865 with a cover printed in colour by Evans.[17] New Aunt Mavor Sixpenny Toys of this date were large octavo with six coloured pages and a yellow or orange cover printed in two or three colours. Three colours (including the key) became standard for Crane covers printed by Evans up until No. 100 in 1872. He followed the yellow back pattern using red and blue with black, then red and green with black, on an orange or yellow paper. Inside there were variations on the number of colour blocks used. These will be discussed in due course.

The stylistic development of Crane's colour work for Routledge reveals increasing fluency and confidence as he learned how to make the most of printed colour and to exploit his own talents as an imaginative and decorative draughts-man. He handled the animal subjects of the first Sixpenny Toy, *The Farmyard ABC*, with his accustomed dexterity, but the ABC aspect involved a design problem which resulted in both this and its successor, *The Railroad ABC*, appearing relatively restrained in comparison with the bright bold designs for Ward Lock.[18] The Routledge format was narrower and Evans's colour printing more limited. Both have key designs in black on a white ground, *The Farmyard ABC* with red, yellow and green, and the *Railroad ABC* with red and blue. The large alphabet letters are not particularly impressive and contribute less than they might have done to a strong page design. He carefully researched railway details for the second book but, despite this, something of the stiffness affecting Crane's drawing of everyday life scenes is still evident.

The next two books, *Sing a Song of Sixpence* and *The Waddling Frog*, were un-hindered by ABCs and Crane found himself dealing with themes open to more lively and imaginative interpretation. The pages are unframed and emphasis is concentrated on the appropriate figures, animals and accessories. Lines from the rhymes appear at the top of each page in thin Gothic lettering headed by a large initial. He considered *Sing a Song of Sixpence* his first successful attempt at more careful design. In *The House That Jack Built* there had already been an opportunity to introduce medieval decorative features and these also add to the quality and characterisation of his deft drawing for *A Song of Sixpence* (see p. 44). This Pre-Raphaelite legacy was one that the young illustrator was to find useful, for many of the picture books, including *The Old Courtier*, the next to be published, are full of details of gothic architecture, mounted knights, falconry and feasting.

The titles issued in 1867 and 1868 show Crane and Evans experimenting with more subtle colour, but the results in *The Old Courtier* are unsatisfactory. Evans printed here using tint blocks of purple, blue and yellow and the effect does not help to unify or give emphasis to Crane's busy designs, which are further confused by the need to accommodate large portions of text. *Multiplication Table* and *Chattering Jack* are less complicated. The 'Ten Steamboats' and 'Twenty-Two Ships' pages of the former are fine designs, probably deriving from studies made on a visit to Plymouth the previous summer. A similar combination of semi-geometrical principles and shallow illusory space appears in parts of *Chattering Jack* like the 'slice' of modern life in the page with a staircase and abruptly truncated foreground figures. Of the Crane Sixpenny Toys issued in the next year,

How Jessie was Lost appeals least, being a feeble story, badly told by Lucy Crane and not visually interesting. On the other hand, the everyday life themes in *Grammar in Rhyme* are quite entertaining and its design is more confident. Pale shades contrast with stronger accents achieved by overprinting the hatched key colour with blue or red. Both these numbers were printed in a dark brown key and three primaries.

It is in the next two toy books, *Buckle My Shoe* and *Annie and Jack in London*, that Crane achieves a fully integrated decorative style. The same colours are used with the addition of a flesh tone, which does away with the striped effect created in earlier books by printing fine red lines to suggest pink, and there are fewer tint effects and more flat colours. Dark accents cover larger areas and are positive factors in creating bold design. A clue to a new factor affecting this change is to be found in a page of *Buckle My Shoe* which has a screen decorated with a design from a Japanese print. The confident outline, diagonal compositions and use of bold page patterns show the important influence of Japanese prints. For the first

Conjunctions join the words together from *Grammar in Rhyme*, 1868, printed in colour by Edmund Evans. By courtesy of Cambridge University Library.

Eleven, Twelve, Ring the Bell, from *One, Two, Buckle my Shoe*, 1868, printed in colour by Edmund Evans. By courtesy of Cambridge University Library.

time Crane is explicit about choosing artistic furniture for his interiors. Blue and white crockery, ebonised clocks and chairs make their own comment on Japanese influences affecting English taste. It is more difficult to see these characteristics in the active pages of *Annie and Jack* – a story by Lucy Crane about children visiting the sights of London – except that they too take on a new assurance with strong outline and confident arrangements of figures against coloured or plain backgrounds. Crane had been given some Toyokuni prints by a naval lieutenant recently returned from Japan. This occurred at an opportune moment because he had not yet resolved the style and presentation of his own picture books. The 'definite black outline and flat brilliant as well as delicate colours, vivid dramatic and decorative feeling'[19] of the woodcuts provided him with the very example needed, and he began to apply these characteristics to the treatment of the historical and humorous subjects of toy books and to the techniques of wood engraving for machine printing.

Almonds in the
hold;

The four books published in 1870, *The Fairy Ship, The Adventures of Puffy, This Little Pig went to Market* and *King Luckieboy's Party* owe an obvious debt to Japan in their new compositional freedom and large areas of bright (but not garish) flat colour. Though still using three primaries, a key and a flesh tint, Evans now set off bright colours against softened blues and greens achieved through subtle texturing of the block and overprinting. Every page of *The Fairy Ship* is delightful, with pompous Captain Duck and his bustling and conscientious crew of white mice attending to the satin sails, and cargo of raisins and almonds. *Puffy*, whose story was written by Lucy Crane, presented greater problems with its longer text. To include this the pages were divided into compartments, a device which possibly also owes something to Japanese methods. The five *Little Pigs* are less elaborate, but distinguished by a truly impressive fleshy grandeur, made all the more ridiculous by their pinafores, ruffs and breeches, and their demure domestic setting (see p. 45). *King Luckieboy's Party* illustrates a rhyme written by Crane himself and based on the idea of the months and the zodiac signs presenting their compliments to Luckieboy. Such a theme, lending itself as it did to fantastic personifications, was to prove a favourite with him. Some of the designs are strikingly impressive with their quaint figures set against backgrounds of flat colour. The effect is bolder than is usual in Japanese prints and in this respect he may also have been influenced by recent English book illustrations like the decorative chromolithographed gift books *Paradise and the Peri* (1860), and *Scenes from the Winter's Tale* (1866), designed by Owen Jones with figures by Albert Warren. Crane's style of around 1869 is even closer to the work of Henry Stacy Marks which he specifically admired for the 'bold outlines and flat tints'[20] of two toy books published as part of Routledge's Shilling Series in 1865, *Nursery Rhymes* and *Nursery Songs*, each including six full colour pages printed by Vincent Brooks. Crane's earliest books have little in common with these designs and it is only in the simplified style of those of a few years later that the connection becomes more obvious. He was brought directly into contact with this work around 1869 when Routledge had him design a cover for a composite volume to contain reprints of the *Rhymes* and *Songs*, called *Ridiculous Rhymes*, which was published for Christmas 1869.[21] In Crane's view the medieval character of these illustrations almost certainly added to their charm. His debt to them can be seen in a page like the 'Old King Cole' design for Cassell's *The Merrie Heart* (1871), a book containing six colour plates printed by Evans with black-and-white work by other artists. This shows, too, how Crane's own tendency to load his pages with decoration and detail has prevailed, in spite of the lessons in economy which he might have learned from Stacy Marks or from Japanese prints.

The excellent sales of Walter Crane's toy books encouraged Routledge in 1870 to begin to issue composite volumes of several titles, and the rapid consumption of these were proof of the artist's well established popularity as a children's illustrator. In 1873 Routledge began the New Series of Walter Crane's Toy Books at sixpence, following it in the next year with the Shilling Series. A new cover was designed for each: one with a Crane in a blossoming tree and an audience of birds with little children's heads printed in green, black and red on buff; the other with an orange tree printed in two shades of blue and orange on white. The pictures inside were produced somewhat differently from the earlier numbers of the original series and instead of a flat flesh tone, Evans used a hatched flesh colour with denser spots for cheeks, while he continued with the same number of colour blocks – a brownish red, a greyish blue, and yellow, with black or brown key. *Noah's Ark ABC* the very last of the original Sixpenny Toys is a puzzling book stylistically, having weaker outline and less assured design than its immediate

55

predecessors. It seems also to represent a transitional stage in Evans's change of flesh tone printing. Here a hatched brown is used to describe the dark-skinned natives and also for the texture of animals' coats.

The preparation of the new Sixpenny Series coincided with Walter Crane's marriage and his visit to Italy, which lasted from September 1871 until May 1873. Several sets of designs were made in Rome during the winter 1872–3 and these included *Old Mother Hubbard*, whose poodle reflects current Roman dog-owning fashion. This book was published in 1874 though the author's statement regarding its design is borne out by a page signed 1873. Once again it is perhaps easiest to follow the numbering of the books as a guide in estimating when they were designed. The earliest, *My Mother*, relates most closely to the original series in its relatively bold uncluttered style. The blissful domestic atmosphere of these illustrations for Ann Taylor's poem may owe something to Crane's newly-wedded state, though they clearly refer to England, not Italy, and some designs may derive from studies made on a visit to his fiancée at Hastings in June 1871. She had already appeared in *King Luckieboy* and is the model for the young mother and daughter-in-law in *My Mother*. While in Italy, Crane benefited from the use Evans now made of photography to transfer drawings on to wood blocks. It was necessary only to send his ink drawings to Evans who returned the proofs ready to be coloured. From this date Crane kept his original finished designs.

Ideas already adopted or invented by Crane are further developed in the picture books of 1873 and 1874: interiors with painted tiles, potted plants and ebonised furniture; elaborate historical costumes and architectural settings; a style involving black as an important decorative element in the rich pattern of the page and the pages themselves framed in a black line with a separate compartment for the text. Animals like the peevish bears who so terrify poor Silverlocks[22] as ever play an important part. Some of the richest effects are achieved through quite unorthodox juxtapositions of styles. Owen Jones's works on ornament, Japanese prints, English MSS, early printed books, Renaissance painting – all may have sown the seeds which blossom in profusion in the picture books; but no child nor even an art-historically anxious adult would wish to alter Ali Baba's orient, or inhibit Valentine and Orson's time-travelling in Dark Age France and the Egypt of the Pharaohs. A fine feature of these toy books is the centre spread for which, in the case of *Cinderella, Valentine and Orson* and *Puss in Boots*, Crane drew splendid sequences. Italian influence, discernible in the glimpses of orange trees, cypresses and heraldic devices in *Valentine and Orson*, is very marked in the Renaissance settings of *Bluebeard* and the Titianesque gowns of his wife and her maidservants. In the last of all the Series, he transfers an essentially Gothic French tale to the Mediterranean. The Sleeping Beauty rests in a Roman palace guarded by a maiden, a harper and soldiers. An owl in a spandrel and poppy in a pot symbolize sleep, while the prince struggles through the thicket, his pose like that of a Michelangelesque slave, clad in leather armour and wearing a sun-decorated mazzocho (see p. 40).

Less dense black is used in the books of 1875, the key is often brown, and a more nervous mellifluous line replaces the confident, sometimes quite angular emphasis of earlier books like *The Three Bears*. A technique, to be seen as early as the *Merrie Heart* pages, where leaves and grass texture are indicated by little dots or strokes, is used more often. Obvious geometry is softened by the text now being framed in a parchment scroll instead of a box. Burne-Jones and Botticelli, whose *Spring* and *Venus* Crane sought out on his visit to the Uffizi in 1871, are sources for this style and the flower-strewn grassy carpets and fruit-laden trees derive from these or other Quattrocento examples, although the exaggerated ideal profiles, rather boneless limbs and fleshy tapering hands suggest the mannerism of the Cinquecento. Even spatial arrangements depending on perspective

Jack tip-toeing past the sleeping Giant, 1875, drawing in pen, ink and water colour, 8¼ × 13½ in. (209 × 336 cm) for the centre page of *Jack and the Beanstalk*. By courtesy of the Victoria and Albert Museum.

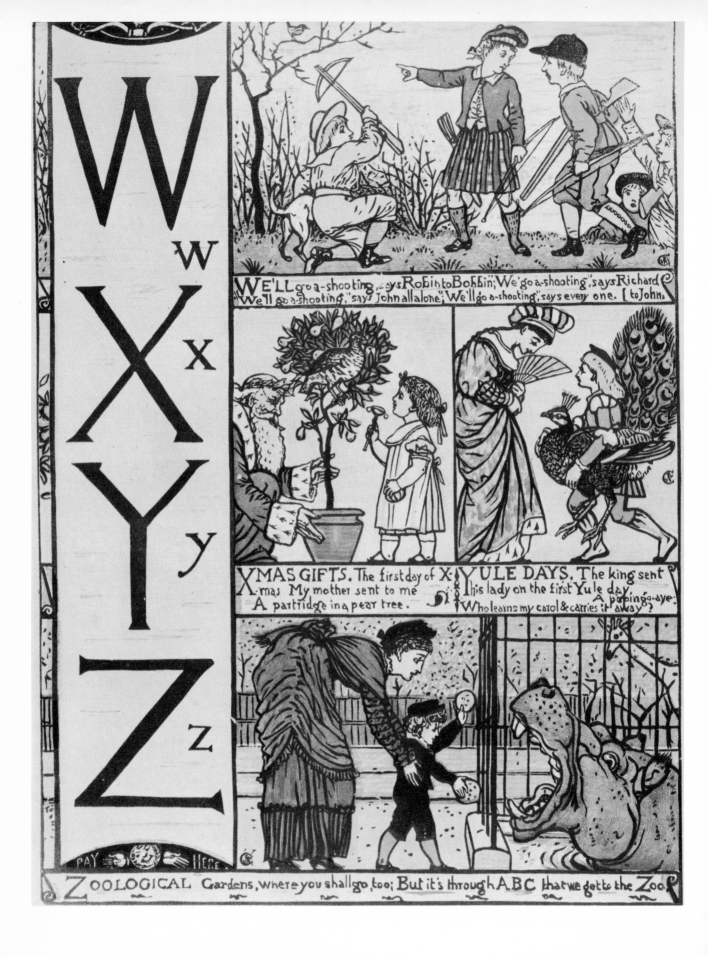

Toutebelle's rescue from *The Yellow Dwarf*, 1875, printed in colour by Edmund Evans. Photograph Peter Adamson.

rather than a frieze system become quixotically extreme in such settings as the centre spread of *The Yellow Dwarf* with its gigantic turkey-cocks, or its final page with the goose-drawn chariot and the tiny figure of Toutebelle by the steel castle.

The Shilling Series is the same as that to which Harrison Weir and Stacy Marks had contributed and in it Crane had greater scope than with the Sixpenny Toys. The format was larger and text was printed on separate pages. The colour range was extended too: in addition to a dark brown key, Evans printed in six colours – usually flesh tone, buff, yellow, red and two shades of blue.

In 1874, *The Frog Prince, Goody Two Shoes, Beauty and the Beast* and *The Alphabet of Old Friends* were issued. Crane designed six pictorial alphabets for Routledge: *The Railroad, Farmyard* and *Noah's Ark* ABCs of 1865 and 1872 which may be said to subscribe to a fairly traditional pattern, and *The Absurd Alphabet* (1874), *The Baby's Own Alphabet* and *Alphabet of Old Friends* (1875) in which he explores different ideas of layout using more flexible subject matter taken from nursery rhymes and stories. The animal characters of the *Absurd ABC* are set in vertical compartments printed in red and yellow, with gold letters, against a black ground. The rollicking mood of these pages is close to contemporary designs by Crane for the coloured covers of Beeton's Humorous Books, also printed by Evans.

Opposite
W X Y Z page from *Baby's Own Alphabet*, 1875 printed in colour by Edmund Evans. By courtesy of Cambridge University Library.

The ABCs of 1875 are less hilarious but still funny and more artistic in colouring than their absurd forerunner. The sixpenny version, *The Baby's Own ABC*, presents a wealth of witty material in scenes organized in comic strip form, their captions below, and letters on a ladder down one side. The sumptuous shilling *Alphabet of Old Friends* introduces many nursery favourites in a variety of page layouts punctuated with gold roundels carrying the capitals. However, it is for the beast fairy-tales in the Shilling Series that Crane produces some of his finest designs: *Beauty and the Beast* and *The Frog Prince* are rich in decorative detail and convey also, in contrast to their obvious glamour, a real sense of horrific fantasy. Beauty's discomfiture, so well expressed by her despairing countenance and lash-frilled eyes, and the control of design in the perspective interior of the page where Froggy visits his beloved, are just two examples of this masterly handling. Crane's uninhibited enjoyment in such pictorial fantasy is equally obvious from the exotic creations of 1875: *Aladdin, Princess Belle Etoile, The Hind in the Wood* and *The Yellow Dwarf*.

When the contract for the Sixpenny Toys ended, Crane offered to continue if granted a royalty but Routledge refused. Together with Evans the artist planned a new book which appeared before Christmas 1876. *The Baby's Opera* marks the beginning of a new chapter in the story of Crane's illustration for children. Editions of the original toy books continued in print for years to come. As late as 1894 Evans had a considerable stock of printed sheets ready for shilling sets, having been in the habit of supplying them to Routledge and Sons. This fact emerges from a correspondence between Walter Crane and John Lane when the latter was negotiating the reprinting of the picture books in composite volumes with new title-pages and end-papers by the artist.[23] These were issued between 1895 and 1914 and it is an amazing testimony to the life of boxwood blocks that these late printings do not seem to be impaired. In August 1909, Crane signed over the rights for twenty-seven Toy Books and all blocks, designs and texts, to John Lane for £300. He continued to expect his publishers to respect his work and wrote angrily about the three 'miniature editions' of 1914, whose end-papers had been coloured in by another hand and block letters, a kind he never used, put in their place. The popularity of the toy books was by no means limited to Britain, but extended to the Continent and across the Atlantic where firms had soon brought out pirated editions.[24]

Picture books were appreciated not only in the nursery but by adults in the parlour and library and even by artists and architects who used them to give clients an idea of the way in which their own homes could be decorated. They were a readily available source of ideas for those following the latest modes of the Aesthetic Movement. Routledge had at first been anxious lest Crane's designs would reflect avant-garde sympathies, and had asked him not to make his heroines look like Pre-Raphaelite girls with masses of long hair.[25] Soon the pages of the picture books were characterized by his own unique blend of detail and decoration in which lively narrative was held captive in brilliant kaleidoscopic designs. Despite the obvious enjoyment derived from this work, it was not a self indulgent artistic exercise. Crane wanted to please the children. He had none of his own when he began to design picture books, but he was not long in forming ideas about what was suitable and these show a sensitive understanding of the child's point of view in keeping with the changing Victorian attitude:

> Children, like the ancient Egyptians, appear to see most things in profile, and like definite statement in design. They prefer well defined forms and bright frank colour. They don't want to bother about three dimension. They

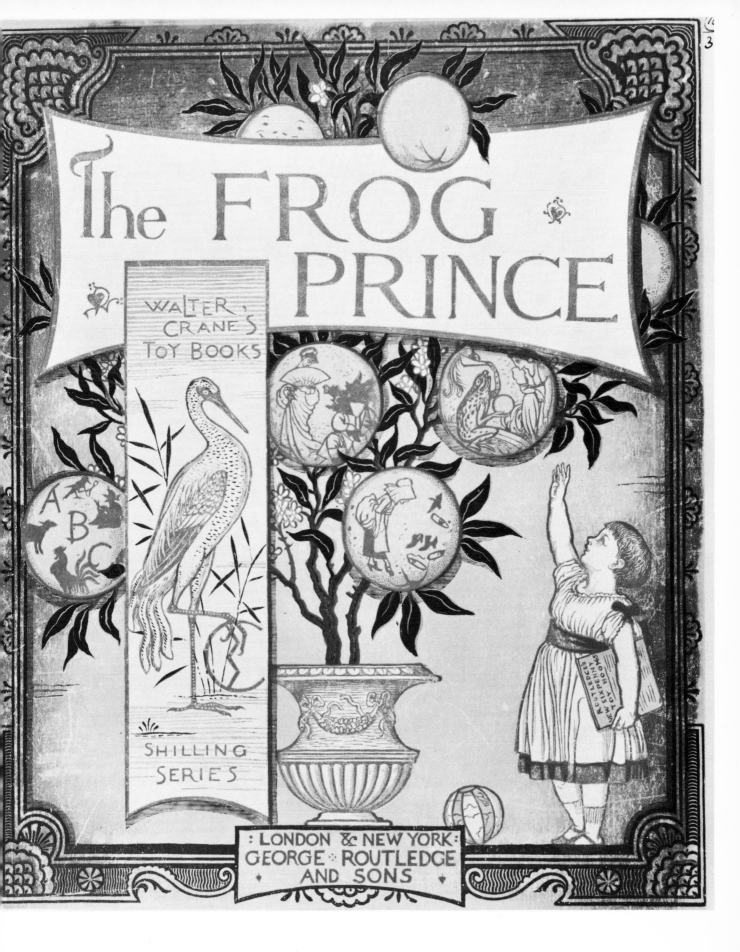

The FROG PRINCE

WALTER CRANE'S TOY BOOKS

SHILLING SERIES

: LONDON & NEW YORK :
GEORGE · ROUTLEDGE
AND SONS

The little disaster from *Baby's Bouquet*, 1878, printed in colour by Edmund Evans.

Where are you going to my pretty maid? from *Baby's Opera*, 1877, printed in colour by Edmund Evans.

can accept symbolic representations. They themselves employ drawing . . .
as a kind of picture-writing, and eagerly follow a pictured story. When they
can count they can check your quantities, so that the artist must be careful to
deliver, in dealing with, for instance . . . 'The Song of Sixpence', his tale of
twenty-four blackbirds.

Educationally, the picture books served a key function because children could
learn 'definite ideas from good pictures' long before they could read or write.
Crane is most characteristically a man of his age in the importance he attached to
the imagination in a child's early development. Later, when artists like Arthur
Rackham peopled their pages of books for the young with Gothic ghouls and
bogeys he was anxious that they should not have too disturbing an effect on the
young, but he put no curb on the artist appealing to a child's imagination 'in a
healthy way'. The imagination freed both the childlike and the artistic spirit:

The best of designing for children is that the imagination and fancy may be let
loose and roam freely, and there is always room for humour and even pathos,
sure of being followed by that ever-living sense of wonder and romance in
the child heart – a heart which in some cases, happily, never grows up or
grows old.[26]

Painting: 1860-80

Crane's first submission to the Royal Academy in 1862, 'The Lady of Shalott' was noticed by Tom Taylor, art critic of *The Times*, as 'the work of a young and rising artist'. It was a promising beginning to a chequered painting career. Only once again, ten years later, was his work accepted at the Academy. He showed at the Dudley, the Grosvenor Gallery, and later at the New and Old Water Colour Societies and the New Gallery but his pictures never became favourites with the English public. Although his work as a designer earned him his living, Crane always claimed that painting was his greatest love.

Early sketchbooks reveal a haphazard art education. He made studies from Charles Bell's popular *Anatomy and Philosophy of Expression* and often referred to books on the history of art and architecture as well as works at first hand in the British Museum, the National Gallery and at South Kensington. Jottings of drapery, figures in modern and medieval dress mingle with carefully transcribed passages from reviews on entirely non-artistic subjects, revealing a diversity of intellectual interests encouraged by Linton and Wise. Crane learned the rudiments of oil painting from his father but in his earlier work he preferred to use water colour and gouache, the medium of 'The Lady of Shalott'.[1] The titles and descriptions of his work before 1867 suggest that interest in the Pre-Raphaelites led him to choose subjects from Tennyson and Keats already depicted by the Brotherhood. 'The Lady of Shalott' was bought by a cloth manufacturer from Selkirk who commissioned a sequel, 'The Lady of Shalott at Camelot' (1863), and after this he bought an 'Eve of St Agnes' (1864),[2] and another Keatsian subject, 'La Belle Dame Sans Merci' (1865). For the costumes, Crane consulted J. Strutt's *Complete View of the Dress and Habits of the People of England* and the Pre-Raphaelites' favourite reference book, Henry Shaw's *Dress and Decorations of the Middle Ages*. Some sketch book drawings, like that of a little minstrel from the Harleian manuscript *Roman de la Rose*, are in colour and have pencilled notes which suggest that he must have checked out this work at the British Museum as well as looking the illustration up in Shaw's second volume.[3] He also visited the Tower of London to study armour. Crane knew about Ruskin's defence of the Pre-Raphaelites and *Pre-Raphaelitism* (1851), *The Elements of Drawing* (1857) and *Modern Painters* Volume I (1843) were in his father's library. For a time eloquent passages from these works encouraged him to try 'little subjects with setting suns in them, groups of cows standing in water, and such like pictorial material', modelled on the Turner steel engravings in Samuel Rogers' *Italy*. From this he went on to attempt to follow Ruskin's ideas about truth to nature by 'drawing trees with every leaf showing'. In his studies of birds and animals he sought a similar kind of scientific naturalism.

Landscape was an equally important preoccupation in these early years. At the time of this first visit to Derbyshire in 1863, he was working on general views and cloud studies, in which the precise colours and times of day were noted. Most of these were in pencil, others in colour wash. His research was quite intensive; sometimes drawings made in the early morning or evening have only a few minutes between them. This procedure parallels Constable's methods as well as those of Ruskin whose final volume of *Modern Painters* (1860) analyzed clouds in enthusiastic detail. However, Crane's perception of nature lacks the passionate intensity of Ruskin's and by 1865 he had generalized the process of landscape painting into a system involving two outline studies: one of basic landscape features on to which the shadow effects of a fleeting moment could be washed in; and one to take general tone and colour. More detailed research was also useful but he noted that 'the picture can be proceeded with after the first two studies . . . This will be a great saving of time should there be much wet weather . . . Last year on wet days I was at a standstill with my pictures because I painted them all out of doors.' He thought it best to finish a painting while still in the neighbourhood for an impression of 'local truth', and that figures and animals should be added afterwards – a procedure calculated to depress any real spontaneity.[4] This method can be seen in the background of 'The Hunt', a water colour of July 1867, which has soft-textured trees and is atmospherically indeterminate. Thus in spite of conscientious aspirations in a Ruskinian direction, Crane began to find himself naturally drawn towards generalisations inspired by a gentle poetry very different from the style of the Turner vignettes or the precision of early Millais and Holman Hunt. The soft forms and opaque technique in 'The Hunt' resemble Burne-Jones's Surrey landscapes of the 1860s and the natural settings of figure paintings like 'The Merciful Knight' and 'Green Summer'.

'The Merciful Knight' was one of four paintings with which Edward Burne-Jones made his debut at the Old Water Colour Society in 1864. These and subsequent exhibits were a revelation to Crane and his friends.

> We had a glimpse into a magic world of romance and pictured poetry, peopled with ghosts of 'ladies dead and lovely knights', – a twilight world of dark mysterious woodlands, haunted streams, meads of deep green starred with burning flowers, veiled in a dim and mystic light, and stained with low-toned crimson and gold.[5]

Most of Crane's group were young artists studying at South Kensington or the Royal Academy Schools and they lived in Bloomsbury not far from his home in Argyle Square. They did not form an official clique but shared the same sort of artistic aims. The results of their labours were to be seen at the annual shows of the Dudley Gallery whose first spring water colour exhibition was held in the Egyptian Hall, Piccadilly, in 1865. Among those on the selection committee were W. S. Coleman, Henry Moore, Poynter, Arthur and Walter Severn and Tom Taylor. The St John's Wood School, including Stacy Marks, joined by invitation in the following year. 'The Dudley' was a welcome exhibiting space for amateurs who were not members of either of the well-established water colour societies, or known at the Royal Academy.

Walter Crane was later invited to join its committee but his first contribution to a Spring exhibition was in 1866, with a scene called 'Twilight'. Next year he showed 'Sunrise – Cawsand Bay, Cornwall' and 'Old Morton Hall, Cheshire' and, in 1868, a topographical view from Hazelford of 'North Leas Hall' as well as three paintings which had lines of verse in place of prosaic titles. It was for this kind of work that Crane and his friends were dubbed the 'Poetry-without-Grammar School'. They even had their own poet, Montgomerie Ranking, whose verse appears in the Dudley catalogue of 1866 accompanying a picture by Robert Bateman, an artist considered by Crane to be the leader of the group. Others in the set were Edward Clifford, Ellis Wooldridge, T. Blake Wrigman, E. H. Fahey and A. Sachaverell Coke. They were enthusiastic about the past and regarded mechanised modern life with horror. Crane's own imaginative pictures were essentially idylls of escape. An *Art Journal* critic of 1868 described him as swooning away 'into delicious sentimentality of colour and morbid mannerism'. In this orgy of poetical sentiment Crane and his friends were emulating Burne-Jones. Their chief source of inspiration was his early gouache paintings. Although he could see his work on exhibition, Crane had not yet met Burne-Jones and his only contact with his circle was Simeon Solomon who was considered by many critics to be one of the most eccentric exhibitors at the Dudley. Crane along with many of the young Bloomsbury painters visited his Charlotte Street studio where he was impressed by the range of invention to be seen in a large sketchbook kept by the artist.[6]

Figure drawings demanded skilful draughtsmanship which could be achieved only after hours of drawing from a model, a training prepared for in the Academy Schools by first working from plaster casts. Crane had none of this experience and after finishing his apprenticeship he tried to make up for it by going to classes at Heatherley's at 79 Newman Street. Until 1860 these had been run by 'dagger Leigh' whose sharp criticism benefited promising young artists like Fred Walker, Stacy Marks and Simeon Solomon. T. J. Heatherley who glided about 'in a ghostly way through the classrooms in slippers and wearing a sort of long gaberdine' was a gentle but not very effectual master. Nevertheless, his teaching certainly helped Crane improve his figure studies and, in the absence of paintings surviving from the early 1860s, this is best judged from drawings like 'Samson and the Lion' and 'Treasure Trove'. Heatherley's also gave him the chance to enjoy the fellowship of young artists working together; something which he had missed as an apprentice but which he soon shared with his Bloomsbury friends. They would occasionally employ their own model and were delighted when they managed to secure the services of Burne-Jones's 'Astrologia', Miss Augusta Jones.

At the Dudley in 1870, Crane showed 'Ormuzd and Ahriman' a painting begun two years earlier. Its subject, the contest between the ancient Persian theological powers of good and evil, was suggested by his reading Max Muller's recently published essays on the science of religion, *Chips from a German Workshop*. But he also wished to convey new philosophical ideas and meant this picture to illustrate the evolutionary principles discussed in the yet controversial writings of Charles Darwin and Herbert Spencer. He read Spencer's *First Principles* shortly after its publication in 1862 and this was probably his first encounter with the idea that history reflects an evolutionary process in which society's development is marked by epochs of conflict alternating with peace and consolidation. In 'Ormuzd and Ahriman' this is seen as an unending combat between good and evil forces represented by the white and black mounted knights. Behind them the River of Time winds past the ruins of ancient civilizations, witnesses of the same struggle in days gone by. Power and beauty are transient and symbolised by the crowned skeleton clutching a sceptre. Reviewing the picture, an *Art Journal* critic considered that it showed 'much thought and poetic imagination' and that its landscape background was 'not unworthy of Perugino, and the more earnest of the Pre-Raphaelite painters'. The developmental approach to history shown in this painting also reflects the theories of the French philosopher, Auguste Comte, the Positivist, whose work had in its turn influenced Spencer and J. S. Mill. It was the work of Mill, discovered through Wise, which, with that of Spencer, Darwin

Ormuzd and Ahriman, signed with
a monogram and dated 1868–70,
water colour and gouache,
10¾ × 29¾ in. (273 × 756 cm).
Collection Charles Jerdein.

and Shelley, set Crane on the road towards becoming a free-thinker. As a painter, young Walter Crane was not concerned with the intricacies of Comte and Spencer's philosophical methods, but he did glean from them the optimistic notion that social progress was possible and he looked around for appropriate images to illustrate it. Shortly after 'Ormuzd and Ahriman', he painted a pilgrim in a similar setting, a work which was later given to another admirer of Comte, Frederic Harrison, who christened it 'The Positivist Pilgrim'.

In other pictures of this time Crane made use of legends more specifically associated with children's stories, where symbolism and colourful fantasy are often vividly united. Fairy tales invariably concern basic human beliefs and fears, with the forces of good and evil personified. An example of this is the water colour 'The Three Paths', exhibited at the Old Bond Street Gallery in Spring 1870, which is based on an illustration completed for a story called 'Charmshine' in *King Gab's Story Bag*. This concerns a princess won by a prince brave enough to take the most difficult path through a dark wood. Although the figures in 'The Three Paths' are more classically attired than in his 'Charmshine' illustration, they were considered to be an example of Crane's ultra medievalism and he was generally held to be one of a band of medieval eccentrics, including Spencer Stanhope, Solomon, Bateman and Wooldridge, who made regular appearances at the Dudley.

His fascination with the northern gothic tradition did not exclude an interest in the classical heritage of the West. In 1865 he looked up various books on sculpture and classical antiquity on his visits to the British Museum Reading Room. This interest may well have been stimulated by the newly restored Elgin Marbles on show at the Museum. Among several young English artists inspired by this sculpture was Albert Moore, whose painting 'The Marble Seat' was on view at the Academy the same year. The work of J. A. Ingres had also impressed Crane in 1862 when he saw 'La Source' at the Great Exhibition, and he may have seen more of his work when he was in Paris in 1866 and went to the Louvre to worship 'at the shrine of the Venus de Milo'. Ingres' death in 1867 and the exhibitions which followed it encouraged a further reappraisal of classicism in

67

English art circles, and it was at this time that Whistler joined Albert Moore in painting Graeco-Japanese pictures[7]. Classical themes were also treated by Burne-Jones who in 1865 began to illustrate *The Earthly Paradise* the epic poem by William Morris – that 'Hellenist of the Middle Age'[8] – whose images of Venus, Cupid and Psyche were to provide inspiration for much of Burne-Jones's later work.

By comparison with Moore's robust images and Burne-Jones's elegant Pygmalian Series of 1868, Crane's own little 'Venus and Cupid' of the same year is a very tentative essay in classicism.[9] Nevertheless, Venus's dependence on Greek proportion is obvious even though she is decorously draped and the smoking fire and woody setting evoke an atmosphere of gothic mystery which is closer in

The Three Paths, signed with a monogram and dated 1869, water colour, 18 × 12 in. (457 × 305 cm). By courtesy of the Victoria and Albert Museum.

mood to Burne-Jones and Solomon than the decorative paintings of Moore or Whistler. The colour harmony of gold and russet with white set against the dark grass and verticals of the trees closely resembles Burne-Jones's colour harmonies at this time. Similar tonal control can be seen in Crane's water colours of the Elements of 1868. The three female personifications, Water, Air and Earth, with their loose, soft hair and wide-spaced eyes are again reminiscent of Burne-Jones or Simeon Solomon. These four units comprise a harmony in blue-green (the basic colour for the female panels) and gold, which is the key for the male personification of Fire – a figure which has a quite surprising Blake-like quality, possibly inspired by Swinburne's new book on the English mystic.[10]

In the late 1860s, one of Crane's painter friends opened a picture shop in Wigmore Street. Here his work attracted the attention of George Howard (the future Earl of Carlisle) who trained under Giovanni Costa and Alphonse Legros at the South Kensington School of Art. The first of Howard's many kind acts was to introduce Crane to Burne-Jones, William Morris, and others among his distinguished artistic circle.[11] Crane is not specific about the date of these introductions, but he remembered their circumstances and both took place before he went to Italy in 1871. George Howard took him along to meet Burne-Jones at the Grange and the visit made a deep impression on the young man.

Morris he probably met in the late summer of 1871 at a dinner given by George Howard. Burne-Jones, Poynter, Sidney Colvin, William de Morgan and Hungerford Pollen were present as well as Philip Webb, the architect of George Howard's new town house, No. 1 Palace Green. Morris had just returned from Iceland. He talked vividly of his experiences there and Crane was pleased to feel he could respond in an intelligent way, having gleaned a certain knowledge of the country from his illustrations for Symington's book.

With this introduction into a circle which he had previously been able to observe only from a distance, Crane must have begun to feel increasingly confident of his artistic future. His name was now associated with his own series of toy books and even his paintings were finding a small but select public. George Howard commissioned several water colours and Crane's Derbyshire landscapes and river views found purchasers among a group of Sheffield business men, members of a fishing club who came to the Derwent each year. The Rev. Stopford Brooke, a friend of Howard, also acquired a considerable collection of early landscapes. Stopford-Brooke's brother-in-law, Somerset-Beaumont, was another generous patron.

When 'Love's Sanctuary' was exhibited at the Old Bond Street Gallery in 1870, it was given a fairly cool reception. This was due largely to its subject, an irreverent interpretation of pilgrimage, in which a fervent youth kneels before the icon-image of the artist's beloved, Mary Frances Andrews.[12] These devotions are accompanied by singers and musicians and on an altar are an illuminated missal and dishes for the celebration of mass. A smoking censer and flaming bowl also hint at pagan ritual, which is depicted in the Greek procession on the frieze above. The benevolent presence of Venus is heralded by a flight of doves, two of whom already bill and coo above the pilgrim. The painting is a surprisingly explicit demonstration of Crane's humanism and his identification with the sensuous aestheticism expressed in Walter Pater's early writings and the work of Simeon Solomon; sentiments made clear also in an accompanying sonnet (see p. 84).

The painting reflects current developments in several ways. The careful arrangement and decorative colour of this picture parallels Crane's own recent toy books. His technique is very meticulous; involving Pre-Raphaelite attention to details, such as the ivy on the pilgrim's staff and the winding path, which have each their

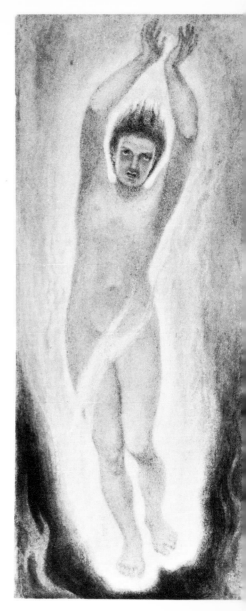

Fire signed with a monogram and dated 1868, water colour, $12\frac{9}{16} \times 5\frac{9}{16}$ in. (32 × 14.2 cm) one of four preparatory designs for a projected oil painting of the elements. Collection the Houghton Library, Harvard University.

part to play in the web of meaning. Exotic patterns like the devices on the frame and the altar cloth resemble those used by Rossetti and the blue and white pot repeats an aesthetic touch introduced the year before in a painting of 'Peacocks on a Terrace'.[13] But the most striking characteristic of 'Love's Sanctuary' is its evocation of the light, decorative ambience of the Quattrocento rather than the grave grace of Greek or Graeco-Japanese styles which also prevailed in the later 1860s. The deep perspective, compartmented space and colour pattern was the result of careful study of Renaissance painting like that of Fra Filippo Lippi.

Walter Crane and Mary Frances Andrews were married at All Souls, Langham Place on 6 September 1871. Three days later they sailed from Harwich to Antwerp. They travelled down the Rhine stopping at Cologne, Coblenz, Mainz, Munich, and Innsbruck, then through the Brenner Pass; and from Verona to Venice and Florence, finally arriving in Rome on 12 October. In the galleries they visited, Crane preferred the intricate, archaic styles. Although they only had a short time in Verona, he made a point of seeing the Mantegnas in Sta. Maria Maggiore and in Venice he took care to note the 'more primitive but not less beautiful conceptions of Carpaccio, Giovanni Bellini and the early Venetian school, tranquil and clear as the luminous air of the sweet morning.'[14]

Leighton's 'Romola' drawings and certain casts at South Kensington had prepared him to some extent for what he would see in Florence. Unlike Burne-Jones, who made a trip to Italy at this time and fell under the spell of Michael-angelo, Crane remained enthralled by the Quattrocento. For him, the Uffizi's most prized possessions were Botticelli's 'Spring' and 'Birth of Venus'; pictures not then in fashion among Italian connoisseurs of Italian art and still skied in minor rooms.

In Rome, the Cranes took lodgings in the Via San Nicolo Tolentino and they soon settled down to the pleasant sociable life led by British and American artists in the city. Among the Americans were a young sculptor, J. W. Swynnerton, and the painter Elihu Vedder. Edgar Barclay, an English painter of Roman peasant scenes, was another good friend. Soon a sketching club was formed and members took it in turns to meet at each others' studios. The Wilbrahams had given Crane introductions to some of the well-established English painters in the city including Charles Coleman, a Yorkshire-born artist famous for his impressive naturalistic renderings of the Roman countryside, its peasants and wildlife. Through Frederic Leighton, whom he encountered shortly after his arrival in Rome, Crane met Giovanni Costa and gained entry to the rather grand social circle of the American sculptor and writer, W. W. Story, who held elegant receptions in his Barberini Palace apartment.

Peasant pictures with topographical settings were obviously saleable commodities and Crane was wary about the commercialism of such subjects. Nevertheless he could not resist portraying picturesque models and introduced a fine couple into the foreground of one of his most ambitious water colours of that winter, 'The Arch of Titus', a tightly painted picture whose minute handling probably reflects the influence of early Italian tempera painting. 'At Home', a portrait of Crane's wife was accepted by the Academy the following year. A charming aspect of this picture is its decorative setting, the painted tiles and tapestry (very like that in Burne-Jones's 'Laus Veneris') in which Mary Crane is represented as Diana the Huntress with Cupid in pursuit of a crane.[15] 'A Herald of Spring' is in a similar style. Here the artist's wife walks barefoot down a Roman street with a basket of daffodils under her arm.[16] Some of Crane's most successful work was done in the summer in the south where he painted numerous landscapes and views such as "Vietri on the Gulf of Salerno', (Whitworth Art Gallery,

Vietri, 1872, water colour and gouache, $7\frac{7}{8} \times 12\frac{1}{4}$ in. (20.1 × 31.1 cm). Collection the Whitworth Art Gallery, Manchester University.

Manchester) which is in a freer style. 'South Italian Farmhouse' now in the Museum of Modern Art, New York, is rather more highly finished and a fine example of this period. The Cranes left Rome for Sorrento and stayed from June to September in Capri. From here they sailed to Amalfi and spent a month on the mainland again, at Ravello and Cava dei Terreni, returning to Rome on 10 October 1872. They settled down for another winter, this time in the Via San Guiseppe. Mary Crane held 'At Home' days and her husband was kept busy with picture book designs and his painting which included a commission from George Howard for a picture based on Shelley's poem, 'The Death of the Year'. When Beatrice was born in February, her father began to find the emotional and bureaucratic implications of such an event in a foreign land a considerable strain and they prepared to return to London, arriving home towards the end of May.

Near their new home, Florence House, in Wood Lane, Shepherd's Bush, lived E. J. Poynter, a painter of considerable achievement by this time. The two families often shared musical evenings and Crane found himself once again introduced to Burne-Jones and his friends, among them Spencer Stanhope whom he had admired for a long time. Walter and Mary Frances Crane welcomed an increasingly impressive list of guests to Florence House, including Luke Fildes (whom Crane had known since Bloomsbury days), Alma Tadema, George Simonds, Mr and Mrs Frederic Harrison, Lyulph Stanley, William Allingham, Comyns Carr and their wives, Miss Greatorex, Mme Bodichon, Mrs Eustace Smith, Mrs Russell Barrington, Sir Charles Dilke and William Armstrong who became godfather to Lionel, born in May 1876.

Apart from the modest reputation acquired through his submissions to the Dudley annual exhibitions, Crane's name in the early 1870s was chiefly associated

The Hon. Mrs Lyulph Stanley, later Lady Sheffield, 1875, gouache, 28¾ × 21¾ in. (73.1 × 55.2 cm). Collection Jocelyn Feilding Fine Art Ltd.

with Toy Books and he enjoyed more and more popularity through the new Routledge series. In this decade, however, he extended his scope as a designer and also gained sufficient prestige as a painter to be invited to contribute to the opening exhibition of the Grosvenor Gallery. Italian elements which appear in the later Toy Books are also increasingly important features of his painting at this time. Many exhibited works were of landscape subjects sketched in Italy, and later in the decade, views of places visited on holidays in England became more frequent, such as those of Whitby and Bamborough. In his imaginative paintings classical and Renaissance motifs predominate. Some of these works were of a general allegorical kind, like the water colour 'Winter and Spring' exhibited at the Dudley in 1874. For others, Crane turned to poetry, often that of Edmund Spenser, as in 'Cupid and My Dame', an oil exhibited at the Dudley Winter

Exhibition the same year. His enthusiasm for Spenser's poetry stemmed from the early Hazelford days when he caricatured himself as Colin Clout and adopted a comical Spenserian style for *Walter's Weekly*. Before leaving for Italy he had exhibited at least one Spenserian subject, 'The Red Cross Knight in Search of Una'. Spenser's writing, rich as it is in visions of fairy knights, flowery meads and classical allusions, appealed to Crane's romantic vision of the past, his delight in decorative detail and concern for a moral thread or story line. 'Amor Vincit Omnia', his unsuccessful Royal Academy submission of 1875, depicts the surrender of an Amazon town to the forces of General Love and is a Spenserian type of fairy tale in Quattrocento and classical styles where the contemporaries of the toy book *King Carabas* gain more sophisticated artistic status through lessons learnt from Parthenon relief and Mantegna's 'Triumphs'.[17] Crane loved processional scenes such as this one. He had already completed 'The Death of the Year' (1872), a counterpart 'The Advent of Spring' (1873), and was to work on several others. In 1875 he began to design wallpapers and two portraits finished at Florence House around this time reveal how up to date he was with the latest ideas in decoration. One represented Mrs Frederic Harrison in her drawing room with its Eastern rugs and Chinese vases, against a background of Morris's Daisy paper. In the other, Mrs Lyulph Stanley (later Lady Sheffield) in a specially designed dress adopts the pose of Whistler's 'Little White Girl'. The portrait, with its folding screen, Morris chair, matting and rug, is a painting about fashionable society and makes an interesting comparison with Whistler's aesthetically influential precedent painted some years before.

Shortly after Lionel's birth the Cranes took over the lease of Poynter's house, Beaumont Lodge, which had a fine garden studio converted from stables by Philip Webb. To avoid the strain of removal, Mrs Howard invited Mary Crane to stay for a few weeks and it was during this time that George Howard asked Crane to complete the Cupid and Psyche decorations begun by Burne-Jones for their dining room at No. 1 Palace Green. In 1872, Burne-Jones had painted small colour sketches for this frieze and started on the large canvases. These consisted of subjects from the set of designs for Cupid and Psyche with which he had previously planned to illustrate the 'Earthly Paradise'. When these canvas panels arrived at the Beaumont Lodge studio, Crane found them in various stages of completion. The procession scene for the west wall of 'Psyche led to be sacrificed to the monster' was 'considerably advanced', but others had hardly even been sketched in. He was lent the colour sketches of 1872 and a set of woodcuts of the 'Earthly Paradise' drawings as a guide. The painting was in flat oil colour with a few details modelled in gilded stucco following early Renaissance work. The scheme no longer survives intact as the canvases were removed when the Palace Green house was sold in 1922. They are now in Birmingham City Art Gallery together with the colour sketches and woodcuts. With the exception of 'Psyche presented to the Gods and Goddesses', which was on a smaller scale and which Burne-Jones wished to finish himself, Crane's work may be identified in all parts of the frieze. Where the master had left much to be completed, he allowed himself considerable freedom, as in 'Psyche at the Shrine of Ceres and Juno'. Here the composition differs from that of Burne-Jones's colour sketch. Crane's figure style although less refined, was naturally influenced by Burne-Jones. These technical differences between them are well demonstrated in 'Zephyrus leading Psyche to Cupid's House', the left side of which Burne-Jones had finished in some detail. The question of shared participation is complicated by the fact that both artists worked together on the frieze after it was put in place. Later, when Morris altered the original white colour scheme of the woodwork to one of green and blue with gold lettering, Burne-Jones heightened the tone of the paintings. Although seemingly not without its unsatisfactory aspects, this project was significant for Crane as it brought him directly in contact with the work of one who he had long admired and provided him with his first experience of painting on a grand scale.[18]

Crane was able to put these lessons into practice entirely on his own behalf in 1877 when Sir Coutts Lindsay invited him to contribute to the first Grosvenor Gallery exhibition where a large number of paintings by Burne-Jones and Whistler were exhibited together for the first time. Many lesser painters who had been unsuccessful at the Royal Academy were also represented. Crane's 'Renaissance of Venus' was the largest oil he had ever planned. Its form and subject suggest the influence of Burne-Jones and Botticelli's 'Birth of Venus' (p. 85), or that of Puvis de Chavannes whose work Crane could have seen on exhibition in London in the early 1870s. He believed that the idea of beauty re-born was relevant to his own time and that society was about to witness a revival of culture such as had been experienced only at rare moments in its history. One such period was the Italian Renaissance which Victorians were becoming increasingly aware of through the work of historians and connoisseurs such as Burkhardt, Crowe and Cavalcaselle, and Pater. 'The Renaissance of Venus' was quite well hung in the west gallery near the Burne-Jones exhibit and William Michael Rossetti commented in *The Academy* that it was 'a charming and delicious picture full of gracious purity'. A rather more astringent, but not ungenerous critic writing in *The Examiner* suggested that:

Mr Crane has still much to learn in the matter of expressive draughtsmanship, as the nude figure of Venus testifies: but the design of his work as a

E. Burne-Jones and W. Crane
Zephyrus bringing Psyche to Cupid's House, 1876–78, oil on canvas, 47 × 49 in. (119.4 × 124.5 cm). Published by permission of the Birmingham Museum and Art Gallery.

whole exhibits a very remarkable feeling for ornamental beauty, and the execution of certain parts of it . . . is a marvel of pure colour and sound workmanship. Of all the younger essays in imaginative painting to be found in the Gallery, this is indeed . . . the most original and most hopeful.[19]

The Triumph of Spring, signed and dated 1879, tempera on plaster mounted on panel, 15⅞ × 58 in. (40.3 × 147.2 cm). Collection the Walker Art Gallery, Liverpool.

Venus's unsympathetic contours were recognised by Frederic Leighton to be those of a young man, Allessandro di Marco, an Italian model in great demand by London artists. He also appears in Burne-Jones's 'Love Among the Ruins' and may well have been Crane's model for the pilgrim in 'Love's Sanctuary'. Crane had been forced by his wife into the somewhat dubious obligation of engaging male models for female roles because she refused to allow him to study from the female nude. The nude had staged a comeback in English art in the 1860s, but it was not a struggle without casualties, and Crane well remembered the Old Water Colour Society's request for Burne-Jones to remove 'Phyllis and Demophoon' because of complaints about its indecency. The artist withdrew his membership as well as his picture and did not exhibit for a number of years.

Encouraged by the success of his first large scale classical picture Crane for a time sent similar works to the Grosvenor Gallery. 'The Fate of Persephone' (1878) is more dynamic in its design than 'The Renaissance of Venus'. Pluto's black stallions make a striking contrast with a fine colour scheme of yellow and white draped figures and flowers.[20] The three dancing figures of 'The Sirens' (1879) are more consciously aesthetic. They gaze out to sea intent on luring Ulysses, whose ship drifts past 'in a diaphanous haze', and the subject is an excuse to depict paragons of Greek perfection on a sea-shore; a theme already handled by Leighton and Albert Moore in pictures exhibited at the Academy earlier in the decade. Crane now achieved a happier control of form. There is more breadth in his classicism, with less of the finnicky picturesque of the Quattrocento. The 1880 version of 'The Triumph of Spring' is a confident attempt to create the relaxed atmosphere of a leisured Golden Age.

Illustration up to 1890

Crane's position in the field of children's book illustration was not long one of splendid isolation. He soon encountered formidable rivals in Kate Greenaway (1846–1901) and Randolph Caldecott (1846–86) both of whom had Evans's collaboration for their colour work. The earliest intimation of this new state of affairs appeared in an advertisement in *The Athenaeum* of 1877 in which Routledge announced a companion volume by Miss Greenaway to Crane's latest bestseller, *The Baby's Opera: A Book of Old Rhymes with New Dresses* which had been issued at Christmas 1876. The nursery songs in this little book were arranged for the piano by Lucy Crane and it was a more ambitious production than previous efforts shared by Crane and Evans. The small quarto format derived from a series of six-inch tiles which Crane had just designed for Maw and Company. Other essentials were worked out during a stay at Evans's home at Witley in Surrey and the printer made up a dummy book for Crane to plan the layout. The experimental nature and success of this venture are clear from the artist's own account:

> ... at first 'The Trade' shook its head, as the sight of a five-shilling book not decently bound in cloth and without any gold on it was an unheard-of thing, and weighing it in their hands and finding it wanting in mere avoirdupois weight, some said 'This will never do!' – but it *did*. The first edition of 10,000 copies was soon exhausted and another was called for, and another, and another. It has long passed its fortieth thousand and, like 'Charley's Aunt', is still running.[1]

This compact little volume is one of Crane's most successful early decorated books. Its pictorial cover deftly introduces motifs from the lively contents. Hubert Herkomer's response to 'the sweet humour, the dainty design, and the good drawing' and his claim that it would be 'a delight for every person of taste no matter what age he or she may be' indicates the approval with which *Baby's Opera* was welcomed in discerning circles.[2]

Randolph Caldecott confined his children's illustration to Routledge's Shilling Picture Books, the series Crane had abandoned in 1876, and he contributed two titles each Christmas from 1878 until 1885, before his untimely death in America early in 1886. When Thomas Armstrong introduced him to Crane in the spring of 1878 Caldecott was already well known for his illustrations to Washington Irving's *Old Christmas* (1875) and *Bracebridge Hall* (1877). Crane found him a gentle and amusing companion. When they first met, the old-established master of the nursery had been glad to give him advice on the series and on his contract, with the result that Caldecott secured a royalty from Routledge, which Crane had failed to get for his own toy books. The firm outlines and bolder decorative shapes of Caldecott's colour designs in his first shilling books, *The House that Jack*

76

Cover of *The Baby's Opera*, 1877, printed in colour by Edmund Evans. Photograph by Peter Adamson.

Built and *John Gilpin*, may be partly indebted to Crane's example although these have still much of the witty, sensitive style of his own earlier black and white work. Crane thought it was Caldecott's ability to appeal to the Englishman's sporting instinct that made his illustration so popular, but his success really lies in its delicate line and deft caricature.

Today, in spite of the recognition given to the robust artistic talents of both Crane and Caldecott, Kate Greenaway's name is the one associated with a magical moment in Victorian publishing – one which, on analysis, would seem to be largely founded on nostalgia. If the world she created evokes a Never-Never Land there was nothing insubstantial about her commercial success. The book which Routledge had the effrontery (in Crane's view) to present as a companion to *Baby's Opera* was *Under the Window*, which had also been prepared with Edmund Evans's help. A first edition of 20,000 was soon followed by one of 70,000. Crane's own best-seller was quite eclipsed. Routledge may have been in the wrong to advertize a companion to *Baby's Opera* without the consent of its designer but Crane had already been asked to produce a sequel and had delayed because he was busy with other work. He also wanted to show a certain independence from the publishers on whom he had had to rely in leaner times. Neither his financial situation nor his reputation could allow him to adopt such a cavalier attitude for long and a true companion called *Baby's Bouquet* was ready for Christmas 1878. This was never to be quite so popular as its predecessor, possibly due more to the selection of French and German songs and less familiar English ones than to any great difference in design. If anything, Crane's style is more restrained and for this the success of Kate Greenaway's demure approach may perhaps be held responsible.

Walter Crane met Miss Greenaway only once. He must have known the work of her father, the wood-engraver John Greenaway, since his apprenticeship days but Kate was a shy and unexceptional person on first acquaintance and clearly Crane never sought to know her better. He was unimpressed by her water-colour portraits, which he knew from the Academy and the Dudley, and preferred the simple outline and tasteful tinting of her book designs. Even here he thought that she overdid her bonnets and that her 'little people were almost lost in their clothes'.[3] Ruskin soon became an ardent admirer of her work, inordinately praising it for its delicate charm. This annoyed Crane who thought that books for the young should also have an educational purpose. In a letter to the *Pall Mall Gazette* in 1886 he criticized Ruskin's views on elementary education and even went as far as to claim that the eye was the 'chief organ for the reception of ideas' – a somewhat extreme position to adopt but one no doubt provoked by his exasperation at Ruskin's over-indulgent enthusiasm for the prim and pretty work of his rival.[4]

However, in public eyes by 1880 Walter Crane was one of the nursery triumvirate which included Kate Greenaway and Randolph Caldecott.

In his Christmas *Punch* cartoons, Linley Sambourne often caricatured Crane, Greenaway and Caldecott together with other designers and companies associated with Christmas publishing. Among these was Marcus Ward and Company, one of the best known firms catering for the rapidly expanding Christmas market. Thomas Crane was later to become Art Director of this business. He was first associated with them early in the 1870s when he began to design greetings cards and

Little Cock Sparrow from *Baby's Bouquet*, 1878, printed in colour by Edmund Evans. By Courtesy of the Trustees of the National Library of Scotland.

calendars, work shared by his brother Walter, Kate Greenaway, Stacy Marks and
Harrison Weir. Thomas Crane confined his activity to floral and ornamental
patterns but Walter's were less conventional and included three sets of New Year
cards, each of four lithographed designs.[5] The first two were folding cards: that
of about 1872 had scenes of children at work and play; the other, of about 1875,
had elegant rustic couples representing the seasons. This was called 'Time's
Garland of the Year' and like the first was in colour with gilding. The third set of
separate cards with fairy motifs may date from as late as 1880. They were printed
on buff paper in brown outline with white highlights. In addition Crane prepared
several cards for *The Graphic* magazine at Christmas 1874 and the following year
a set to advertize pantomimes at the Crystal Palace. These are closer in style to
contemporary toy books than his work for Marcus Ward.[6] In 1876 this firm
published eight Valentine designs by Crane and Kate Greenaway in a book called
The Quiver of Love but Crane was very critical of its general design, especially the
'lithographic-mealiness' of the colour printing.

The previous year, however, Marcus Ward let him plan the presentation of his
own semi-satirical fantasy rhyme *Mrs Mundi at Home*; an invention similar to
King Luckieboy but more sophisticated. To her terrestrial ball (an event possibly
suggested by Mrs Crane's entertaining) Mrs Mundi invites the planets and
elements, gods, goddesses and mortals. Monkeys decline for the reason that
'decent men from their stock were long ago selected'. First to arrive is Lord Sol
with twenty four in hand. Jove follows, festooned in sections of *The Times* 'like
a champion sporting his belts'. Urania leads in midget versions of Tennyson,
Morris, Rossetti and Swinburne, and the Queen of the Air is borne aloft by long-
winded Ruskin with the help of a cloud and copies of *Fors Clavigera*. The twenty-
four full page plates are printed in brown ink on cream paper. Crane also designed
the title-page and cover. The text was printed on separate pages and for this reason
the book was relatively easy to arrange. One of the most difficult problems in the
design of illustrated books was that of incorporating decoration and long passages
of text because the use of standard type-face almost inevitably introduced a
mechanical element alien to the quality of a drawn line. Crane was to be much
pre-occupied with this problem in his work over the next few years.

In 1875 Crane designed illustrations for *Head of The Family* and *Agatha's
Husband* by Dina Maria Muloch, both of which were published by Macmillan and
Company. This year marked the beginning of a steady and fruitful association
between Crane and this publishing house, which already had a reputation for its

THEN THE QUEEN OF THE AIR FLUTTERED INTO THE ROOM,
SIROCCO IN WAITING, AND THE SULTAN SIMOOM

ÆOLVS

THEY COULD HARDLY ENDURE ALL HER GRACES AND AIRS.
AND WHILE SHE WAS FANNING COULD SCARCE KEEP THEIR CHAIRS.

The Queen of the Air from *Mrs Mundi at Home*, 1875. By courtesy of Cambridge University Library.

Opposite
Swan, 1877 dado design in water colour and gouache, 21 × 21 in. (5.33 × 5.33 cm) planned to accompany the *Iris and Kingfisher* filling (see endpapers of this volume). By courtesy of the Victoria and Albert Museum.

fine illustrated books and decorated bindings.[7] At this time too Crane made black and white designs for *Tell Me a Story*, the first of eighteen books by Mrs Molesworth which he was to illustrate for Macmillan.[8] The series followed an octavo format with a red cloth cover printed in black and gold, six full-page illustrations, a frontispiece and a small picture for the title page. Within this scheme there was only limited scope to experiment with cover design. His black and white style for Mrs Craik's books is rather mannered with very formally posed figures. This is also the case with the frontispiece to *Tell Me a Story*. In the better pictures for Mrs Molesworth's books he succeeds with a relatively simple and sympathetic interpretation of the various domestic dilemmas and imaginative adventures of her little heroes and heroines. Crane's handling of children is more appealing than his treatment of adults and it must be concluded that despite the enormous popularity of these books their illustrations often fall below the mark. *The Adventures of Herr Baby* (1881) (an exception for the series because it was produced in quarto and had an attractive pink cloth with a design printed in brown) has illustrations which suffer badly from their expansion to a larger format. Best among the earlier books are *The Cuckoo Clock* and *The Tapestry Room* and the happiest results are to be found in the later books like *Christmas Tree Land* (1884) whose illustrations are treated in a more linear technique and are full of lively assurance. Apart from work for Macmillan which kept Crane regularly occupied, he also designed two frontispieces for Robert Louis Stevenson's *Inland Voyage* (1878) and *Travels with a Donkey in the Cevennes* (1879) published by Kegan Paul. The first of these is remarkably restrained in comparison with the earlier outline style of *Mrs Mundi* or that of contemporary colour work like *Baby's Opera*.

And I will o'er your sports and revels reign.
And in my justice-court will pardon grant
For all your sins, except love's perjuries,
For who 'gainst love against forgiveness sins,
Or would do so, but love forgives all things.

SONG OF THE CHILDREN.

Nightingale change night for day,
All your sorrow throw away;
Robin leave your half-built nest,
Gallant, with rose at your breast;
Skylark, skylark, mount aloft,
Cloudward to your organ-loft;
Join in chorus all to-day,
Welcome to our Queen of May!

Come, all creatures, here to-day,
Hedgehog, hare, mole, fieldmouse play;
Squirrel leap with all your might,
'Till birds envy you your flight;
Glitter, insects, scale on scale!
Dance, thou knight in armour, snail!
Come all creatures here to-day,
Welcome to our Queen of May!

Forest animals from *The First of May, A Fairy Masque*, 1881, p. XLI, pencil drawing reproduced using photogravure by Goupil and Co. By courtesy of the Trustees of the National Gallery of Scotland.

Crane responded more imaginatively when he was using material of his own choice as in the *Baby* books. With Evans he had learned what it was like to have complete control over all design aspects of a book's production and, in the future, he wanted to plan his own format, binding, endpapers and page layout. Up to this time, apart from the single colour outlines of *Mrs Mundi*, his black and white work was chiefly limited to the frontispiece or a few full page pictures set opposite pages of type. His chance to take fuller advantage of his developing ideas on design in monochrome occurred with the commission of a book for his old friend John Wise. *The First of May, a Fairy Masque*, which was dedicated to Charles Darwin, was published by Southeran and Company in 1881 in a lavish oblong folio edition of two hundred copies and one of three hundred in a smaller format.[9] Most of the illustrations were done in 1878 and 1879 during a series of visits to Sherwood Forest, the setting chosen for Wise's fairy-tale adventure in a Mayday variation on 'A Midsummer Night's Dream'. Fifty-two pencil designs were finished the following spring. These were reproduced by Goupil and Company using photogravure, a process Crane found highly satisfactory.

It is delightful as an inventory of imaginative design: little studies of animals and birds, grotesques, frogs, flowers and elves woven into a delicate interlace or set against grassy carpets, numerous fairies in déshabille and dressed for amateur theatricals, even troupes of smocked and bonneted babes and miniature rustics – more decorous, pretty and Kate Greenaway-like than ever before. Burne-Jones greatly admired this gift book. Indeed, the pencil medium may have been suggested by his *Aeneid* drawings. Many other details reflect the influence of the older artist's work such as the flowing bands of drapery of the Rainbow Guardian in the 'Procession of Spring', Crane's androgynous nudes and various perpendicular compositions which echo the gentle spiral of 'The Golden Stairs', one of Burne-Jones's major works of the decade. Although Crane was freed from the geometry which had been imposed by musical notation in the case of *Baby's Opera* and *Baby's Bouquet*, he chose to keep a compartmented page layout here also. A similar page layout was also to be used in the songbook *Pan Pipes*. In *The First of May* he introduced little motifs around the text, which was harmoniously incorporated into the design by being hand-written and not, as in the case of the earlier books and *Pan Pipes*, in type. His style at this stage combines fluency with considerable restraint. As the decade advanced it was to become more abandoned and gain the organic linearism generally associated with his maturity.

An energetic line characterizes many examples of his earlier work (in *Mrs Mundi* for instance) but it was only during the 1880s that Crane in the company of other English designers evolved stylistic characteristics which are usually associated with Art Nouveau.[10] This development may be studied in an analysis of the illustration of two books issued by Macmillan in 1880 and 1882 and of three illuminated poems reproduced in the *English Illustrated* Magazine during 1884 and 1885. The first of the Macmillan books was *The Necklace of Princess Fiorimonde* by Mary de Morgan. Her brother, the ceramic designer William de Morgan, had illustrated her previous book *On a Pincushion*, published by the same firm in 1877. Crane followed this example by including headings and tailpieces as well as full page illustrations. However, where de Morgan chose a deliberately primitive style for the small text embellishments, Crane's were derived from early printed books. His full page illustrations are confidently planned around stable horizontal and vertical axes. They are more relaxed in effect than the earlier frontispiece for R. L. Stevenson's *Inland Voyage*, with more fluent treatment of forms and drapery. *Princess Fiorimonde* has a fine grey cloth cover with devices stamped in black and gold. Crane's skill in handling headings and tailpieces is more vigorously demonstrated in the next Macmillan book, the *Household Stories of the Brothers Grimm* which Lucy Crane translated at the suggestion of Mr Craik. Crane was delighted with the subject. He tackled the vivid and grotesque fantasies of the text decorations with the enthusiasm of a gothic illuminator let loose on his marginalia. The influence of Renaissance printed books, particularly the work of Dürer and Holbein which had already played its part in the development of Crane's drawing style, is very obvious in the full page designs which are given elaborate geometrical and semi-architectural frames. The flowing rhythms apparent in *Princess Fiorimonde* develop a new urgency in the Germanic pages of the Hausmärchen. The angularity of the seated figure of 'The Goose Girl' is broken down by the hatching lines of the grass, the folds of her dress, her fluttering hair and fleeing Conrad.[11] This new spontaneity is proclaimed with a flourish in many tailpieces. The red and green cover incorporates the design of a fantastic house and there are endpapers with motifs from the stories.

Crane's interest in illuminated manuscripts and early printed books was a natural result of his work as an illustrator. His study was directed essentially towards an understanding of the unity of design and how this could best be applied to modern conditions of book manufacture. In 1883 Macmillan sponsored the *English Illustrated Magazine* and Crane was invited to design a cover.[12] This venture

The Renaissance of Venus signed and dated 1877, oil on canvas, $54\frac{1}{2} \times 72\frac{1}{2}$ in. (168 × 183 cm). This, Crane's first large-scale painting, was exhibited at the Grosvenor Gallery in 1877 where it attracted the attention of G. F. Watts, who bought it several years later. Collection the Tate Gallery.

Love's Sanctuary, signed with a monogram and dated 1870, oil on canvas, $30\frac{3}{8} \times 21\frac{3}{4}$ in. (773 × 548 cm). Collection the William Morris Gallery, Walthamstow.

was planned to compete with the American periodicals *Harpers* and *Scribners* and its aims were artistic as well as literary. The first editor, J. Comyns Carr, was chosen because of his knowledge and interest in woodblock printing and engraving. Crane already knew Comyns Carr from his association with the Grosvenor Gallery. He must also have known his lectures on 'Book Illustration Old and New' given at the Society of Arts in the Spring of 1882, where the design of early manuscripts and printed books was discussed and the principles of

The Goose Girl, wood engraving from *Household Stories of the Brothers Grimm*, 1882. Photograph Peter Adamson.

different printing techniques, including the latest lithographic processes, were explained.[13] Crane cannot have heard much that he did not already know but it is clear from Comyns Carr's praise of wood engraving and his emphasis on unity of conception in page layout that they shared the same ideas. Presumably when Crane came to prepare his own contributions for the new journal he took pains to demonstrate these principles as best he could. Decorated versions of his poems 'A Herald of Spring' and 'Thoughts in a Hammock' appeared in April and November 1884. Each incorporated a handwritten text and the effect is more like manuscript than his decorations for *The First of May*. The similarity to illuminated books is most obvious in the second poem where forms break the bounds of their frame and curl into leaves and scrolls reminiscent of the Byzantine blossom of Romanesque manuscripts. Naked figures disporting among weeds and waves suggest also a more recent source in the Germanic style of the illustrator John Franklin, whom Crane had admired since his youth.[14]

His third contribution to *The English Illustrated* was 'The Sirens Three', by far the longest and most ambitious poetical effort Crane had so far attempted. It was published in instalments over six months from April to September 1885 and then in book form by Macmillan the following year. Its decoration is remarkable for the way in which Crane's hand-written verses are swathed in vital linear patterns of weeds, waves, winged figures and motifs to illuminate their highly picturesque if loftily vague meaning. There are no longer any traces of a Germanic style. Here Crane's graphic inspiration came chiefly from the work of William Blake, whose influence is apparent in the whiplash rhythm of the very first page.

As Professor Robert Schmutzler has shown, Blake's influence on the later style of Rossetti as well as the work of Edward Burne-Jones and designers like Mackmurdo, Selwyn Image and Crane played a vital part in the evolution of a proto Art Nouveau style in England in the 1880s.[15] Crane's familiarity with Blake's achievement dates from at least as early as his apprenticeship days when he was struck by the beauty of the designs Linton prepared for Gilchrist's *Life of Blake*, but with the exception of the study for 'Fire' painted in 1868 there is little evidence in his early work that he looked to Blake for ideas. Comyns Carr, an acknowledged authority on the English mystic, may have encouraged him in this, but the most obvious spur to renewed interest in the 1880s was the publication in 1880 of a second revised and enlarged edition of Gilchrist's book with a cover design adapted by Frederick Shields. This remarkable design (actually from one by William Blake's brother, Robert) set an example of flowing pattern derived from plant form, which is considered to be a source for some of the earliest English Art Nouveau designs by A. H. Mackmurdo including the cover for *Wren's City Churches* published in 1883.[16] Morris, with whom Crane was becoming more closely associated at this time, was interested in the printed book, and began to add early examples to his collection of manuscripts. He generously allowed Crane to refer to these and use illustrations from them for the Cantor lectures on 'The Decorative Illustration of Books' given to the Society of Arts in 1889. In this fairly detailed historical account Crane assessed Blake's contribution as one of major significance for the modern revival: 'William Blake is distinct and stands alone. A poet and seer as well as a designer, in him seemed to awake something of the spirit of the old illuminator. He was not content to illustrate a book by isolated copper or steel plates apart from the text . . . When he came to embody his own thoughts and dreams, he recurred quite spontaneously to the maker of the MS books. He became his own caligrapher, illuminator, and miniaturist, while availing himself of the copper-plate (which he turned into a surface printing block) and the printing press for the reproduction of his designs.'[17]

'Yes, said Thaw!', drawing in ink
and water colour from the Black
Book *Lancelot's Levities* October
1884, $6\frac{1}{2} \times 5\frac{11}{16}$ in. (16.5×14.4 cm).
Collection the Beinecke Rare Book
and Manuscript Library, Yale
University.

Then lilies, turned to Tigers, blaze

Amid the garden's tangled maze.

Lilies turned to tigers from *Flora's Feast*, 1889, colour lithograph.

The opening page of *The Sirens Three*, 1885, wood engraving. By courtesy of the Trustees of the National Library of Scotland.

THE·SIRENS·THREE

LOST on a sleepless sea, without avail
My soul's ship drifted wide, with idle sail
    And slow pulsating oars, that night's blue gulf
Beat noiselessly to Time's recurring tale.

The rolling hours like waves broke, one by one,
Upon the tide of thought time's sands outrun,
    And cloudy visions hovered o'er my bed,
Piled to the stars, full soon like cloud undone:

As, like the wan moon through her fleecy sea,
My spirit clove their rack unceasingly,
    And struck at last upon an unknown ground,
More still than sleep, more strange than dreamlands be.

Blake's struggles in adversity and his spiritual integrity heightened Crane's admiration for the man whose poetry and art he so esteemed. It is appropriate that it was in 'The Sirens Three', his first poetic manifesto of Socialism, that Crane should have been inspired by Blake. The two shared a vision of a more simple humane life and Crane saw in 'the extraordinary suggestiveness' of the other's work and in the freedom of his thoughts, a progressive spirit in close sympathy with the aspirations of the later Victorian age.

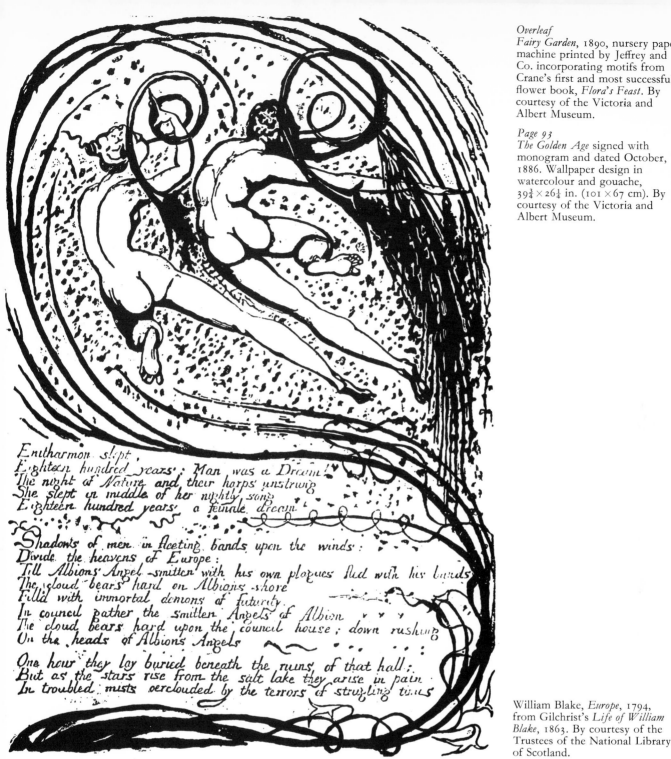

Enitharmon slept,
Eighteen hundred years: Man was a Dream!
The night of Nature and their harps unstrung
She slept in middle of her nightly song
Eighteen hundred years, a female dream!

Shadows of men in fleeting bands upon the winds:
Divide the heavens of Europe:
Till Albions Angel smitten with his own plagues fled with his bands
The cloud bears hard on Albions shore
Filld with immortal demons of futurity.
In council gather the smitten Angels of Albion
The cloud bears hard upon the council house; down rushing
On the heads of Albions Angels

One hour they lay buried beneath the ruins of that hall;
But as the stars rise from the salt lake they arise in pain
In troubled mists oerclouded by the terrors of struggling times

As his young family grew up Crane would invent and illustrate stories for them
in little picture books. These were strictly for home consumption. Only *Legends
for Lionel* and *Lancelot's Levities* were published in Crane's lifetime. The family
knew these as the 'black books' from the shiny covers of the notebooks bought
for the purpose. Their author described these sketches as 'the offspring of the
odd half hours of winter evenings'[18] and a glance at almost any one of the twenty-
nine books at Yale and Harvard (listed in the Appendix) reveals a delightful

succession of fact and fancy. The early ones are the most inventive. From 1879 to the *Notebooks for Beatrice* of 1882 Crane used pencil and water-colour wash, from *Beatrice's Bearings* of 1883 the medium was ink and water colour. It is fascinating to see how he adapted ideas to suit the characters and taste of his children: fairies and flowers for Beatrice; adventurous and artistic incentives for Lionel; and mostly pure fun for Lancelot, whose chubby form equipped him for a variety of roles.

The earliest surviving 'black book' is one completed for Beatrice's sixth birthday on 20 February 1879, *Beatrice in Fairyland*. Accompanied by her good fairy the little girl explores the heavenly bodies and the mountains of the moon, and is encouraged up the ladder of learning – as inevitably were all the little Cranes. She falls into the clutches of mis-spelling, is rescued by friendly letters of the alphabet and sails on a sea of ink to the kingdom of sums. That same year Lionel

Colour printed page of designs from a private picture book for Crane's daughter, *Beatrice, Her Book of Beauties*, 1886. By courtesy of Liverpool City Libraries.

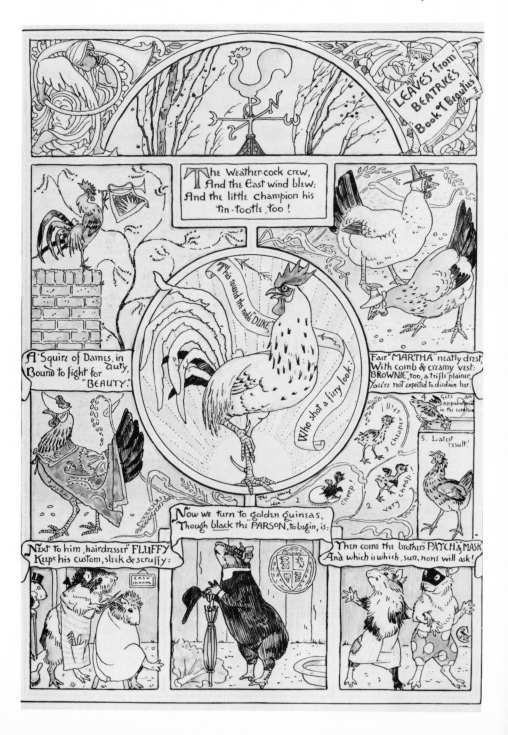

With a bouncing B to follow from *Pothooks and Perseverance*, 1886. By courtesy of the National Library of Scotland.

has lessons in ABC and drawing, in his *Primer and Copy Book*. He ascends the steps of knowledge to find himself in a painter's paradise where he is taught the primary colours by Major General Red Coat, Miss Daffodil and Bluebell, and then meets Rainbow who introduces him to her band of colours represented by Scarlet Poppy, Orange, Leaf Green and Violet girls. Designs from *Beatrice Her Book of Beauties* were worked up for publication in two large pages with images arranged like those of comic strips.[19] Some idea of the later books may be had from *Legends for Lionel* and the charming *Mouse's Tale*, which was published by Yale University in 1956.

These private picture books were the testing ground for ideas developed in three publications of the mid-1880s, *Slateandpencilvania* (1885), *Little Queen Anne* (1886) and *Pothooks and Perseverance* (1886). They were issued by Marcus Ward and Company separately and in a composite volume under the title *The Romance of the Three R's* (1886). By this time Thomas Crane was Art Editor of the firm. The designs were drawn on zinc lithographic plates using a very fine brush but Walter Crane was not so pleased with the colour of this printing as he had been with the results Evans achieved.[20] *Slateandpencilvania*'s theme was first explored in *Lionel's New Picture Book* of November 1880. *Little Queen Anne* appeared initially only shortly after this in the opening page of *The Adventures of Beatrice* of 1881, where she receives an invitation to meet the occupants of a great house – the Library of Learning. Sir Percyvere's hobby horse tilting at pothooks has its earliest precedent in Lionel's charge at a canvas in a notebook of 1880.

It led up to a little wood of cyclamen,
c. 1887, ink, water colour and
gouache, 6 × 5 in. (17.2 × 14 cm)
from the manuscript containing
the story, *Mr Michael Mouse
Unfolds his Tale*. Collection the
Beinecke Rare Book and
Manuscript Library, Yale
University.

The wind and sun from *Baby's Own Aesop*, 1887, printed in colour by Edmund Evans. By courtesy of the Trustees of the National Library of Scotland.

Stylistically this last of the Marcus Ward series is notable for its development of flowing rhythms and flourishes and in this respect may be compared with the last of the triplets, *Baby's Own Aesop*, which was published by Routledge in 1887, a decade later than *Baby's Opera* and *Baby's Bouquet*. These delicately coloured and compact volumes set the precedent for a series of highly successful 'aesthetic little quartos' published by Warne and Marcus Ward in the early 1880s and designed by J. C. Sowerby, Thomas Crane and a cousin of the Cranes, Ellen Houghton.[21] Thus, *Baby's Own Aesop* had to face more serious competition than *Baby's Opera*. Crane used a text devised by his old master W. J. Linton but this was not very suitable for young children. From a commercial point of view the *Aesop* was the least successful of the *Triplets*, as these three Crane-Evans productions were called when they were published together in 1899.

In the spring of 1886 Crane was asked to design a book to commemorate a theatrical event based on new translations of Homer and Aeschylus by Professor Warr of Kings College, London. The first part of this entertainment, 'The Tale of Troy' was performed in 1883 and was repeated, together with 'The Story of Orestes' at a performance at the Prince's Hall in 1886. Crane's *Echoes of Hellas* was published by Marcus Ward in the following year. Many designs were based on stage settings devised by well-known artists; that of 'Aphrodite's Pledge Redeemed' for example from a tableau by Sir Frederic Leighton. This project allowed

97

WOMEN.

The races of men are born and die as the leaves of the forest;

As the dead leaves fall betimes in the wind, but anon with the springtide

The greenwood is quickened again, and the leafage appeareth in season,

So hath the seed of man its time to increase and to perish.

Crane to indulge his love of the antique. Several designs are close to contemporary work by Leighton, Alma Tadema and Poynter.[22] Greek themes were fashionable in aesthetic London circles. *Echoes of Hellas* was printed by lithography in black and brick red and Crane tried to overcome the variation in style between the more three-dimensional designs derived from stage settings and his own decorative inventions by framing them all with pattern. He had also to incorporate large passages from Professor Warr's text which were printed in type. Some of the finest pages are very simple and reveal an economy rare in Crane's work. The classical theme encouraged the portrayal of statuesque figures moving with noble calm and heroic gesture but, as in the page of 'The Furies', he occasionally relaxed into a more abandoned linear style. Fluent draughtsmanship, originally developed in 'The Sirens Three' appears in several books of 1887 apart from certain sections of *Echoes of Hellas* and *Baby's Own Aesop*. Most noteworthy perhaps is *Four Winds Farm* by Mrs Molesworth. This highly personal graphic expression culminated the following year in Crane's designs for *Flora's Feast*, one of the most remarkable contributions to herald the decade of Art Nouveau. *Flora's Feast, A Masque of Flowers*, was published by Cassell and Company in 1889. It contains forty unframed colour-lithographed pages illustrating Flora calling the flowers from their winter sleep, each one appearing according to its place in the yearly cycle.[23] The idea of

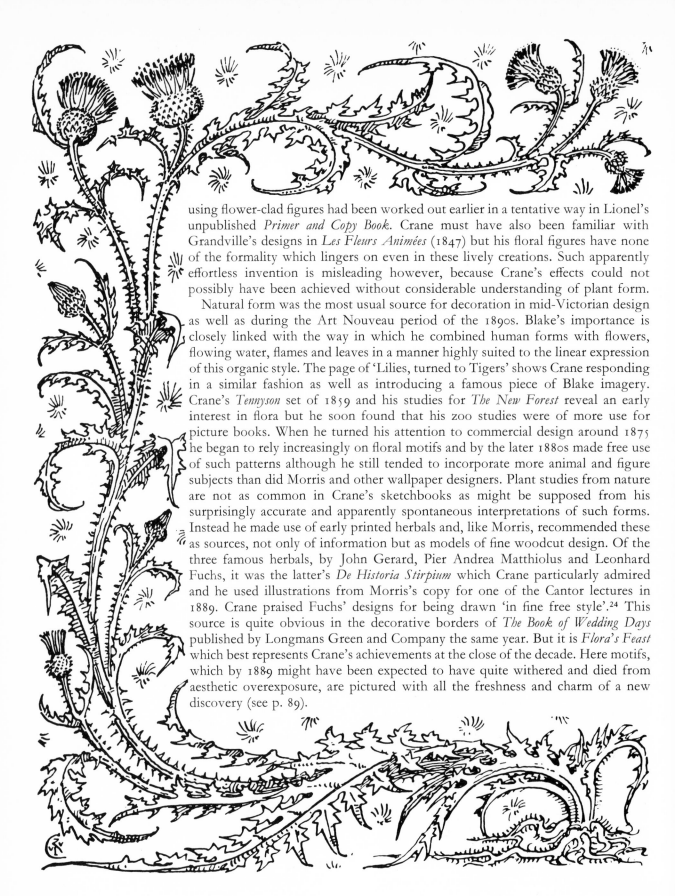

using flower-clad figures had been worked out earlier in a tentative way in Lionel's unpublished *Primer and Copy Book*. Crane must have also been familiar with Grandville's designs in *Les Fleurs Animées* (1847) but his floral figures have none of the formality which lingers on even in these lively creations. Such apparently effortless invention is misleading however, because Crane's effects could not possibly have been achieved without considerable understanding of plant form.

Natural form was the most usual source for decoration in mid-Victorian design as well as during the Art Nouveau period of the 1890s. Blake's importance is closely linked with the way in which he combined human forms with flowers, flowing water, flames and leaves in a manner highly suited to the linear expression of this organic style. The page of 'Lilies, turned to Tigers' shows Crane responding in a similar fashion as well as introducing a famous piece of Blake imagery. Crane's *Tennyson* set of 1859 and his studies for *The New Forest* reveal an early interest in flora but he soon found that his zoo studies were of more use for picture books. When he turned his attention to commercial design around 1875 he began to rely increasingly on floral motifs and by the later 1880s made free use of such patterns although he still tended to incorporate more animal and figure subjects than did Morris and other wallpaper designers. Plant studies from nature are not as common in Crane's sketchbooks as might be supposed from his surprisingly accurate and apparently spontaneous interpretations of such forms. Instead he made use of early printed herbals and, like Morris, recommended these as sources, not only of information but as models of fine woodcut design. Of the three famous herbals, by John Gerard, Pier Andrea Matthiolus and Leonhard Fuchs, it was the latter's *De Historia Stirpium* which Crane particularly admired and he used illustrations from Morris's copy for one of the Cantor lectures in 1889. Crane praised Fuchs' designs for being drawn 'in fine free style'.[24] This source is quite obvious in the decorative borders of *The Book of Wedding Days* published by Longmans Green and Company the same year. But it is *Flora's Feast* which best represents Crane's achievements at the close of the decade. Here motifs, which by 1889 might have been expected to have quite withered and died from aesthetic overexposure, are pictured with all the freshness and charm of a new discovery (see p. 89).

Decorative Art

Of late years . . . a kind of revival has been going on, as a protest against the conviction that, with all our modern mechanical achievements, comforts and luxuries, life is growing 'uglier every day' as Mr Morris puts it. Even our painters are driven to rely rather on the accidental beauty which, like a struggling ray through a London fog, sometimes illumes and transfigures the sordid commonplace of everyday life . . . The true root and basis of all Art lies in the handicrafts. If there is no room or chance of recognition for really artistic power and feeling in design and craftsmanship – if Art is not recognized in the humblest object and material, and felt to be as valuable in its own way as the more highly rewarded pictorial skill – the arts cannot be in sound condition; and if artists cease to be found among the crafts there is great danger that they will vanish from the arts also, and become manufacturers and salesmen instead.

In this passage from his introduction to the catalogue of the first Arts and Crafts Exhibition of 1888, Crane (with an aside directed at Whistler) briefly put his case for the lesser arts. The founding of the Arts and Crafts Exhibition Society was an important step in the history of the revival of the decorative arts in England not only because it celebrated 'the fateful marriage' of the words 'Arts' and 'Crafts',[1] but, as Gillian Naylor observed in her history of the movement, it gave designers the opportunity to display their work and a platform for publicizing their philosophy.[2] Each exhibition included a series of lectures and demonstrations, and essays were published in the catalogues. The Exhibition Society was formed by a splinter group protesting against the non-exhibiting policy of the Arts Workers' Guild founded in 1884, a year after Mackmurdo's Century Guild. Crane's earliest association with such a group was with The Fifteen who since 1882 had held monthly meetings 'in response to a feeling for more fellowship and opportunity for interchange of ideas on the various branches of their craft'.[3] His contemporary, Lewis F. Day, was secretary and among the others were the painters and designers Henry Holiday, Hugh Stannus, T. M. Rooke, G. T. Robinson; the architects James D. Linton and J. D. Sedding; and the sculptor George Simonds. They met in different members' houses where the host of the evening supplied refreshments and gave a paper or launched a discussion. The origins of the Art-Workers' Guild itself did not stem directly from Ruskin's St George's Guild but from the St George's Art Society formed in 1883 by pupils and assistants of the architect Norman Shaw. Wishing to improve relations between architect, artist and craftsman, these young men proposed the idea of a 'Guild of Handicraftsmen and Designers in the Arts' and invited various people including The Fifteen to a meeting in January 1884, when the principles of the new Guild were established, many of them proposed by William Lethaby. Crane

101

Membership card of *The Fifteen*,
c. 1882, wood engraving, 4 × 4 in.
(10.1 × 10.1 cm). By courtesy of
Liverpool City Libraries.

was elected a member during the first year and several of the original Fifteen were
to make up the hard core; its first three masters being George Simonds (1884–5),
J. D. Sedding (1886–7), and Crane himself (1888–9). Thus united, handicraftsmen
and designers, artists and architects looked to a new era of co-operation and shared
interest. Dissent arose over the matter of publicity which the Guild had originally
decided to avoid. Several members hoped that their group could acquire enough
weight and significance to counteract the professional bodies of the Institute of
British Architects and the Royal Academy but this was a difficult matter for a
society which remained more like a private club. In 1886 Crane was involved with
George Clausen and Holman Hunt in promoting the idea of a National Exhibition
of fine and decorative art where artists could be free to choose the committees
responsible for the hanging and selection of their work.[4] Most painters and
sculptors, including Clausen and Hunt, really thought of this in terms of a
reformed Academy rather than the more radical notion of a National Exhibition,
but Crane found supporters for an independent exhibition among the Art-
Workers' Guild, some of whom welcomed the prospect of an opportunity for a
public representation of design and decorative art. A committee was formed and
circulars distributed with the heading 'The Combined Arts' suggested by W. A. S.
Benson. By the time of the first exhibition in the Autumn of 1888, at the New
Gallery in Regent Street, T. J. Cobden Sanderson's title 'Arts and Crafts' had
been adopted and the Society was known officially as the Arts and Crafts Exhibition Society. In addition to those already mentioned the most active members were
Heywood Sumner, Emery Walker, Henry Longden, J. D. Sedding and Day.
Morris was on the original committee but he was sceptical about the outcome of
the venture; doubtful of the public support it might expect and of the effectiveness
of publicizing the names of maker, as well as designer, as a means of furthering
the interests of the workman. However, the first two exhibitions were very
successful and it was only with the lower standard of the third exhibition held in
1890 that it was decided to hold one every three years. This concentration gave
the venture new vigour and its impact was felt abroad as well as in Britain. Crane
was president from the outset with the exception of the term from 1893 to 1896
(when William Morris took over) until 1912 the year of the last exhibition before
World War I. He was well represented in every exhibition. In 1896 he became the
first master of the Junior Art-Workers' Guild.

By the time of the founding of the Art-Workers' Guild the aims of the
decorative art revival were confused by commerce and fashion. During the
increasingly prosperous decade of the 1870s enterprising business firms filled the
market with 'art manufactures' and the public followed various aesthetic crazes
encouraged by lively satire in the press and on the stage. Crane found it 'amusing
to see the travesties of ideas which had been current in artistic circles for long
before, now proclaimed as the new gospel of aesthetic salvation'.[5]

> To trace the genesis of our revival he explained we must go back to the days
> of the pre-Raphaelite Brotherhood . . . by their resolute and enthusiastic return
> to the direct symbolism, frank naturalism, and poetic or romantic sentiment
> of medieval art, with the power of modern analysis superadded, and the more
> profound and intellectual study of both nature and art which the severity of
> their practice demanded, and last, but not least, their intense love of detail,
> (they) turned the attention to other branches of design than painting . . . The
> late D. G. Rossetti, the poet, painter, and perhaps the central and inspiring
> luminary of the remarkable group, evidently cared greatly for decorative
> effect, and bestowed the utmost pains upon tributary detail, designing the

frames of his pictures, the cover and lining for his own poems, and various title pages.[6]

Henry Shaw's research into medieval art and the work of the Gothic revivalist architects A. W. Pugin and William Burges also served to focus attention on the beauty and invention of the accessories of daily life in medieval times, while Ruskin was a vital force whose teaching stimulated 'sincerity and Gothic freedom in the arts . . . a strong protest against Academic convention and classical coldness'. Early Victorian taste was a subject Crane always enjoyed discussing:

An illustrated catalogue of the Exhibition of 1851 will sufficiently indicate the monstrosities in furniture and decoration which were supposed to be artistic. The last stage of decomposition had been reached, and a period of, perhaps, unexampled hideousness in furniture, dress and decoration set in which lasted the life of the Second Empire, and fitly perished with it. Relics of this period . . . take the form of big looking-glasses and machine-lace curtains, where the furniture is afflicted with curvature of the spine, and dreary lumps of bronze and ormolu repose on marble slabs at every opportunity; where monstrosities of every kind are encouraged under glass shades, while every species of design-debauchery is indulged in upon carpets, curtains, chintzes and wallpapers, and where the antimacassar is made to cover a multitude of sins. When such ideas of decoration prevailed, having their origin or prototypes, in the vapid splendours of imperial saloons, and had to be reduced to the scale of the ordinary citizen's house and pocket, the thing became absurd as well as hideous. Besides, the cheap curly legs of the *uneasy* chairs and couches came off, and the stuffed seats, with a spacious show of padded comfort, were delusions and snares. Long ago the old English house-place, with its big chimney-corner, had given way to the *bourgeois* arrangements of dining and drawing-room . . .
Enter to such an interior a plain, unvarnished rush-bottomed chair from Buckinghamshire, sound in wind and limb – 'C'est impossible!'. And yet the rush-bottomed chair and printed cotton of frank design and colour from an unpretending and somewhat inaccessible house in Queen Square, may have said to have acted as the sling and stone which have slain the false ideals of vulgar smartness in domestic decoration – at least wherever refinement and feeling have been exercised at all.[7]

Crane first saw the work of Morris's firm at the Great Exhibition of 1862 where the Chaucer wardrobe painted by Burne-Jones and Philip Webb's St George cabinet with its paintings by Morris were on display.[8] The earliest evidence of contemporary design in Crane's own illustration is in *The House That Jack Built* which has Gothic gables, finials and painted decoration (including a frieze of dogs and cats chasing mice) like that on Burges's polychromatic cabinets. But a real interest in the modern interior is not apparent until the books published in 1869, as can be seen by comparing *Chattering Jack* and *How Jessie was Lost* issued the year before, with their successor *One, Two Buckle My Shoe*. Interior decoration had become a matter of importance and serious consideration for designers, painters and architects alike. Since their move to new premises at 26 Queen Square in 1865 Morris's firm began to gain a wider reputation not only for its stained glass but for wallpaper and furniture suitable for quite modest middle-class homes. Crane had followed the critical and constructive views on design in

Charles Eastlake's early essays which were published together in 1868 as *Hints on Household Taste*.[9] The interiors of *One, Two Buckle My Shoe* are bright and relatively uncluttered. They are not at all Gothic. Instead, the ebonised furniture and oriental details reflect the kind of taste that was soon to be dubbed 'aesthetic'. Lucy probably encouraged her brother's enthusiasm. Her own interest later led her to lecture on the subject. These talks were published soon after her death in 1882 in *Art and the Formation of Taste* with illustrations by her brothers Walter and Thomas. Eastlake's highly successful attempt to give popular guidance had by this time been copied by many others. Macmillan, the publisher of Lucy Crane's lectures, issued the first of their Art at Home Series in 1876.

Crane occasionally worked for Wedgwood in the 1860s but it was not until after his marriage and subsequent visit to Italy that he began seriously to extend his range as a designer. He was encouraged to do this by people who recognized the potential of the invention and detailing in the toy books. Shortly after Crane's return to England in 1873, the architect E. J. Tarver asked him to paint a frieze of birds and animals for a house in Palace Gardens belonging to a Mr de Murietta.[10] Later, probably in the summer of 1875, Poynter lent his Beaumont Lodge studio to allow him to paint another frieze, of white cockatoos on a gold ground connected by scroll work in bronze-green and red, for Mrs Eustace Smith's boudoir at No. 52 Prince's Gate. These led to more private commissions of an increasingly ambitious kind. Embroidery, textiles, ceramics, plaster and gesso relief, mosaic and stained glass were soon claiming his attention but of all the branches of decorative art at which he was to work with apparently ceaseless energy in the coming years, Crane's wallpapers are among his finest inventions.

Metford Warner, the proprietor of Jeffrey and Company, asked Crane to design his first cartoon for a paper based on toy book motifs in 1874. It was issued the following year and was the first of a total range of over fifty patterns manufactured by the firm in the artist's lifetime (see Appendix). He met Warner through the Scottish architect-trained designer, Bruce J. Talbert, one of several leading designers including Burges, Godwin, Eastlake, Harrison Weir and Owen Jones, employed by Jeffrey and Company in the later 1860s. After 1866 the firm had begun to widen the range of its designs not only in expensive hand-made, block-printed hangings but in the cheaper papers machine printed from rollers.[11]

All seven of Crane's nursery papers were machine printed and derived from picture books. In the first, the 'Queen of Hearts' scenes from the rhymes 'Queen of Hearts', 'Little Boy Blue', 'Bo-Peep' and 'Sing a Song of Sixpence' are set against a coloured ground and arranged in three vertical strips separated by a band of decoration. The 'Humpty Dumpty' paper of 1876 was more of a departure from the pages of the toy books, having a lighter ground and variety of nursery motifs arranged about a scroll pattern. In 'Froggy Would A'Wooing Go' of 1877, animals are set in framed squares alternating with squares of ornamental design. Two years later the delightful 'Sleeping Beauty' paper came out and, after an interval, 'The House that Jack Built' (1886) and then 'The Fairy Garden' (p. 92), which was based on *Flora's Feast*. These three are more sophisticated than the early papers and yellows predominate. Last of these machine printed designs is 'Mistress Mary' which is in a flat, formalized style developed from that of the late picture book *A Floral Fantasy*. This paper was shown at the Arts and Crafts Exhibition of 1906.

Crane emphasized the importance of understanding manufacturing techniques and the limitations of material. In the essay 'Of Wallpapers' printed in the catalogue to the Arts and Crafts Exhibitions of 1888 he recommends designs with 'a certain flatness of treatment' and well-constructed pattern which 'will repeat satisfactorily over an indefinite wall space without running into awkward holes and lines.' His first block-printed paper, 'La Margarete' (1876) owes an obvious debt to Morris's earliest design, the 'Daisy'. Crane's work is more simple with one daisy plant and slender garlands looped across a light blue or soft ochre field. This simplicity assured 'La Margarete's' popularity for a long time. It could also be incorporated into a more elaborate scheme with alternative friezes, a dado, and a ceiling paper. A three-part division of wall surface had been recommended by Eastlake and became fashionable in the 1870s. Jeffrey and Company manufactured a series of schemes of frieze, filling, border and dado papers for which they won a medal at the Fine Arts Exhibition at the Albert Hall in 1873. 'La Margarete' won recognition at the Philadelphia exhibition of 1876, the first of many honours Crane brought the firm through his designs. Its 'Alcestis' frieze expanded the Chaucerian theme of the daisy:

'As she that is of alle floures flour
Fulfilled of alle virtue and honour
And ever alike fair and fresh of hue'

with six caryatid figures symbolizing the winged God of Love, Alcestis (the queen of wives) and her attendants; the domestic virtues Diligence, Order, Providence and Hospitality. The other frieze had doves and baskets of daisies. The dado of lilies and doves continued the theme of purity and innocence echoed in the ceiling paper, a geometrical arrangement of doves and suns in squares. Though the daisy filling and Chaucerian theme are in sympathy with Morris, the classical character of the 'Alcestis' frieze and Crane's use of figures are not. He went further too in giving meaning to a decorative scheme and this use of symbolism occurs often in later work in papers such as 'Corona Vitae' (1890) and 'Trio' (1893) which, like 'La Margarete' were advertized with long iconographic explanations. Thus Crane's first hand block-printed paper shows both a debt to Morris and divergence from his example. He was already showing something of the eclecticism of the toy books. Stylistically the geometrical format of the 'Dove' ceiling reflects a more controlled decorative trend than Morris's naturalism. Other early Crane patterns

Humpty Dumpty wallpaper, 1876, machine printed by Jeffrey and Co. This was Crane's second nursery paper.

like 'Iris and Kingfisher' (1877) and 'Almond Blossom and Swallow' (1878) hint at contemporary English Japanese taste evident in those L. F. Day prepared for Jeffrey and Company. Metford Warner, the driving force behind the firm's artistic papers, allowed designers considerable freedom, being content often only to suggest motifs. Crane's earlier block-printed hangings used several colours. Only in two of 1894 did he begin to restrict himself to four blocks apiece.[12] His range and remarkable facility in pattern making is clear in such designs as the stairway paper, 'Awakening Day' (1880) or 'Billow' (1879) with its 'Mermaid' friezes. 'Briar Rose' (1880) was basically 'The Sleeping Beauty' design without figures and its delicacy made it perfectly suited to bedrooms and drawing rooms. 'Peacocks and Amorini' (1878) was a more formal paper and was used by Morris in St James's Palace. This hanging, the dignified 'Golden Age' (p. 93) and rich 'Peacock Garden' (1889) were among several produced in an embossed and gilded range designed to simulate expensive Spanish leather wall-coverings and were suited to grand reception rooms and public buildings. The light self-coloured walls and Japanese taste of *One, Two Buckle My Shoe* suggest a desire to promote simpler styles in decoration but Crane would probably have found the white and grey interior of E. W. Godwin's scheme for Oscar Wilde's Tite Street house of 1884 too austere.[13] He loved rich effects and unlike Morris was not shy of Italianate splendour. Nevertheless, when he did indulge his quasi-baroque exuberance, the designs continued to be carefully controlled with close colour tones and shading carried out frankly with little dots and strokes which explain form rather than give too illusionistic an impression of roundness. In one of her lectures Lucy Crane warned against 'the mock-aesthetic colouring which ... is all deadness, darkness, dullness'.[14] Her brother's wallpapers reveal a masterly handling of colour, varying from high bright keys for nurseries, dainty drawing rooms and morning rooms; middle tones and deeper effects for more important apartments. But even in a relatively sombre example like 'Fig and Peacock' (1895) the colour combines richness and variety and Crane's vital drawing line increases the effect, so suitable to a large wall-surface decoration, of dynamic force at rest. Within the three years from the regimental rushes and irises of 1877 to the delicate briars of 1879 it can be seen how Crane quite faithfully adapted nature to design. After an interval, in 1886 he produced 'Woodnotes' (see p. 116), combining figures and curling acanthus in a way that may have been influenced by the 'Mermaid' paper designed by Morris and Burne-Jones about 1880. Like Morris, Crane often found ideas for designs in the art and decoration of the past. 'Woodnotes' manages to combine echoes of East Anglian manuscript illumination with Mediterranean pagan mischief. 'Corona Vitae' was influenced by 'a textile motif somewhat after the manner of the Sicilian silk hangings of those sumptuous brocades one sees spread behind royal seats in early pictures and woodcuts'.[15] From 'Woodnotes', when his foliage drawing style was close to that of Morris, Crane evolved a more spontaneous linear technique in keeping with the development of his own graphic art. In 1888 he declared that 'suggestion' of natural form was 'better than any attempt at realisation'.[16] His interpretation of sources whether from art or nature becomes more and more free as his style develops richness and fluency. The clearly delineated acanthus scrolls of 'Woodnotes' begin by 1889, in 'Peacock Garden', to look more like rippling seaweed – a tendency also apparent in 'Corona Vitae' and 'Cockatoo' of the next two years. With this loosening of the conventional bonds of decorative form some of Crane's later designs evolve the 'swirl' and 'blob' pattern defined by Tschudi Madsen as so characteristic of Art Nouveau.[17] This can be seen in 'The Peacock Garden' issued in 1889 the year of Crane's first and finest flower book, *Flora's Feast*.

At the outset of the official decade of Art Nouveau more vertical emphasis is apparent in 'The Fairy Garden' (1890) and even in the later 'Lily and Rose' (1894). His works after this vary between the oddly overripe 'Seed and Flower' (1894) and 'Artichoke' (1895), the dainty 'Meadow' (1896) with its 'Maytree' frieze, and highly original 'Day Lily' (1898) with its slow-curving stems set against great sun patterns on an orange-red or purple-blue ground. The year 1900 saw the production of the 'Rose Bush' paper whose long stems and knots of flower may reflect the vertical emphasis of the Glasgow style. Its 'Lion and Dove' frieze, however, has an obvious source in the Ionides' 'Forest' tapestry and with this Crane once more asserts his allegiance to Morris. Some of the very late designs are surprisingly conventional such as the 'Marathon' and 'Classic' series of 1910 but 'The Formal Garden' (1904; p. 117) and 'Macaw' (1908) are very different yet fine and individual patterns. This individualism has so far prevented Crane's papers from enjoying the popular acclaim now given to those by Morris and admittedly many are too elaborate for modern taste. Nevertheless, these comprise a significant contribution to Victorian design. Their present neglect is all the more remarkable because wallpapers were an aspect of his art fully appreciated during Crane's lifetime even by his severest critic P. G. Konody.

When he began to work for Jeffrey and Company, Crane also became associated with the Royal School of Art Needlework, founded in 1872 with the philanthropic purpose of giving work to poor gentlewomen. This school was the home of an 'art' industry which aimed at raising the standard of secular needlework. In 1875

Embroidery Hangings designed by Crane and worked at the Royal School of Art Needlework. Shown in the United States at the Philadelphia Centennial Exhibition of 1876.

the School employed over one hundred workers and engaged the services of leading designers, among them Morris, Burne-Jones, Selwyn Image, G. F. Bodley, Frederic Leighton, E. J. Poynter and Alexander Fisher.[18] One of its early triumphs was the exhibit sent to the Philadelphia Centennial in 1876, which included hangings designed by Bodley and Morris, and a set by Crane. This last was worked in crewel wools and consisted of four figure embroideries representing Music, Painting, Architecture and Poetry, framed in an architectural setting with the inscription 'ARS LONGA VITA BREVIS' above. Below hung a valance of the Three Fates, Clotho spinning, Lachesis weaving and Atropos with her shears, and two long panels with classical figures of welcome and farewell. On the outside were banners with a pilaster design and inside there were identical, reversed, decorations of inhabited cornucopiae, and fruit and foliage scrolls branching from a central pedestal supporting a flaming bowl. Various features of the whole complex relate to wallpapers like the 'Alcestis' frieze and 'Peacocks and Amorini'. The cornucopia designs formed the basis of another work by the School in 1879, a large folding screen of five panels which is now in the Victoria and Albert Museum. A description of part of this refers to the subject as The Four Elements, which may explain the happy association of such disparate decorative motifs as fruit, fire, birds and mermaids. The workmanship is rich and intricate, embroidered in crewel wools on a dull gold ground, imperial in its effect rather than medieval.[19] Individual motifs from these panels could be used for smaller embroideries. Late in the 1870s he designed a heraldic portière for the Duke of Bedford's Eaton Square house[20] and this was probably also made by the School – many smaller designs by Crane continued to be worked long after the period of his most active participation in the 1870s.[21] His wife shared his interest in contemporary art and decoration with an enthusiasm which she could exhibit with great 'panache', being 'capable of shocking her respectable Kensington neighbours by such wild eccentricities, for those days, as driving herself alone in a horse and buggy to pay her visits and leave her cards, appearing in the streets in a chintz dress covered with some of William Morris's most extravagant flowers'.[22] Her own embroideries were designed by her husband and often on view at the Arts and Crafts Exhibitions. The first of these were an embroidered waistband and memoranda pockets and needlework panels for an ebonised cabinet.[23] Other items included cushion covers and the fine Burne-Jonesian panel of 'The Vision of Dante' exhibited in 1893.

After his initial contact with the Royal School of Art Needlework, Crane turned his attention to patterns for woven and printed fabrics. Morris had been so impressed by 'The Goose Girl' design for *Household Stories* when he saw it in the Beaumont Lodge studio that he asked to have a large cartoon prepared for the first arras tapestry woven at Merton Abbey in 1881. Unfortunately this did not lead to further work in the same line. Crane's earliest repeating pattern for a woven fabric was for a Manchester firm and represented 'Luna and the Stars', with a deep border of arabesques and figures. Then Edmund Potter of Manchester commissioned the 'British Empire Print' and a 'Fantasy of Fashions' for the Jubilee Year of 1887 and about three years later George Wardle of Leek printed the 'Four Seasons', a design framed in leafy borders like those forming the ogee patterns of 'Corona Vitae'. Crane's impressionistic style of the early 1890s was well suited to damask weaving and his designs for John Wilson and Sons were very successful. They include a set of dessert doilies called 'Flora's Retinue', which was issued in colour as well as ivory white, and a tablecloth of 'The Five Senses' designed in 1891.[24] When he planned 'The National' wallpaper in 1897 Crane began a series of heraldic textile hangings, beginning with a block-printed

The Four Seasons, *c.* 1890, japon silk printed by Thomas Wardle and Co., Leek, 35¼ × 29¾ in. (89.5 × 75.5 cm). Collection Oslo Decorative Arts Museum.

worsted containing the emblems of Scotland, Ireland, England and Wales in ogival repeats framed by branches of thistle and shamrock. This was followed by the wool tapestry of jousting knights, 'England and France', woven by the firm of A. H. Lee of Manchester (p. 121); and the 'Pax' design of 1902.[25] Other printed textiles were 'Golden Pheasant' (1901–2) and 'Iris'.[26] He even attempted carpet design. In 1896 the Glasgow firm of Templeton manufactured 'Lily, Pink and Columbine' and 'Daffodil and Bluebell' in Brussels pile. Elements in each relate them to the 'Meadow' and 'Day Lily' wallpapers but Crane probably found that the technical limitations imposed by carpet making inhibited the linear freedom of his style.[27] Unlike Morris he had little inclination to plan small or regular repeating patterns which would look well in floor coverings or in textiles hanging in folds. Although he produced some very striking patterns for printed and woven fabric, Crane did not take up and consistently develop his design in these media in the way he did for wallpaper.

The distinction between 'art' and ordinary industry was nowhere more marked than in pottery. By the 1880s big stores in London like Howell and James, W. B. Simpson and Liberty commissioned artistic ceramics from various manufacturers, very different to the traditional lines of fine porcelain and heavy kitchen ware produced by England's long-established firms, some of whom led the way with their own 'art' pottery. Decorated tiles had become a fashionable feature, not only of fireplaces, stairways and interiors but were used on 'art' furniture. One of the best known ceramic designers was William de Morgan who began his art career working for Morris's firm in the 1860s, but there were many versatile artists like Stacy Marks, Day, Poynter and Crane who made effective contributions to Victorian ceramic decoration.[28]

Crane's earliest commissions date from after 1866 when his Cheshire friend Mrs R. Wilbraham introduced him to the Wedgwoods of Etruria and over the four years from 1867 he supplied them with several designs.[29] In this context Crane describes drawings of the Seasons and the Ten Virgins for vases in cream-coloured ware done 'in a light sort of treatment with a pen in purple-brown using a medium composed of oil and turpentine and glycerine', and 'a kind of encaustic inlay' border for a chessboard in Wedgwood's Henry II ware.[30] This cream-coloured ware, and most likely also the vases, were on view at the Paris Exhibition of 1867. He next designed tiles for the Shropshire firm of Maw and Company and these, like the early wallpapers, relate to the toy books. The first set dating from 1874 or 1875, were each 6″ square and had on them Boy Blue, Bo-Peep, Tom Tucker and other nursery characters. Another set of similar or slightly later date is 8″ square with figures personifying the Seasons and Times of Day. This was a more classical scheme than the nursery tiles having an elegance and sophistication similar to the cover for Routledge's new Railway Library edition of Bulwer Lytton novels issued in 1877. Both series were etched on copper in outline, painted, transferred to the tile, then coloured by hand. A third set of four 6″ tiles with figures of the Elements in circles was produced a little later. This format influenced that of *Baby's Opera* but, basically, it can be said that Crane's work for Maw and Company reflects the picture books, whose strong outline and flat tints were well suited to tile design. This was acknowledged at the time. Howell and James, for example, sold blank tiles and recommended enthusiastic amateurs to use appropriate models, such as Crane picture books, for tiles to decorate a nursery. Similar advice was given by the American Clarence Cooke in his book *The House Beautiful* (1878) for which Crane designed a coloured frontispiece. American commercial firms took up the idea too. Both the American Encaustic Tiling Company, founded in 1875 (better known as A. E. Tile), and the Mosaic Tile Company, founded in 1894, were to use designs from *Baby's Own Opera* and *Baby's Own Aesop*.[31] Early in the 1890s Maw and Company issued a blue and white 6″ tile of 'Little Boy Blue' and may also have been responsible for the blue and white double tiles comprising single figure designs used in the decoration of Bedford Park's Tabard Inn.[32]

In 1880 Crane became Art Superintendent of the new London Decorating Company, a firm which specialized in encaustic tiles. His next work of this kind was a large panel, produced in collaboration with Day and shown at the Paris Exhibition and at the Arts and Crafts Exhibition in 1889. Crane's three panels, two horizontal ones representing 'Ploughing' and 'Reaping' and a central upright section of 'Sowing', are in red and cream lustre. Their bold line and silhouette may owe something to William de Morgan who was responsible for reviving the use of lustres and Maws was one of the first firms to adopt these techniques under industrial conditions. The inspiration behind the seven pots Crane designed for Maw and Company around 1889 is vaguely Greek or Italian but the chief impression they create is one of striking originality. He gave section drawings to the thrower and then painted the design on a biscuit pot. This was afterwards copied on duplicate vases in ruby lustre.[33] Crane's decorative instinct, at a peak at this date, responded with great sensitivity to the slender tensions and bulgings of each form covering, but not overloading them, with fluent pattern. In the 'Swan' pot the Victorian grotesque, so popular in the work of the Martin brothers, takes on a new dynamism and rugged grace. Crane's utopian ideal was to return to conditions where all pottery would once again be made and finished on the wheel. He hated 'the hard mechanical false finish of the lathe'.[34] Ironically, however, the kind of individual treatment which allowed a potter to see to each stage of production could only be lavished on expensive ornamental ware such as his own designs for Maws. Given such treatment ordinary cups and saucers would soon

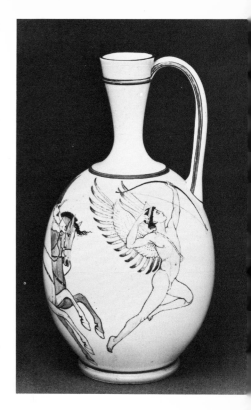

Imagination jug, 1868, manufactured by Wedgwood. Collection the Wedgwood Museum, Barlaston, Stoke-on-Trent.

Nox, c. 1876 tile manufactured by Maw and Co. at their Benthall works in Broseley, Shropshire, 6 × 6 in. (15.2 × 15.2 cm).

Swan vase, 1889, manufactured by Maw and Co. By courtesy of the Victoria and Albert Museum.

Opposite
Advertisement for tiles *c.* 1876 designed by Crane and manufactured by Maw and Co. at their Benthall works in Broseley, Shropshire. By courtesy of Liverpool City Libraries.

have been far beyond the reach of the working man's pocket. This was an all too familiar paradox for artistic socialists like Crane and Morris.

In 1900 Crane designed two sets of tiles for the newly formed Tile and Pottery Company belonging to Pilkington, one called 'Flora's Train' with flower figures clad in coloured petals, in 'cuenca' technique of moulded ware filled in with coloured glazes; and one of 'The Senses'. After this came a series of designs which date originally from between 1904 and 1906 but which were used repeatedly until 1938. For this work Crane would visit the factory to discuss the painting of the designs which was carried out by Pilkington's own artists William Mycock, Richard Joyce and E. Charles Randall. These patterns decorate much less unusual vase, bowl and flask forms than was the case with Crane's work for Maws. The designs are more elegant and suited to the finer texture of the clay body. The 'Sea Maiden' vase and 'Lion' bowl are reminiscent of de Morgan patterns and are in darkly glowing silver ruby and red blue lustre. Finest of all this work for Pilkington's are three plaques; one with a splendid 'Peacock'; another with figures and a sunburst, representing 'Night and Morning', and the 'St George' plaque of 1906, with its mounted knight 'un chevalier sans peur et sans reproche' and sinuous serpent rim painted in silver lustre by Richard Joyce (see p. 120).[35]

Apart from a youthful attempt at modelling using clay from a London brick-field, Crane's early art work was chiefly two-dimensional and it was only around 1874 when he was commissioned to design decorative panels for the frieze of a dining-room that he thought to build up the surface, using a paste made of plaster of paris and glue applied to canvas, 'after the manner of the early Florentine School'. He developed this idea in the saloon of Dr William Spottiswood's Palladian country house, Combe Bank, at Sundridge, near Sevenoaks. At Combe Bank Crane met the celebrated scientists of the day and he took pleasure in arranging the decoration of the saloon (in which the Royal Society met from time to time during Spottiswood's presidency) to suit its owner's interests. This work was carried on after the 'Psyche' frieze was finished between 1878 and 1880.[36] An existing moulding on the ceiling had to be allowed for as well as a painted

PICTURE·TILES·DESIGNED·BY·
WALTER·CRANE·

frieze of putti with fruit and animals, which Spottiswood had brought from abroad. The ceiling scheme includes figures of the Seasons and Planets arranged in square and circular compartments around a central motif of the sun and zodiac signs. Crane added a few of his own less rotund putti to the frieze and an embossed and gilded version of 'Peacocks and Amorini' covered the walls. Painted decoration on the lintels and on canvas applied to the panels of doors and window-shutters contains lightly draped and nude figures illustrating the Senses, Arts and Sciences and Welcome and Farewell. The shutter panels relate to the first two of these and represent nude boys at innocent pursuits such as fruit-picking and blowing bubbles, and several at more scientific activities, one with a camera and another with a telescope. The quality of Crane's painting varies although the general effect of black ground, white and pink drapery, flesh colour and touches of red is an agreeable accompaniment to the general scheme with its green stained woodwork, gold walls and gold and silver ceiling. Crane also designed the fire grate and irons, and the brass plaques on the jambs as well as the high wooden casing for the fireplace itself, with its decorated pilasters, gold niches and stucco relief of the Three Fates, reminiscent (as are other motifs here) of Crane's hangings for the Philadelphia Centennial. Most of the stucco work is on the ceiling.

Because it was so much a medium of design in the classical tradition stucco was not a medium encouraged by Gothic revivalists but through Crane's example it became more popular in the Arts and Crafts movement of the 1890s. He was familiar with the famous English ceilings such as those at Blickling Hall and Audley End and the many examples of Italian stucco relief in South Kensington Museum. In a discussion on the subject held by the Royal Institute of British Architects in 1891 he emphasized the importance of the decorative plasterwork of the High Renaissance, when Raphael and Giovanni da Udine revived the delicate technique of Roman stucco. These sources lie behind the scrollwork and classical forms of the Combe Bank ceiling, which are painted in gold and white metal.[37] The relief consisted of plaster of paris, size and cotton wool built up directly on to fibrous plaster panels. Crane was helped by Osmund Weeks his assistant in several later works in stucco. The method and recipes they perfected over the next ten years were published in 'Notes on Gesso' Crane's first contribution to the new *Studio* in May 1893.

The Combe Bank commission was followed by another from Alexander Ionides, the Greek Consul-General and financier well known in London as a generous patron of the arts. He employed the architect Philip Webb and Thomas Jeckyll, Morris and de Morgan to make alterations and to decorate the interior of No. 1 Holland Park which he moved into at the time of his marriage in 1875.[38] His taste was wide-ranging and the Ionides collection included Japanese paintings and prints as well as work by Whistler, Burne-Jones, Sandys and at least five water-colours by Crane.[39] The latter's work at No. 1 Holland Park was begun in the early 1880s and consisted chiefly in an elaboration of the decoration of the dining-room, for which Webb had already designed new woodwork, including a sideboard and mantelpiece. Crane later covered the panels with raised designs in gesso modelled with a brush. But the main part of his work comprised the gesso reliefs for ceiling and frieze, which were silvered and tinted in copper-coloured lacquer. The ceiling theme was that of the vine of life described in the Rubaiyat of Omar Khayyam, a quotation from which framed another relief over the fireplace. An inverted Greek wine-cup was also placed at the intersection of the ceiling coffering framing the squares of vine pattern. The deep frieze below contained square panels illustrating fables alternating with vertical ones with arabesques, including a lunette of 'The Lion in Love' above Webb's sideboard. Crane also designed a set of finger plates in lacquered gesso, two light fittings with grape clusters and an overmantel for the drawing-room to house Aleco Ionides' collection of Tanagra figurines. It was a double-tiered affair in black marble with a central pediment, two side sections above, and gold niches in the lower story. All the compartments were framed between red and yellow Siena marble columns – certainly a dramatic setting for the terracottas and one in accord with Ionides' rich and exotic taste.

Crane used plaster relief for a large fireplace for No. 1 Cumberland Place, which was completed early in 1884.[40] His most important work in this medium after Holland Park was for Sir Frances Wigan's house, Clare Lawn, at East Sheen in Surrey possibly begun as early as 1886. Panels from this were shown at the Arts and Crafts Exhibitions of 1889 and 1890.[41] Aston Webb, the architect who was partly responsible for this commission, found Crane further work in the spring of 1897, a plaster frieze for the dining room of Sir Weetman Pearson's country house, Paddockhurst, near Crawley in Sussex. The house is now Worth Abbey and the relief still survives, set above rather oppressive wooden panelling. It describes the history of transport from primitive times, when the Indian squaw carried her child in a papoose and horses were harnessed to man's needs, up to the present day whose progress is celebrated by bicycle and motor car, and by the grand concepts of 'The Genius of Mechanical Invention uniting Agriculture and Commerce' and 'The Genius of Electricity uniting the Parts of the Earth'. The use of antique personifications to illustrate such a futurist view may nowadays strike the onlooker as quaint but this is a remarkable manifestation of Crane's progressive outlook.

Dining Room at No. 1 Holland Park, the home of Alexander Ionides. Crane's decorative gesso work was applied to panelling designed by Philip Webb. Photograph by courtesy of the late Mrs Penelope Hotchkis.

Left
Woodnotes, 1886, wallp
blockprinted by Jeffrey
and Co. Collection the
Whitworth Art Galler
Manchester University

Right
The Formal Garden, 19
wallpaper, block print
by Jeffrey and Co.
By courtesy of the Vi
and Albert Museum.

The Genius of Electricity Uniting the Four Corners of the Earth, 1897, plaster relief. Part of a scheme illustrating the history of transport and communications, Worth Abbey, Crawley, Sussex.

Despite his admiration for the achievements of antiquity and the middle ages he looked ahead to the new century with an eager anticipation founded on his respect for science and optimism for Socialism.

With artistic gifts which so obviously inclined towards linear rather than three-dimensional expression it is not surprising that Crane's sculptural activities were limited chiefly to reliefs. However he did produce a model of 'Europa and the Bull' based on his painting of this subject, and design figure sculpture for the entrance porch of the Victoria Law Courts in Birmingham, a building constructed during 1887 and 1891 to plans by the London architects, Sir Aston Webb and Ingress Bell. In addition to the work for specific decorative schemes were a number of reliefs on a smaller scale including a plaque for the Art-Workers' Guild and little colour panel of a 'Sea Maiden'. In several Arts and Crafts Exhibitions he showed repoussé work, plates for moulded versions of his wall-papers and individual themes such as the copper shield with divers exhibited in 1893. In this year he took up his duties as Director of Design at Manchester School of Art and this led to a commission to design a mace for the city.[42]

During the 1870s several London houses became famous for their interior decoration. Before the dining room at No. 1 Palace Green was eventually completed by Burne-Jones and Crane the public had been invited to view Whistler's Peacock Room in F. R. Leyland's house at No. 49 Prince's Gate. Entirely different but unique in its own way was Frederic Leighton's Arab Hall. This extension to the Academy President's Holland Park House was designed by George Aitcheson, who asked Crane to prepare a mosaic frieze for the interior (1877–9) which had walls covered in ancient Persian, Islamic and modern tiles selected and designed by de Morgan, a mosaic floor with a pool in the centre and a dome above. Light filtered in through wooden grilles and small coloured glass windows on to the exotically glinting surfaces as it might in a painting by John F. Lewis. Crane's frieze enhances this Arabic delicacy with a Byzantine splendour controlled in strictly formal designs which at Leighton's request were based on the mosaics in the twelfth century Norman Sicilian Palace, La Ziza. Confronted peacocks with tails of coiling arabesques, cockatoos and deer in acanthus run around the walls and in the window recesses are roundels with sun, moon and winged beasts, separated by formalized trees and shrubs. Leighton kept a check to see that his designer's plans agreed with his own fastidious taste and was so pleased with

Crane's work that he hoped to have him and Burne-Jones design a mosaic for the dome but this idea was given up because of the expense involved. At Aitcheson's suggestion Crane also provided mosaics for Mr Stewart Hodgson's house at 5 South Audley Street.[43] His last mosaic scheme never materialized. It was to have been a huge frieze seventeen feet high and sixty-five feet wide for the outside of Harrison Townsend's Whitechapel Art Gallery. In comparison with the truly decorative fancy of his work for the Arab Hall this was to have been a more ponderous and predictable Victorian effort, too close to the manner of W. B. Richmond.[44]

Crane's earliest stained glass designs were small panels for the library of 'Vinland' near Newport, R.I., and probably date from late in 1883. They were made at Merton Abbey as were also two glass door panels of 1889 for the picture gallery at Clare Lawn, each representing a classical figure holding the symbols of an artist's inspiration 'Speculum Naturae' and 'Sphaera Imaginationis'.[45] Shortly after this he designed a large three-light window of 'St Paul Preaching at Athens' for a church in Newark, New Jersey, which was carried out by the New York firm of J. and R. Lamb. This was destroyed in 1936.[46] A complete set of windows by Crane do survive however in the Cathedral Church of the Good Shepherd, then known as the Church of the Agapemone, at Stamford Hill – a Gothic building designed by Joseph Morris and Sons of Reading. It is distinguished by its decoration rather than any special architectural merit, having sculpture by A. G. Walker on the lowest offsets of the tower buttresses and Walter Crane's glass within.

The Sun of Righteousness, 1896, stained glass, the central west window of the Church of the Agapemone, Stamford Hill, London.

St George Plaque, 1806, diameter
11 7/16 in. (29 cm), designed by
Crane and painted by Richard
Joyce for Pilkington's, Royal
Lancastrian Ware. Collection the
Whitworth Art Gallery,
Manchester University.

Right
England and France, 82 × 56 in.
(234 × 143 cm) wool and cotton
woven hanging designed by
Crane for the Franco-British
Exhibition at Earl's Court in 1908
and made by A. H. Lee for
Warner and Sons Ltd. Collection
the Whitworth Art Gallery,
Manchester University.

There are eight double-light aisle windows, four on each side, with motifs of Lily, Vine, Plum, Poppy, Rose, Fig, Pomegranate and Olive against a cerulean background. Over the entrance at the west is a four-light window of The Sun of Righteousness and at either side double-lights of Sin and Shame and Disease and Death, elongated images consumed and tortured by flames and snakes and made more lugubrious by the use of deep red, blue-greens and purples. At the east above the altar are the Dove of Peace and Lion of Judah flanked by the Translation of Enoch and Elijah.[47] The work was carried out by J. Sylvester Sparrow who made use of various kinds of 'antique' or pot metal glass made by Britton and Gibson, and Powell's of the Whitefriars Glass Company – one of the earliest in the country to revive ancient techniques of stained glass manufacture. This had also preoccupied Rossetti and Burne-Jones who tried in their work for Morris's firm to evolve styles appropriate to the rich mosaic effects obtained by using small pieces of glass rather than the large areas which had become usual in the previous century. Crane too saw stained glass in terms of 'a network of jewelled light'.[48] His lead lines are more closely packed than they appear to have been in the Newark window and he uses them here more as he might his pen in black and white work – for expressive as well as decorative effect. Vigorous swirling patterns and ribbons of flame-like shapes match the intense mood evoked by the glowing and eerie gloom of the variegated glass in contrast to the more classical and logical conception of 'St Paul Preaching in Athens'. At least one further example of later glass survives, a five-light window of 1897 for Holy Trinity Church, Hull, also executed by Sparrow.[49] But it is clear from this that the Psalms of David did not appeal to Crane's imagination as much as did the apocalyptic subjects for the Church of the Agapemone.

Other designs which do not fit the categories described above include a set of painted panels for an ocean liner called *The Ophir*, four for the Chicago World Fair, an inlaid wood floor for the new South London Art Gallery and one in mosaic for a bank in Cleveland, Ohio.[50] With all this work it cannot but be wondered how Crane managed to continue for so long in his official post as President of the Exhibition Society. Ashbee recalled that he was 'a shockingly bad chairman'[51] but there were few who could compare with his record as an indefatigable art worker and the obvious pleasure he derived from being an official prevented his friends and colleagues from voting him out. Some were to regret this lenient attitude when, after two very successful decades, the society began to founder. Rather late they wished for a more decisive character able to give a firm lead to designers in the knotty matter of how arts and crafts were to cope with the machine age. Crane's attitude to the machine became quite accommodating but he had not the temperament of a designer whose style lent itself to a machine aesthetic. The splendid example set by his many designs was wholly in the arts and crafts tradition, full of the 'living and tender detail'[52] that was the hallmark of English craftsmen of his generation.

Late Work

When his ideals and philosophy clarified in support of socialism, Crane's position as an artist became paradoxical. He vigorously promoted the lesser arts and yet put his own most ambitious effort as painter and philosopher into pictures pregnant with myth, personification and an assortment of quaintly original and exploratory metaphors. In this way he gave support to the long-established notion that Fine Art in its highest form was the product of skill, culture and intellect. These endeavours were beyond the comprehension of the average British workman, and aroused much less enthusiasm among art connoisseurs. But he continued to persevere with at least one major work for the annual Grosvenor summer exhibition. A glance at the unlikely and phlegmatic 'Abduction of Europa' of 1881 reveals little development from the Grosvenor Gallery exhibits of 1877 and 1879, his 'Anadyomene' and 'The Sirens'. Whether due to their hermaphroditic genesis or the artist's reticence, Crane's nudes, unlike Burne-Jones's, lacked the allure of sensuality which increased their marketability. A few works of the early 1880s were in a more romantic, north Italian vein. The oil, 'The Laidly worm of Spindleston Heugh', was exhibited with 'Europa'. Its subject, from an old legend which Crane heard on a holiday at Bamborough in 1877, told of a princess transformed into a serpent by a wicked stepmother and restored to her ladylike form by a brotherly kiss, and contains the same successful basic ingredients as the toy-book fairy-tales. His choice of this source reflects the taste of the Pre-Raphaelites and their followers (Swinburne wrote a version of the same ballad) but it was also the kind of narrative which became generally popular with Victorian painters on the look-out for dramatic narratives.

Graham Robertson's boyhood recollections of pleasant afternoons spent with the Cranes at Beaumont Lodge convey a sensitive picture of their domestic life; with the master not very masterful but surprisingly young-looking and shy, his handsome hospitable wife, their brood of 'stout and placid babies' and a blossoming garden of resident rabbits and guinea-pigs.[1] This happy atmosphere was clouded early in 1882 by the death of one of the children, a third son born in June the previous year. To escape the memories of Shepherd's Bush the family took a house for a few months at Wickhurst, near Sevenoaks. Here news came of the death on 31 March of Lucy Crane, who had taken ill with heart trouble while on a lecture tour in the north of England. In the face of these family tragedies Crane threw his energies into a new painting. 'The Roll of Fate' was exhibited at the Grosvenor Gallery that year, accompanied by a verse from the Rubaiyat of Omar Khayyam, expressive of the artist's sad and baffled feelings:

> Would that some winged angel ere too late
> Arrest the yet unfolded scroll of Fate . . .

Came first the glowing Rose in view,
With crimson pennon fluttering new;
With glittering spines all armed he came,
With lance and shield - a rose aflame;
With tossing crest and mantling free,
On fiery steed, - a sight to see!

Cloth binding for *The Shepheard's
Calender* stamped in gold and
colour, 1898. By courtesy of
Glasgow School of Art,
photograph Peter Adamson.

*Left
The Rose Knight* from *Queen
Summer*, 1891. By courtesy of
Glasgow School of Art,
photograph Peter Adamson.

The Roll of Fate, 1882, oil on
canvas, 28 × 26 in. (71 × 66 cm).
Collection Arch. Alberto Galardi,
Milan.

Deep emotions here tempted Crane to venture from the cool glades and limpid
pools of classical myth to scale loftier peaks of Victorian high art. The angel is the
most impressive nude yet to come from his brush. But in spite of wings and astral
portents this work remains a literal interpretation of an evocative text, rather too
substantial and earthbound.

The previous Christmas Crane had visited Italy with a friend but, apart from
the inevitable sketchbook jottings, had had little time for much serious work.
He went to Venice, saw Turin, Genoa and Ravenna for the first time, and also
Piero della Francesca's frescoes at Arezzo, but stayed in Rome only long enough
to renew a few old friendships before returning home early in January. In the
following September when he took the whole family to Rome his plans for
working were agreeably frustrated by the commission from a rich American, Miss
Catharine Wolfe, to paint a frieze for the dining-room of her house at Newport,
Rhode Island. 'Vinland' was a brownstone villa built in 1883 by Peabody and
Sterns. Architecturally speaking the house has little to do with English styles of
the period but its interior contained wallpapers and fabrics from Morris's firm
as well as stained glass manufactured at Merton from designs by Crane and Burne-
Jones. Only Crane's frieze survives in what is now the library of Salve Regina
College. It depicts Longfellow's ballad 'The Skeleton in Armour', a romantic

Viking tale spun round an ancient circular tower at Newport which was believed to have been built by Norsemen. This exciting subject afforded Crane scope for dramatic action, especially the episode of Hildebrand's pursuit of the hero, with its scenes of mounted warriors and battling longships. The work was carried out in flat oil on four large canvases, each about three feet by twenty-four feet. The technique is broader than usual and the cool blues and silvery tones, set off occasionally by warmer colours and rich Venetian reds, are pleasantly contrasted by light oak panelling beneath. Most of the work was finished and shipped directly to the United States before Crane left Rome in the Spring of 1883.[2] Two sections, 'The Viking's Bride' and 'The Viking's Wooing', were brought back to England and exhibited at the Grosvenor Gallery that summer with a portrait of his wife and the oil 'Diana and the Shepherd' which is now in Dundee Art Gallery. In place of Allessandro young Graham Robertson posed as the huntress holding in leash one of the family's larger, leaner pets. The Vinland commission prevented Crane from immediately pursuing the philosophical line of 'The Roll of Fate'. He returned again to the style in 1884 with an elaborate double allegory of 'The Bridge of Life'. It was exhibited at the Grosvenor together with a poem on its frame and a lengthy catalogue note describing the familiar dramatis personae of Love, Life, Death, Hope, the Fates and Fame. Crane was clearly making a bid for the kind of acclaim which greeted Watts, Leighton and Poynter but it eluded him and Sir Coutts Lindsay began to give his pictures less prominence.

When the innocent allure of his 'Sirens' was developed and invested with a more overt socialist meaning in *The Sirens Three*, Crane began to lose earlier sympathizers. The conclusive image of this poem is one of Earth emerging 'renascent from the sea of crystal air'. This description of the climax of Earth's rebirth has its counterpart in 'The Renaissance of Venus'. Images decorating *Sirens Three* also appear in contemporary paintings such as the large oil of 'Freedom' exhibited at the Grosvenor Gallery in the summer of 1885: and a smaller water colour of 'Pandora'. The delicate colour and setting of a collonaded hall with tossing cypresses

The Bridge of Life, 1884, oil on canvas. One of several important paintings by Crane, which were bought by the German dealer and art collector, Ernst Seeger, during the 1890s. Present whereabouts unknown.

*The Laidly Worm of Spindleston
Heugh* signed with a monogram
and dated 1881, oil on canvas,
28 × 67 in. (71.1 × 170.2 cm).
Collection Dr Emilio Bertonati,
Galleria del Levante, Milan.

Neptune's Horses, 1893, oil on
canvas, 34 × 84 in. (86 × 215 cm).
Collection Neue Pinakothek,
Munich.

The Chariot of the Hours, 1886–87, water colour, present whereabouts unknown.

beyond made this a pleasing work in spite of Pandora's abandoned posture which was condemned by critics for being as formless as a jellyfish.[3] A collection of holiday views of St David's and Swanage were submitted to the next Grosvenor exhibition but another image with its genesis in *Sirens Three* appeared in 1887, 'The Riddle of the Sphinx'. Instead of man questioning the secret of life Crane's riddle has a more revolutionary, and presumably socialist, significance as it is accompanied by a passage from Carlyle on the nature of Justice.[4] In contrast with this enigma his other major work, 'The Chariot of the Hours', brought with it a dash of the vitality more common in his illustration. It was based on the description of the flight of the Hours in 'Prometheus Unbound' and on studies of horses and riders made at chariot races at Kensington Olympia. Even Shelley's allegory could not revive Sir Coutts Lindsay's waning interest and the picture was skied. A worse fate befell 'The Riddle of the Sphinx', which was put behind a pillar in a corridor. Crane withdrew it and never again submitted work to the gallery.

His contributions to the Dudley dwindled to a few designs and ceased after the spring exhibition of 1881. As a committee member of this water colour society he had been invited to join the reorganized Institute of Painters in Water Colour and use their galleries in Piccadilly, where he exhibited 'La Belle Dame Sans Merci' in 1884. The following year he helped plan a tableau for a ball celebrating the inauguration of the new society. Crane took the part of Cimabue in his tableau of 'The Art of Italy' where Mary Crane was Laura, Lionel Giotto, Beatrice 'an early Italian angel', Lisa Stillman Fiametta, and W. A. S. Benson Nicolo Pisano. Henry Irving commissioned a painting of the group and this is now in Manchester City Art Gallery. Its exhibition at the Grosvenor in 1886 caused some dispute at the Royal Institute and led to Crane's resignation. Two years later Poynter proposed him for associate membership of the Old Water Colour Society with whom he exhibited until the end of his life.

He was not alone in his dissatisfaction with Sir Coutts Lindsay's management of the gallery. In the summer of 1887 Comyns Carr and Charles Hallé resigned their directorships and set about planning a rival concern. Crane conveniently transferred his allegiance to the New Gallery for the opening exhibition in the summer of 1888. Thanks to the support of well-established figures like Burne-Jones, G. F. Watts, and Alma Tadema its security was well assured. A less adventurous policy was pursued than in the days of the early Grosvenor Gallery.

Instead of being considered among the dangerously innovatory products of an avant-garde, Burne-Jones's work was now much in demand and the one-man show of loan paintings mounted by the New Gallery in the winter of 1892–3 was a sound business investment.

In 1889 Crane scored his first continental success by winning a silver medal at the Paris Universal Exhibition for a little water colour of 'A Diver', which had been shown previously at the Royal Institute. Sea themes became fashionable in British painting at this time, a vogue which Burne-Jones helped to promote with his unique Royal Academy exhibit of 1886, the glaucous fantasy 'The Depths of the Sea'. Among Crane's paintings at the New Gallery in 1888 was 'A Water Lily',[5] a personified plant picture paralleling those of *Flora's Feast*, upon which he was then working. But he was also to explore another oceanic theme in the grand elemental metamorphosis, 'Neptune's Horses', shown at the New Gallery in 1893. This commanding vision has a dramatic force, reminiscent of Swinburne's descriptions of the sea, although Crane stated that the idea of a wave breaking into a frieze of aquatic stallions was suggested by the Atlantic 'white horses' he watched at Wauwinet, Nantucket, in 1892 (p. 128). It was his most successful imaginative picture of the decade. In 'Swan Maidens' of 1894,[6] the transformation of swan into maiden is much less convincing than the previous metamorphosis of spume into stallions. Wagnerian themes had for some time been popular with continental symbolists and in England Burne-Jones was an early follower of the fashion. Crane's first contribution to the cult followed a visit to Bayreuth in 1893 where he saw Löhengrin, Tannhauser, and Parsifal.

In 'The Rainbow and the Wave' of 1895 he was more successful in raising his idea from a purely literal to a poetic level. Watery and nebulous elements are united in a delicate, intimate way owing more to Watt's manner than to the frank

The Mower, 1901 described by the artist as in tempera but it is painted on canvas, 31½ × 46 in. (80 × 117 cm). Collection Staatliche Kunsthalle, Karlsruhe.

The Dance of the Five Senses, signed and dated 1891–93, water colour, 18 × 38 in (46 × 97 cm). Collection Squarzina, Milan.

treatment of that more sensuous master of the water-sprite and nereid, H. J. Draper. 'In the Clouds' (1894) and 'The Crest of the Wave' (1903) are other examples of such themes.[7] One of Crane's oddest inventions (which may be a reminder of nature's transience of just an eccentric message for conservationists) is 'The Mower' of 1901, in which a field of elfin daisies shiver beneath the menacing scythe of Death.

In addition to these phenomenal metamorphoses the familiar forms of Eld and Father Time, angels of Peace and Labour, Britannia, Beauty, Youth, Spring and a host of gallant knights people his later paintings. Their function, as ever, is to symbolize ideas relating to the plight of Humanity and Art. 'England's Emblem',[8] shown at the New Gallery in 1895, is a medieval subject with a modern message. St George charges a lowering beast, a symbol of greed which belches fire and crouches over a desolate land in which the inevitable river meanders past a neglected plough and the 'pale cliffs of Albion'. Against a lurid sunset are silhouetted the black smoking stacks of factory chimneys. 'Britomart by the Sea' (1896) was based on one of the headings to Book III of the *Faerie Queene* and she was succeeded in 1897 by 'Britannia's Vision' which featured an equally homely armour-clad maiden. This picture aroused more than the usual criticism because its vision of an empire tolerating greed, poverty, and unemployment was thought to be in bad taste for Victoria's Jubilee Year. Although Crane had by this time more or less abandoned his grand style of the previous decade, philosophical notions continue to sustain apparently romantic conceits as in the above patriotic efforts or the 'World's Conquerors' of 1898.[9]

One of his cherished visions was of an England whose happy communal life was expressed in pageantry and folk festivals. And when he planned the entertainment 'Beauty's Awakening: a masque of Winter and Spring' he felt the need to convey a message. This event was staged by the Art-Workers' Guild in London's Guildhall in June 1899. Originally it was Crane's idea but he was helped in final versions of text, costumes and stage design by various guild members including Ashbee, Selwyn Image, Joseph Pennell, Halsey Ricardo, Harrison Townsend and Henry Wilson, most of whom also took part in the masque itself. Crane played the part of Dürer. His designs for the Dance of the Five Senses were reproduced in colour in the special *Studio* summer number devoted to 'Beauty's Awakening' and were also used for a painting.[10] It is a charming invention with all the light decorative qualities of Crane at his best. The theme around which these fantasies were woven was that of the revival of art in a new age, described using a Sleeping Beauty allegory in which Fayremonde, the spirit of Beauty, is awakened by the knight Trueheart, who struggles against Aschemon's demons, representatives of the faults and malpractices attributed to London's City Council. Eventually the seven lamps of architecture, Fayremonde's attendants, are rekindled and England's capital is allowed to join her court with the other fair cities of the world. Crane never discovered how the city fathers took this criticism which was directed at them under their own roof. Despite its arty disguise there was a good deal of pointed protest, particularly where Ashbee gave vent to his feelings when he called Bumbledeadalus out for a wigging:

> Room of the London of old Bumblebeadalus!
> The London of vestries, of jobs and of lies,
> Of puffs and of posters, of signs in the skies,
> Of crawling busses and crowded trains,
> Of river monopolies, unflushed drains,
> Would you be-wheedle us old Bumblebeadalus?
> Our London, the joyless, the reckless of brains,
> The sleepy, the smoky, the sooty remains!
> And what if a tub-thumping socialist boggles
> At your mace and your furs and your gloves and your goggles,
> Old Bumble grows bigger, his heart merely hardens
> As he crawls from the Mansion House into Spring Gardens . . .[11]

In the 'Masque of the Seasons' and Glasgow Art Gallery's 'Briar Rose' triptych both of 1905 Crane continued with familiar imaginative subjects. His late painting is without any very purposeful direction and even his missionary spirit seems to have been somewhat quelled. However, he did return to Wagner with a dashing 'Valkyrie's Ride' in 1903, and, in a final grand gesture expressive of his old zeal, produced a 'Prometheus Unbound' for the New Gallery show of 1906.

Crane never grew out of the habit of recording views and holiday experiences. He and his wife were enthusiastic travellers and their journeys abroad became increasingly exotic. For James Baker's article 'In the Peleponnesus', printed in *The English Illustrated Magazine* in 1889, he contributed Greek sketches. A Bohemian set from a tour of 1890 was published in *Pictures from Bohemia* by the same author. Water colours from these and other holidays were on view at the Fine Art Exhibition of 1891 and the Doré Gallery show of 1902. At Dowdswells' in 1907 there was an exhibition of work from his Indian tour of the previous winter. Much of this was used for Crane's book *India Impressions*, published the same year.[12] In 1910 they visited Egypt. A further exhibition of drawings was put on to accompany the special viewing in the Leicester Galleries in 1912 of the self-portrait commissioned by the Uffizi, and, finally, the memorial exhibition of 1920 provided a comprehensive selection of paintings of American, Scandinavian, various British, French, Italian, German and Indian subjects.

Crane's chaste avoidance of even the most delicate sexual implications and his persistent plugging of a humanitarian message preclude any claims of decadence. As a symbolist his place is a minor one although he nevertheless exerted an influence on younger artists which will be discussed in the last chapter. Outside the fairy realms of folklore and floral fantasy he perhaps handled pictorial imagery too literally. He saw himself as a painter of 'inner vision' and yet swept away all the cobwebby mysteries which make such visions intriguing.[13]

Crane's urge to intellectualize and relate literature to painting accompanied all his major pictorial enterprises in the form of verse and often copious catalogue entries. Spiritual food was best administered by gods and goddesses, knights and fairies even although such characters were almost complete strangers to an uneducated public. Crane believed that an artist's aim in depicting ordinary life should be to infuse it with improving factors like dignity, devotion and heroism. Unlike Baudelaire and Manet he saw little romance in the chimney pot hat and tubular clothing of the modern citizen. Hence his condemnation of Degas's 'L'Absinthe' in 1893 as a vulgar affront to sensitive minds and his declaration that he could certainly never live with such an object – a criticism which earned him doubtful fame as the originator of 'Walter Crane's co-habitation test'.[14]

The loose brushwork and apparent lack of compositional structure, a factor for which he chiefly criticized Monet, were other elements of Impressionism that offended Crane's sense of artistic propriety. He had never experienced the satisfaction of evolving a truly painterly style and it was unlikely that he could sympathize with the freedom of the modern movements. It was characteristic of his preference for meticulous details that he should have experimented with tempera at this time in his career. His oils consistently deny the lush possibilities of the medium and even in water colour he insisted on adding gouache to achieve an opaque effect instead of exploiting its luminous potential. In these things Crane followed the example of others, including Burne-Jones. Writing after the Grafton Galleries Exhibition of 1910–11, he cautiously welcomed Roger Fry's Post-Impressionism, acknowledging in its diversity a trend towards more conscious formal design, a possible 'indication of a return to sanity and a desire to restore the art of painting to an art of design',[15] but was sensitive to the difficulties facing sophisticated idealists – he would be thinking of the Pont Aven painters rather than of Cézanne – who wished to express the naiveté of primitive life.

The earliest important black and white commission of Crane's final quarter century were illustrations to *The Story of the Glittering Plain* by William Morris, published by the Kelmscott Press in February 1894, a press founded as a result of discussion between Emery Walker, Morris and Crane during the Arts and Crafts Exhibition in 1888. A small quarto edition with text decoration by the author had been the first work issued by the Press in May 1891 and the idea that Crane should illustrate the poem originated at this time. Crane had not Morris's passionate interest in the minutiae of type design. He had worked earlier in different calligraphic styles as can be seen from the texts of *The First of May* and *Sirens Three* although these are not as fine as the Roman and italic scripts developed by Morris in his illuminated manuscripts of the 1870s, and so Crane's contribution to the press was to be limited to illustration only. Every Kelmscott production was planned by Morris with scrupulous care, from the choice of suitable hand-made paper to the laborious process of designing type, the first of these being the Roman Golden type followed by the Gothic Troy and Chaucer (a large and smaller version of the same design). The large quarto *Glittering Plain* was printed in black and red, in Troy with a list of chapter headings in Chaucer. Morris contributed initials and borders, and Crane twenty-three drawings engraved on wood by his cousins A. and E. Leverett.[16]

Although he later doubted that these designs were ever 'quite Gothic enough in feeling' to suit Morris,[17] it is clear that in preparing them Crane made definite concessions to the other's taste. His style here is not as angular and elongated as Burne-Jones's Kelmscott *Chaucer*, but it is distinctly medieval and different to the lighter linear treatment of his own more recent graphic work such as the frontispiece to Effie Johnson's *In the Fire and Other Fancies* of 1892. Several details in *The*

BUT on the morrow the men arose, & the Sea-eagle and his damsel came to Hallblithe; for the other two damsels were departed, and the

Glittering Plain illustrations are reminiscent of the Cupid and Psyche woodcuts of the 1860s but it is distinguished chiefly by a richer texture of black and white pattern and fewer forms in outline.

The *Glittering Plain* designs impressed F. S. Ellis, the publisher of Morris's earlier books and his friend and assistant on many Kelmscott matters. He asked Crane for drawings to decorate his edition of William Caxton's *History of Reynard the Fox*, a small quarto printed at the Chiswick Press and published by David Nutt in 1894.[18] This work included headings, tailpieces and a full-page frontispiece illustrating 'Reynard at the Court of the Lion King', which like the title-page opposite, was framed in a border of ivy-leaf tendrils, a motif used by Morris for several of his early illuminated books. In Crane's case its derivation from late Gothic manuscripts is more obvious and this indicates how the historical implications involved in Kelmscott and related publications encouraged designers to look to the past rather than to rely on their own inventiveness.

About the same time as he began the *Glittering Plain* project Crane started a series of illustrations to three Shakespeare plays, 'The Tempest' (issued in 1893) 'Two Gentlemen of Verona' and 'The Merry Wives of Windsor' (both issued in 1894). Each of the eight designs were printed using a new facsimile process created by Duncan C. Dallas[19] but Crane's interpretation of these familiar scenes is weak.

Crane's most important work in terms of quantity were the illustrations to Spenser's *Faerie Queene*, edited by T. J. Wise and published by George Allen in nineteen parts from 1894 to 1897. He designed a cover for the series and at least one full-page illustration, heading and tailpiece, for the twelve cantos of each book. Both Konody and Berlepsch praise this as a major achievement among Crane's later black and white work but it is disappointing as was indicated at the time by poor sales. The text decorations are lively and inventive without the obvious historicism of the *Reynard* edition of 1894. They continue the fine development of such motifs in *Household Stories* and the more recent colour work for Hawthorne's *Wonder Book,* except that he now extends the tails of initials to partly frame page layouts which are less pretentiously archaic than some Kelmscott books. There is a good balance of text and decoration, and blank paper is allowed to act as a foil to the design. Unfortunately when faced with a full-page illustration Crane too often suffered from a *horror vacui*. His borders are original enough (Morris came increasingly to depend on designs from earlier works or to repeat his own) but this elaboration seldom enhances the central drawing. From these unwieldy volumes of *The Faerie Queene* it must be concluded that despite his deep affection for Spenser's allegory Crane found it difficult to sustain enthusiasm and a spontaneous response.

The little volume of Spenser's *Shepheard's Calender* of 1898 presents a much more satisfying unity. It was printed at the Chiswick Press and for the cloth cover Crane evolved one of his most restrained and charming designs. The Kelmscott Press had recently issued an edition of the same book and although Crane's style shows no trace of the clean-cut angularity of A. J. Gaskin's illustrations he may have been influenced by the simple presentation of this book to reduce the decoration in his own. The illustrations are framed in a double line as in the Kelmscott version with the addition only of one or two emblem roundels and the name of the month in the designs introducing the twelve eclogues. Stylistically there are more woodcut mannerisms than in the pages of *The Faerie Queene* (see p. 125).

Recognition of his international status as a graphic artist came with the commission to design all the text ornament, covers and five full-page illustrations to Genesis for a Bible to be issued by the Illustrated Bible Society. Crane worked at

The Witch creates a snowy Lady
Like to Florimell;
Who, wrong'd by Carle, by Proteus sav'd,
Is sought by Paridell.

this between 1897 and 1900 and among others involved in this ambitious project were Burne-Jones, Alma Tadema, Frank Dicksee, the French artists Puvis de Chavannes, Gerôme and Tissot, the Germans Max Klinger, Uhde and Lieber-mann, Joseph Israels of Holland, the American E. A. Abbey, the Russian Repin and the Italian Segantini. As a whole Crane considered the Bible a compromise because the styles of individual contributors were too diverse and the publishers did not follow his suggestions for a heavier type and unglazed paper.[20]

Flora's Feast was the first of a series of flower books designed by Crane between 1888 and 1906. The second, *Queen Summer or the Tournay of the Lily and the Rose,* was also published by Cassell and Company and appeared in 1891. It had forty colour

The Snow Lady from Spenser's *Faerie Queene*, 1894-7.

Love in a mist from *A Floral Fantasy in an Old English Garden*, 1898. By courtesy of the Trustees of the National Library of Scotland.

Though LOVE IN A MIST may hide, When Time's in the garden weeding.

designs which, unlike the previous book, were framed and included the text written on scroll placards. The theme is that of a flower masque and tournament of suitors for Queen Summer's favour. The style is medieval (see p. 124); a kind of decorated Gothic of Crane's own devising, based on a more impressionistic principle than the simple outline and flat colour of *Flora's Feast*. An intermediary stage of stylistic development between this and *Flora's Feast* is to be seen in the nervous line drawing in *A Book of Wedding Days* of 1889. With *Flora's Feast* Crane had followed the procedure of his children's picture books and painted in the colours on a pull of the key proof but colour and outline must have been worked out together for *Queen Summer*, as they contribute equally to the overall effect of the designs resulting in a fluent and variegated surface pattern. This sequel to *Flora's Feast* is a very different but equally delightful fantasy. Of three important colour commissions resulting from his American trip, Margaret Deland's *Old Garden and Other Verses* (Osgood, McIlvaine and Company, 1893) may be classed as a flower book. Crane embellished the poems with a wealth of floral and figurative motifs. The style is a development of the *Queen Summer* technique but the drawing is all in colour and unframed. The darkest accents are provided by the black Gothic type of the text. Some designs have a prim and dainty quality which hint at Greenaway, others more vividly suggest Blake. *A Floral Fantasy in an Old English Garden* of 1899 illustrates the more formal trend of Crane's graphic style at the end of the century, one visible already in the very last few designs for *The Faerie Queene*. The idea for *A Floral Fantasy* originated in the summer of 1898 when Crane rented an Elizabethan farmhouse in Kent from Ford Maddox Hueffer. Pent Farm, with its trimmed lawns and hedges, and neat flower beds, provided the setting for the familiar theme of 'flowers masquing like women and men'. There is no single key outline, the designs being drawn in various colours with infilling of flat wash. The geometrical principles so obvious in the later 'Mary, Mary' wallpaper are most clearly demonstrated in the endpapers for this book. Not every page is laid out with such regularity. 'Love in a Mist' is a tangle of flowering tendrils delicately expressive of her fright at seeing 'Time in the garden weeding' on the opposite page.

In his last three fantasy books, all of which were published by Cassell, *A Masque of Days* (1901), *The Flower Wedding* (1905) and *Flowers from Shakespeare's Garden* (1906), the emphasis becomes distinctly fashionable. Bizarre costumes look like ideas for fancy dress. Indeed the 'young spark' giving dinner to the days of the year in Elia's *Masque of Days* may be Lancelot and the whole event represent the celebration of his coming of age. Four years previously a memorable Fancy Ball was arranged in Lionel's honour at the Crane's Holland Street house and required a temporary one-way traffic system to accommodate the carriages of seven hundred guests in the narrow Kensington streets.[21] Many there distinguished themselves by the inventive variety of their costumes but few could have rivalled Crane's own bird outfit with its beaked hat and triple-toed feet or the bold figure his statuesque wife must have cut in the topical guise of a sunflower.

Crane's fantasy flower books occupy the place taken earlier by his picture books for children. In both he had complete freedom with regard to content and design. He also continued to work on more specific colour commissions in several publications for older children. The earliest and best of these was Hawthorne's *Wonder Book*, whose designs he completed while in Florida in the early summer of 1892. It has sixty colour drawings, including nineteen full-page plates, endpapers and a fine white cloth cover printed in green and brown. The headings and tailpieces are in one or two colours only but the main illustrations use six. A brown key ensures a soft and rich effect. The lithographs were admirably printed for

'Twas now impossible to fly from the anti-meat-eating satire *Rumbo Rhymes*, 1911. By courtesy of the Trustees of the National Library of Scotland.

Houghton Mifflin at the Riverside Press. Crane was less fortunate with regard to Judge Perry's version of *Don Quixote*, issued in 1900. The colour designs here have much of the lithographic mealiness he had so disliked and a hard wiry black outline. Although he tried to enter into the spirit of the story his characterizations of Sancho Panza and Don Quixote are predictable. There is little about this volume to raise it above the level of the many good colour illustrated books which were by this time being produced for the children's market.

Martin Hardie, in his study *English Coloured Books*, published in 1905 considered that the 'collector may cherish an acquatint, a chromolithograph, a coloured wood engraving, but a process plate never'. By this date, however, photographic colour half-tone printing had been in use for a decade. Crane's first book with colour plates was Arthur Kelly's delightful *Rosebud and Other Tales* of 1909. These show him beginning to take advantage of the subtle effects the process afforded but the bright colour and strong design, plus the way in which they are mounted on dark paper, ensures that they do not detract from the unified concept of the whole book. Even in Alfred Calmour's anti-meat-eating animal satire *Rumbo Rhymes* of 1911 there are reminiscences of Japanese prints which indicate Crane's continuing sensitivity to harmonious page design. His capitulation to pictorial illusionism is to be seen in Henry Gilbert's *King Arthur's Knights* (1911) and *Robin Hood* (1912), each of which had sixteen full-page illustrations in the first edition. If anything the designs for *Robin Hood* are even more illusionistic than those to *King Arthur's Knights*, as Crane seems to have become increasingly interested in depicting atmosphere with coloured shadows dappling sunlit woods. The brighter local colours and stronger contrasts and outline of his plates for Mary MacGregor's *Story of Greece* (1913) suggest that he tried to check these painterly tendencies in favour of stronger design but the results are still a surprisingly unexceptional compromise for an artist who had once created the brilliant pages of the toy books. By this time his popularity as a fashionable illustrator had passed to men like Arthur Rackham and Edmund Dulac who relied on a more stylized idiom to preserve decorative feeling.

From the 1880s onwards Crane was often busy with various commissions ranging from book plates for private individuals,[22] to menu cards, tickets, cover designs and advertisements for business firms. Many of the covers were for left wing magazines and are listed in the following chapter. Others include *Atalanta* (1889), *The Art Journal*, *Harper's Round Table* (1897) and those designed for publishers' catalogues put out by Joseph Hughes, The Caxton Head and Houghton Mifflin. He also continued to produce advertisement material for the wallpaper manufacturing firm of Jeffrey and Company. Among his best known designs were those for insurance companies: The Scottish Union and National; Economic Life Office; Metropolitan Assurance; Law Union and Crown Insurance; and particularly the Scottish Widows Fund for which he began to work in the early 1890s. The design 'Take Time by the Forelock', where Bellerophon grasps the mane of a magnificent Pegasus, that of the Viking warrior keeping 'The Wolf from the Door' and many more appeared on calendars, posters and bookmarks issued by this firm. Other advertisement series were designed for Pears soap and Sanatogen.[23] Crane and his colleagues in the Art-Workers' Guild often protested against the way in which advertising spoiled the environment. The American tour of 1892 helped to confirm his fear of the threat presented by posters, which he saw as symbolic of the successes of commercialism. To an audience of Manchester students in 1893 he observed: 'I am afraid the modern triumph, such as it is, is pictured for us in the rampant posters which pursue us in and out of stations, up and down streets, and even along the railway lines, which last vantage has hitherto

Cover of *Atalanta*, August 1889. By courtesy of Liverpool City Libraries.

Advertisement for Pears Soap *c.* 1900. By courtesy of Liverpool City Libraries.

been the prerogative of our American cousins. I do not say the poster has no place in art. Under considerable restraint and chastening it might be possible to make the announcement of useful wares and theatrical events at least inoffensive, perhaps; and it may be that the mere working of competition will produce a demand for more refined productions, since when all shout together no one voice is likely to be heard and the accepted theory of a poster is that it *must* shout; but at any rate let us keep it out of our scenery. Anyway, the subject is important, since our hoardings are evidently the most obvious public education in pictorial and typographical design.'[24] Crane's own first poster of any consequence was derived from the drawings of the Chariot races at Kensington Olympia in 1887 which he had made to illustrate a souvenir booklet, but he produced very few others.[25] An intriguing contrast between the continuing virtuous tone of the Victorian era and light-hearted indulgence of the Edwardians is provided by his somewhat inconsistent designs for a Dutch temperance campaign and for Hau and Company's champagne. Crane recognized that the turn of the century was the epoch of the pictorial poster and later praised it as 'the most original, flourishing and vigorous type of popular art existing', one which often revealed remarkable artistic ability as well as the great resources of modern colour printing. Nonetheless he regretted that such energy should be spent on ephemeral purposes and concluded in a socialistic vein, endorsing the views of William Morris: 'The same ability under different influences and inspired by different ideals might serve to make eloquent the bare walls of our schools and public buildings with painted histories and legends of our country and race, which might foster the public spirit of our future citizens.'[26]

Socialism

Oh! men and women true, once more take hands,
Join hearts and heads, and clear the crooked maze:
Set Love and Justice up o'er these our lands:
Let Truth be honoured, honest work have praise.
And bring joy back to human days again:
Lift from Life's daily round its sordid cloak;
Draw Beauty near, nor common Use disdain;
Unite in one great cause the struggling folk.[1]

'I imagine that as people can be roughly divided into Socialists and Individualists so they can be sub-divided into conscious Socialists and unconscious Socialists. I believe I really belonged to the latter class long before I knew I belonged to the former.' This was how Crane introduced a discussion of his conversion to Socialism, published in *Justice* 30 June 1894. From his apprenticeship days he had been familiar with a situation of collaboration between artist and craftsman. Respect for economic and technical limitations was a natural part of his training as an illustrator designing for a mass market rather than for an elite. The acceptance of a painting at the Academy may have encouraged dreams of success in the loftier spheres of fine art but the expansion and development of his activities in the decorative arts kept him in close touch with the workshop practice. By the early 1880s, when he became a socialist he was already an established figure and champion of the 'lesser' arts.

W. J. Linton was an inspiring if eccentric character – a man with a complete disregard for material wealth and firm commitment to causes he considered just. Although he seems never to have forced his view on his pupils, Crane knew about his Chartist activities in the 1840s, of his concern for various international liberal movements and his friendship with foreign exiles in London, including Mazzini. To Crane the 'really heroic figure' was Garibaldi. Before the Italian leader's visit to London in 1864 Linton had helped send out the English volunteer contingent supporting Garibaldi's Sicilian campaign. He confided at the time how difficult it was to restrain young enthusiasts from renouncing their responsibilities and joining the red-shirt corps and may, in doing so, have forestalled any such request from his own young apprentice. An aura of revolutionary ardour surrounds Crane's description of his master. Walter regarded the events of 1848 and the Crimea in the same vague, exciting light as the American Civil War which he associated with slavery and different British class allegiances but which made most direct impression through 'John Brown's Body', a popular marching tune with the Volunteers. Linton not only aroused enthusiasm for noble endeavour but he taught tolerance. Crane felt himself mildly reprimanded for having a superficial outlook and being over impressed by outward appearances. Wise had encouraged him to deepen his knowledge of current affairs and the ideals guiding them. Crane's own description of how the writings of J. S. Mill, Darwin and Herbert Spencer helped him become a free thinker suggests almost too carefully planned an idealogical basis for a budding socialist. He was to become a Fabian and Edward Pease in his Fabian history includes Mill, Darwin and Spencer in his discussion of influential forces behind Fabian Socialism. Utilitarianism, with its ethical basis derived from Bentham of 'the greatest good of the greatest number' and Mills's political ideas regarding liberty and equality occupy a key place in later histories of nineteenth century socialist movements. The evolutionary theories of Darwin and Spencer encouraged socialists to believe that not only was reform desirable but that historical evidence existed to prove that its progress was inevitable. Crane appears to have had little difficulty in accepting this standpoint despite the doubts of his former mentor, Ruskin. His careful note-taking habits leave no room for doubt that he studied these ideas closely in the early sixties and was not merely recounting in his memoirs impressions of his youth which he later found relevant to Socialism. Comte's 'religion of humanity', which had as its primary aim the spiritual reorganization of society from which it was believed political reorganization would follow naturally, presented a gradual and peaceable solution which likewise recommended itself to intellectual reformers such as the Fabians. Crane's sketchbooks of 1865 and 1866 also reveal his interest in theory and constitutional reform; matters of hot discussion at this critical period when Russell and Gladstone prepared to introduce their unsuccessful Reform Bill of 1866. Among the speakers whose meetings he attended then were those of J. S. Mill, John Bright, Henry Fawcett and Sir Charles Dilke.

As well as efforts to master theories relevant to the current debates on parliamentary reform, the extension of franchise and trade unions Crane also witnessed the protest rallies of workers which greatly alarmed those mid-Victorians so comfortably cushioned into a false sense of complacency during the Palmerston era. Edmond Beales, a barrister who led the new Reform League was responsible for many demonstrations culminating in the Hyde Park 'Riot' of July 1866 when a mass of workers broke down the railings, having been refused entry to this traditional rallying ground. Crane sympathized with the workers' demands and was genuinely surprised at the intolerance of the 'country house reaction' of a clergyman at Rhode Hall who remarked roundly at breakfast after family prayers that he should like to throw a brickbat at Beales. No moderately observant and reasonably well-read Londoner in the 1860s could fail to be aware of the miserable plight of the poor or ignorant of the appeals for action implicit in the writings of Dickens, Thackeray, Kingsley and, more recently, George Eliot and Mrs Gaskell. Among the painters whose work conveyed a social message, Crane had immense respect for Ford Maddox Brown whose picture 'Work' he saw on view at 191 Piccadilly in 1865. Here Carlyle and the Christian Socialist founder of the Working Men's College, F. D. Maurice, are the observant and critical bystanders in an allegory on the dignity of labour.

Had he found realism more suited to his talents, Crane might himself have persevered with everyday subjects and become a painter of the people. But just as his literary inclinations avoided the nitty-gritty of Grub Street and tended to higher philosophical planes, his preference for imaginative painting led to a more poetic vein and the use of symbolic imagery. In the later 1860s he conceived a picture on the theme of 'Freedom', inspired by Swinburne's poem 'The Era of Revolution' in which a winged figure, clad in flowing drapery and wearing the 'bonnet rouge', rescues humanity symbolized by a youth chained in prison and guarded by a king in armour and a cowled priest. A large painting of this subject was exhibited at the Grosvenor Gallery in 1885. The winged figure of Freedom became one of Crane's most familiar socialist images.

The belief that the artist had a vital role to play in the social revolution was endorsed by Comte. The French Revolutionary cry 'Liberty, Equality, Fraternity' had been taken up by the English Romantic poets whose writing inspired a devoted following among the Pre-Raphaelites and their friends. Even more influential, however, was the emphasis given to this theme in the work of Shelley whom Crane particularly admired.

In Shelley's aspirations for humanity Crane found a philosophical standpoint which resisted religious dogma, sympathized with the methods and achievements of science and yet promoted the creative imagination above all else as the force which could redress the balance in the materialistic new era.

It was in an essentially poetical and non-political way that Crane pursued his ideologies in the next decade with paintings like 'The Renaissance of Venus', 'Truth and the Traveller'[2] and poems echoing themes of the pursuit of Beauty and Goodness. His collaboration with Wise on the *Fairy Masque* suggests that the erstwhile students of Mill and Spencer had resolved to devote their reforming efforts entirely to fairyland but by the time *Sirens Three* was published Crane had entered the Promethian struggle in earnest and ranged himself alongside Morris in the cause of Socialism.

It was as the artist of Socialism that Crane made his greatest contribution to the movement. The images he invented to convey its ideals soon became an indispensably powerful means of propaganda. So familiar were his compelling forms that they continued in use well into the present century when his style had long been superceded by more modern modes of artistic expression. Crane's early cartoons were published together in 1896, the year Morris died, but he continued to design for the Cause right up until his own death in 1915. He did not confine himself to cartoons however, but – especially during the early years – was much occupied with socialist theory and in trying to bring others round to his point of view. The ideals he expressed in his poems and lectures inevitably largely follow those of Morris, the man personally responsible for his conversion.

Only in 1876, over the Eastern Question, had Morris begun to take an active part in politics and reform. Soon he grew disillusioned with the Liberals who since coming to power in 1880 carried out few of the policies which had earned them his support. He then associated himself with men of more radical views, joining the Democratic Federation (one of the earliest Socialist societies, founded in 1881) in January 1884. Two years later this adopted its full title of Social Democratic Federation, popularly known as the S.D.F. Morris pursued his new ideal with characteristic ardour, helping in 1884 to launch (and keep afloat) the Socialist weekly *Justice* and lecturing all over the country, often in London. Crane had shared Morris's liberal affiliations in the 1870s and was alike influenced by Ruskin's economic writings, following in the seventies *Fors Clavigera*, his monthly *Letters to the Workmen and Labourers of Great Britain*. These were to become increasingly idiosyncratic but nevertheless Ruskin's indignation at social systems in which four fifths of the population lived lives of poverty and ugliness naturally won the sympathy of sensitive men like Morris and Crane. Since their first meeting in 1870 Crane had had little opportunity to become closely associated with Morris although this situation changed in 1881 when he prepared the cartoon for the 'Goose Girl' tapestry woven at Merton. Previous to this he paid close attention to Morris's letters to newspapers against imperialist foreign policies and, on the home front, his work for the Society for the Protection of Ancient Buildings (Anti-Scrape) founded in 1877. His activity in 1884 on behalf of the S.D.F. cannot have come as a great surprise to Crane, following as it did the quickening mood in favour of reform at the outset of the decade. Not every Morris admirer was to be so easily persuaded however, as Crane observed after hearing a lecture by him at this time: 'Some of his old friends (who looked upon him as a prophet in decorative art, though but few could follow him as a socialist) were present, and were a little startled and flustered by some of the things he said, and I remember one saying rather apprehensively, as we came out, "He bears the fiery cross" '.[3] Crane had few misgivings about taking this up – especially a fiery cross held aloft by such a personable prophet. He had recently read Morris's pamphlet *Art and Socialism* and wrote him a letter in which he stated all that occurred to him against the movement, to which Morris replied in full: 'The result was that the difficulties disappeared, and from the verge of pessimism as regards human progress, I accepted the Socialist position, which became a universal solvent in my mind. It was the question which swallowed all other questions – "Like Aaron's Rod", as Morris said at the time'.[4] The new convert was advised to read Maurice Grünland's *Co-operative Commonwealth*, Hyndman's *Historical Basis of Socialism* and *Das Kapital*. H. M. Hyndman had been converted to socialism after reading *Capital*. Morris also considered Marx the originator of the socialist movement in England. The historical basis of Marxism which set out to demonstrate that socialism was the natural outcome for a developing society must have been readily acceptable to Crane familiar as he was with the theories of Comte and Spencer. It is doubtful if he could have made much of the French translations which Hyndman and Morris used but articles on *Capital* were published in *Justice* and *The Christian Socialist* during 1884. After this exchange of letters, Crane attended the S.D.F. meetings where he met Hyndman, John Burns, Tom Mann, H. H. Champion and other socialists. In December 1884 the executive of the Federation split. Morris left, taking with him Edward Aveling, Eleanor Marx Aveling, and Belford Bax and leaving the leadership to Hyndman. This disagreement arose partly out of frustration at the latter's desire to be master, caused by the following Morris naturally attracted; and partly from the antagonism of Morris's party to Hyndman's policy of working directly towards parliamentary representation. By Christmas, Morris had formed his own group, the Socialist League, whose journal *The Commonweal* came out in February 1885.[5] Having taken the fatal step of thwarting united progress toward socialism he declared his intention of avoiding direct rivalry with the S.D.F. and emphasized his belief in 'an educated movement. Discontent is not enough . . . The discontented must know what they are aiming at when they overthrow the old order of things.' This, he maintained, following Marx could only be done by force 'and for that reason it is all the more important that the revolution . . . should not be an ignorant but an educated revolution.'[6]

Crane loyally joined the new League and in March contributed headings for *The Commonweal*. He often went to the Sunday meetings of Morris's Hammersmith Branch which took place in the lecture room converted from a coach house at Kelmscott House, Morris's London home since 1878, and was among the privileged friends afterwards invited for supper 'in the famous dining room on the oaken board'. These evenings of comradeship and conversation around the Kelmscott fireside proved immensely enjoyable. Morris attracted to his circle men of calibre and great personal charm, like the Russian prince and Anarchist-Communist Pierre Kropotkin. At one of these gatherings Crane first met the young journalist George Bernard Shaw who had joined the Fabian Society late in 1884.[7] There were few clear differences in the aims and beliefs of the early socialist societies. Crane's decision to join the Fabians as well as the other two groups says much for his enthusiasm but little about his allegiance to specific socialist principles. Presumably Crane felt at home in the intellectual and middle class atmosphere of the Fabians as well as being familiar with theories sympathetic to their general ideology.[8] The relative youthfulness of the Society, among whom Shaw, Sydney Webb, the Blands, Graham Wallas and Annie Besant were then the most lively members, was another factor. Crane was thirty-nine years of age when he joined the socialist movement, younger than the average on the S.D.F. executive and eleven years younger than Morris. Shaw's humour may have been alluring too though it was to be employed at Crane's expense when Corno Di Bassetto later functioned as an art critic.

Crane's first socialist address entitled 'Art and Commercialism' was given before the Fabian society on 16 October 1885 just before he became a member. On 2 July 1886 he chaired a special meeting when Morris agreed to the invitation of the Fabian executive to lecture on 'The Aims of Art'.[9] Crane found lecturing very demanding. Shaw wrily remarked of these performances that they 'were bearable only when he took up the chalk and showed what he meant on the blackboard',[10] but although he lacked the eloquence of his tall Irish comrade many people enjoyed his talks. Bruce Glasier, describing a meeting in which Crane addressed a Glasgow audience, emphasized how favourably his blackboard demonstrations were received and gave a less pithy, but perhaps more accurate, account of his lecturing style. 'He had little flow of language, no vigour of statement, and spoke in rather a jerky fashion. But there was a certain archness and occasionally an epigrammatical flavour in his remarks which, together with much gracefulness of gesture, made it pleasant to listen to him. In appearance he was almost ideally the artist. His finely shaped head, beautiful face with clear kindly eyes and handsome moustache and short pointed beard, together with his finely proportioned and mobile figure, gave him the look of a troubadour who had stepped out of some medieval page.'[11]

Crane's early papers were published together in *The Claims of Decorative Art* in 1892. Not surprisingly, with art as his theme, his views relate closely to those of Morris. The preface explains that his guide was 'that new-old view of art . . . revived during the last quarter of our century, which regards it not only in relation to use and material, and seeks for its vital root in the handicrafts but also in its connection with common life and social conditions'. Modern society was the victim of commerce. Without economic freedom there could be no political freedom. As long as there were monopolies of land and the means of subsistence there would be slavery and poverty. Art could not flourish. The cheap and nasty products of the industrial age were geared to competitive business interests catering for a public expected to conform to one grim average. Steam machinery symbolized this impersonality, 'intended for the service of man and for the saving of human labour' it had 'under our economic system enslaved humanity instead, and become an engine for the production of profits, an express train in the race for wealth, only checked by the brake of what is called over-production'.[12] Such a system prevented the free expression of art making it 'the mere toy of wealth' 'the superficial bedizenment of fashion'. Only under Socialism could Use and Beauty be re-united. 'We want a vernacular in art . . . no mere verbal or formal agreement, or dead level of uniformity but that comprehensive and harmonizing unity with individual variety which can only be developed among people politically and socially free.'[13]

Architecture was the primary expression of art in a healthy happy community. Crane shared Ruskin and Morris's respect for the monuments of the past and, like Morris, looked to the future and a united society whose co-operative effort would create magnificent buildings. They would grow from humble beginnings: 'It is deep down in the life of the people that we must dig the foundation and out of common speech and common labour and handicraft must be shaped that architecture of art. Without such foundations, and without the cement of fellowship, without due recognition of the equality and unity of all art-workers; and their mutual independence in building the great structure we shall raise no monument to be a delight to ourselves and a memorial to those who come after . . . most of the efforts to revive the arts and crafts among the people without reference to their economic condition are like so many attempts to grow the tree leaves downwards'.[14] On art and labour Crane proposed the idea – which was Morris's theme in his lecture 'Art and Socialism' and one for which he was again indebted to Ruskin – that work is a necessity of human life, not merely as a means to earn a living but for health and happiness. This was not true of factory labour but of all kinds which allowed for invention, judgement, discretion; a freedom to exercise individual skills which the simplest kind of work shared with art itself.[15] In advocating his new art of living, Crane was not blind to essentials. He was the first to agree that the best decoration for a hungry home was a flitch of bacon and that artistic activity could only develop as conditions eased, emerging first in very simple and sincere forms of construction and ornament. People would gradually have more time for cultivation and enjoyment. The machine would be rightly used to save tedious labour and thus contribute to the short working day.

'Let our aims be the *abolition of class* and the establishment of a truly human society of equals' Crane stated in his lecture 'Art and Social Democracy'.[16] Such references to the class struggle and the exploitation of the capitalist system illustrate how he accepted the Marxist precepts fundamental to Morris's socialism. He seldom sounds quite as revolutionary as Morris, however, and 'The Architecture of Art' of 1887 is one of his most aggressive papers, while 'Art and Social Democracy' reflects his usual moderation. Here mention of the class war is not, as was so often the case with other writers, backed up with militant allusions to the Paris Commune of 1871 which early Marxist socialists took as a significant manifestation of the kind of popular force needed to bring about the Revolution. In his designs and poetic expression Crane was less inhibited, producing cartoons to commemmorate the Paris Commune in 1887 and in 1891.[17]

Crane shared Morris's dislike of the futurist mechanical urban utopia of Edward Bellamy's *Looking Backward 2000–1887*, preferring the idyll envisaged in the prose romance *News from Nowhere* (1890) in which Morris expressed his passionate identification with nature. With rather less eloquent conviction Crane enlisted nature's help in the cause of art and life: 'There is nothing . . . like close intimacy with nature and fact to strengthen the character all round, and clear the mental vision of morbid states; and as for art, like the wrestler, it always gains new vigour every time it touches the ground – the ground of nature and of common life'.[18] The poem 'The New Era' is another of the many parallels between Crane and Morris. It is close in form and sentiment to Morris's 'Message of the March Wind' the prelude to 'Pilgrims of Hope' of 1885. The softening and subtle influence of natural forces which both admired inclined them to a less authoritarian point of view than Marx. Crane and Morris emphasize man's right to individual expression and the importance of a moral and often implicitly Christian standpoint.

Shaw remembered Crane as

a pleasant soul without a trace of quarrelsomeness which did no harm to the Labour Movement . . . quarrelsome as Labour leaders are, they are angels compared to artists, who are apt to get into little cliques hating each other . . .

146

The combination of art clique and Labour faction makes their society almost impossible. I never saw any trace of this in Crane.[19]

This character made him a natural Fabian, preferring education to active revolt. When Crane joined the society they could adopt a fairly combative front. Their first tract 'Why are the Many Poor' of 1884 fiercely condemned middle class complacency and greed. By 1889 when *Fabian Essays* was published, with a cover and frontispiece by Crane, they were bent on democratic procedures; an egalitarian society brought about constitutionally with the consent of a majority who believed in its moral value. Its realisation had to be gradual and 'prepared for in the minds of all'.[20] Morris too had come to realise that the social revolution could not, as he had earlier believed, be achieved in his lifetime. He was reluctant to abandon his conviction that a revolution was inevitable but grew wary of reckless action in the face of experiences like Bloody Sunday. He began to resent constant appeals for such by the increasingly restless anarchist faction of The League. It was this section who voted him out of the editorship of *The Commonweal* in 1890. Morris withdrew from The League and formed his own independent Hammersmith Society, which Crane joined. In his rejection of a pure anarchist standpoint Morris was willing to admit a transitional period of 'state-socialism' and in 1892

Cover of the shilling edition of *Fabian Essays*, 1889, representing the fat figure of Privilege plucking fruit and perched precariously on the ladder of Capitalism, which is supported by the stalwart figures of Labour. By courtesy of Liverpool City Libraries.

guardedly accepted the position he had long resisted by admitting that the ballot box might be an easier means to socialism than open revolt. Crane instinctively preferred the idea of constitutional democracy and this began to seem more possible by 1889 as trade union leaders succeeded in gaining seats on local councils. The 1892 general election saw three independent Labour MPs returned with a Liberal victory. In December 1892 the Hammersmith Socialist Society discussed the possibilities of a Socialist Federation 'to promote the alliance of socialist organizations in Great Britain', each, on Morris's advice, to remain autonomous. The S.D.F. and Fabians were approached and a manifesto drafted but the Fabians withdrew.[21] Morris would probably also have invited the Independent Labour Party to join but for Hyndman and S.D.F. opposition. In the few years left until the end of his life Morris was anxious for a united front but little was achieved by 1896. That year Crane made an unsuccessful bid to have the anarchists accepted by the Socialist (Second) International.[22] Like all those who had worked with William Morris he was deeply affected by his death on Saturday 5 October, the day of the private view of the Fifth Arts and Crafts Exhibition. At Cobden Sanderson's suggestion, Crane's sonnet was placed among the display of Kelmscott books. Though lacking the power and grace Morris himself might have given the lines this is nonetheless a moving tribute to the manifold loss they all felt:

On The Death of William Morris
How can it be! that strong and fruitful life
Hath ceased – that strenuous but joyful heart,
Skilled craftsman in the loom of song and art,
Whose voice by beating seas of hope and strife,
Would lift the soul of labour from the knife,
And strive 'gainst greed of factory and mart –
Ah! ere the morning, must he, too, depart
While yet with battle cries the air is rife?
Blazon his name in England's Book of Gold
Who loved her, and who wrought her legends fair,
Woven in song and written in design,
The wonders of the press and loom – a shrine,
Beyond the touch of death, that shall enfold
In life's House Beautiful, a spirit rare.[23]

To the working man Crane remained a much less well known personality than Morris. He never spoke before mass rallies but confined his lecturing to artistic and left wing societies. One of the few moments when he may have experienced what it was like to be a public hero was at the May Day celebration held at the Crystal Palace in 1899 for which he designed a firework display. Lit up it revealed four workers blessed by the angel of liberty and the words 'The Unity of Labour is the Hope of the World'. It was greeted 'by the hearty cheers of a vast multitude' already very familiar with such designs.

The Twentieth Century Press published *Cartoons for the Cause* as a souvenir of the International and Trade Union Congress of 1896. Among these twelve designs Crane's earliest political cartoon, dating from December 1884, was printed for the first time. Called 'The Party Fight and the New Party' it showed two knights with shields marked 'Liberalism' and 'Toryism' who look up from their combat to an armour clad angel carrying the shield of 'Socialism'. This was a very tentative effort compared with his next, the impressive 'Capitalist Vampire', designed at the suggestion of the S.D.F. member, H. H. Champion, in which the freedom figure of Socialism attempts to waken a slumbering workman whose lifeblood is being sucked by the monster of exploitation. This was originally published in *Justice* in the summer of 1885 ready for a big rally of workers and socialist sympathisers in Hyde Park. That winter more protests followed and the S.D.F. played an active part in organizing marches of the unemployed. On one occasion John Burns (holding red flag aloft) led the people to the Park, much to the alarm of the fashionable crowds gathered there, and then down Piccadilly. Several windows were smashed. Burns, Hyndman and Williams were arrested to be subsequently acquitted amid useful publicity. The middle classes and poor alike were beginning to sit up and take notice of the now quickly expanding socialist societies. The fear aroused in bourgeois bosoms by the February demonstration gave Crane the idea for his other famous early cartoon 'Mrs Grundy frightened by her Own Shadow' which was printed in the first weekly issue of *Commonweal* in May 1886.[24] This year and the next he also produced designs supporting League policies against war in the Sudan and Irish coercion.

The police had not interfered at the mass meeting of February 1886 but they were soon to do so and, with the appointment of Sir Charles Warren as chief of the Metropolitan force, the Socialists began to recognize that an important part of their struggle would involve fighting for the basic privilege of free speech and public meeting. This was all too evident on Bloody Sunday, 13 November 1887, when a mass meeting of workers organized in protest against death sentences unjustly conferred on the Chicago Anarchists[25] was barred from congregating in the centre of Trafalgar Square by a 'hedge of policemen six deep'. Warren's force had already dispersed the many processions making their way to the square, including that of Morris and his League. Annie Besant was reported to have hurled herself at the phalanx and Cunninghame-Graham, Hyndman and Burns

Below left
The Capitalist Vampire, 1885, one of Crane's earliest socialist cartoons reprinted in *Cartoons for the Cause*. By courtesy of the Victoria and Albert Museum.

Below
Mrs Grundy frightened by her own Shadow, a cartoon, first published in William Morris's *Commonweal* in May 1886 and later in *Cartoons for the Cause*, in which Crane mocked the fears aroused among the better-off at the increasingly forceful protests of early socialists. By courtesy of the Victoria and Albert Museum.

William Morris speaking at a May Day Rally in Hyde Park, 1 May 1894, pencil sketch, $5\frac{1}{8} \times 4\frac{3}{8}$ in. (13×11 cm). Collection the Houghton Library, Harvard University.

broke through but were arrested. Many innocent onlookers were injured by police clearing the square. Crane himself narrowly escaped and was shocked at the bloodshed: 'I never saw anything more like real warfare in my life – only the attack was all on *one* side. The police, in spite of their numbers, apparently thought they could not cope with the crowd. They had certainly exasperated them, and could not disperse them, as after every charge – and some of these drove the people right against the shutters of the shops in the Strand – they returned again'.[26] The Guards were called out and he long remembered that gloomy November evening with the row of red tunics and glistening bayonets ranged before the National Gallery, while the magistrate was fetched to read the Riot Act. At this point he had not met R. B. Cunninghame-Graham but he responded to the spirited appeal of his wife to an 'At Home' at Bond Street Police Court after which the accused was given bail and later, with Burns, a sentence of six weeks. That December Crane was a willing helper ready if required to bail out friends who fell foul of the law for the Cause. On the Sunday following the fateful thirteenth an innocent bystander, Alfred Linnell, a young radical law-writer, was ridden down by police intent on preventing further popular gatherings in the square. He sustained fatal injuries and a great funeral was planned by the Socialists. Morris wrote a death song which was set to music by Malcolm Lawson and printed with a cover design by Crane of Justice and Liberty defending Linnell against the attack of a ferocious mounted policeman. This was not reprinted in *Cartoons for the Cause* which mainly consisted of designs of general relevance to socialism, but it is illustrated in the *Reminiscences*.

The labour festival of May Day was a fruitful theme with which to promote liberty, equality and fraternity. Old colonial allegiances are given emphasis in his design of 1888 with its figures representing Africa, India, America and

Australia. Most ambitious of all is 'The Triumph of Labour' planned to commemorate the first International May Day 1891. It was done at the suggestion of the engraver Henry Scheu and was adapted with mottos in different languages for distribution throughout Europe. To the workers of 1891 it gave promise of future abundance at an optimistic moment in the early years of the movement. Morris told Crane that this was the best thing he had done. It certainly merited praise in the Ruskinian terms of sheer work involved. Some of Crane's later May Day designs are still intricate, 'The Worker's May Pole' (*Justice* 1894) is a graceful evocation within decorated Gothic framework of the labourers' paradise envisaged in Morris's prose romances. Both the triumph procession and this design illustrate the kind of community celebration which Morris and Crane welcomed as one of the great pleasures of the new era. 'A Garland for May Day' published in a special May Day number of *The Clarion* on 27 April 1895, enshrines labour's promise of the rural idyll in a delightful way.[27]

A Garland for May Day, 1895, reprinted in *Cartoons for the Cause*. By courtesy of the Victoria and Albert Museum.

·A·GARLAND·FOR·MAY·DAY·1895·
· DEDICATED·TO·THE·WORKERS·BY·WALTER·CRANE ·

The Triumph of Labour, 1891, cartoon engraved by H. Scheu, designed to commemorate the first International May Day. Like most of Crane's cartoons it was available separately, although here different versions were printed with the slogans in French, German and Italian for European comrades. Reprinted in *Cartoons for the Cause.*

Crane's non-sectarian approach is well demonstrated in the many headings he made for different socialist societies. Morris set an example with his little woodcut design for the S.D.F. After the split, Crane did likewise for the Socialist League and the Socialist Union, a breakaway group led by James Macdonald and C. L. Fitzgerald which for two years tried to steer a middle course between the Federation and the League. All these may be seen together in a new monthly called *The Practical Socialist* for which Crane drew an elaborate title decoration with the figure of freedom holding a lamp in whose flame shone the motto 'all for one and one for all'. This was first issued in January 1886 and included Morris on 'The Aims of Art' and 'The Labour Question', Tom Mann (still an S.D.F. member in 1886) on the 'Eight Hour's Working Day' and various papers by Fabians including Pease and Webb. The Fabian Conference of June that year was significant for many weighty reasons but Shaw considered it a useful opportunity on which to show off 'our pretty prospectus with the design by Crane at the top, our stylish looking blood-red invitation cards and other little smartnesses on which we then prided ourselves. We used to be plentifully sneered at as fops and arm-chair socialists for our attention to these details; but I think it was by no means the

least of our merits that we always, as far as our means permitted tried to make our painted documents as handsome as possible . . .'[28] The Fabian emblem was in regular evidence in the sixpenny monthly *Our Corner* (from 1886 until 1888) for which Crane also designed a cover. This was edited by Annie Besant who had been elected to the Fabian Executive only a few weeks after joining the society in 1886, remaining there until 1890 when she took up theosophy. In 1888 he designed a seal for the Socialist Co-operative Federation of London. Soon the familiar ladies of liberty and rustic workers were to be seen on the covers of many left wing journals. Among them were *The Political World* (1889), *St Jude's* (1889), *Work* (1889), *The Pioneer* (1889), *Time* (which had a new Crane wrapper in 1890), *The Labourer* (1895), *Free Russia* (1905), *The British Esperantist* (1905), Mary Macarthur's *Woman Worker* (1907), *The Reformer's Year Book* (1908) and *Concord* (1911). He produced a prospectus cover for the International Socialist School in Fitzroy Street, run by the ardent Communist Louise Michel and a frontispiece for *Chants of Labour* (1892) edited by Edward Carpenter and for *The New Party* (1895) edited by Andrew Reid. There were also fine headings to the chapters of Crane's own book *The Claims of Decorative Art*.

WORK

EDITED BY FRANCIS YOUNG,
Author of "Every Man his Own Mechanic."

Heading for the socialist paper
Work, 1889. By courtesy of
Liverpool City Libraries.

'Nobody, not even William Morris', wrote the S.D.F. President and editor of
Justice, H. M. Hyndman, in his obituary of Crane, 'did more than he to make Art
a direct helpmeet [*sic*] to the Socialist propaganda. Nobody has had a greater
influence on the minds of doubters who feared that Socialism must be remote
from, and even destructive of the sense of beauty'.[29] In 1895 Crane's 'Donkey
and the Common' cartoon was published in *Justice* together with an explanation
of the meaning of this 'Little Holiday: or a day Off for All Parties' where Labour's
brutish mascot is shown unseating the top-hatted gent of Capitalism having
already thrown his rotund companion, Landlordism, to the ground. This turned
out to be a unique experiment because Crane generally relied on conveying the
full message within the cartoon using only a few slogans. After this he designed a
large May Day cartoon for *Justice* every year. Like many of the earlier cartoons
these were also for sale separately printed on strong paper by the Twentieth
Century Press. Here Crane's heroines – his comely version of the French Marianne,
Britannia, and the Angel of Liberty – upheld their principles against labour ex-
ploiters: the 'bag barons' of rent, profit and interest;[30] and the bogeys of commercial imperialism, militarism and the inevitable increased taxation. The ghoulish
capitalist vampire makes its appearance again in a fine drawing 'Britannia's Best
Defence' (a plea for home grown corn for the people) prepared for *Justice* on 25
June 1898, as propaganda for a demonstration to be held the next day in Trafalgar
Square. The 'Triumph Car for May Day' design of 1911 uses the theme made
popular in 1891. These later compositions more often lack the simplicity and
vigorous design of earlier versions but Crane never ceased in his ingenious
attempts to appeal to the popular imagination as can be seen from his May Day
specials 'John Bull's Creditor's' (1900), 'The Goal' (1904) and 'A Posy for May
Day and A Poser for Britannia' (1910). Other designs include Christmas cards
and greetings and one for the *Daily Chronicle* on 27 February 1897, where he
depicted the Easter Crisis in terms of Perseus (Greece) liberating Andromeda
(Crete) from Turkish oppression, while the lion of England and various birds of
prey representing other interested parties watch from cliffs nearby. The same
design was used that year as a frontispiece in G. H. Perrins' book *The Eastern
Crisis of 1897*.

Crane like many socialists believed that wars were more often begun by
capitalists for reasons of commerce than for idealism. When the Fabians failed to
oppose British participation in the Boer War of 1900 he resigned his membership
along with eighteen others including Ramsay Macdonald, the future Labour

M.P.s George Barnes and Pete Curran, and Mrs Pankhurst.[31] The theme of peace often recurs at this time. 'A Stranger', the large oil now at the William Morris Gallery, represents a winged figure hovering over earth holding out an olive branch. A similar form appears in his cartoon to commemorate the end of the Transvaal War published in *The Daily News* on 2 June 1902. Crane's grief at the wasted lives and England's hypocrisy were expressed in the poem modelled on Swinburne's 'A Watch in the Night', called 'Watchman, What of the Night?' published on 23 December 1901.[32] These efforts continued unabated up to his last years. On the eve of the great war he pleaded for a better understanding among German and English people and in a letter of 1911 to John Galsworthy (in which he promised to sign an appeal against the use of flying machines in warfare) he reiterated: 'my chief hope for the cessation of war . . . lies in the break down of the capitalist system and the adoption of socialism'.[33] With such an aim he saw little point in internal squabbles and wrote to *The Clarion* on 3 November 1911, describing the recent formation of the British Socialist Party as 'the most important and encouraging event which had happened to the movement for a long time' adding that he had felt unity on main principles so important as to 'reconcile membership of the S.D.F., the Socialist League and the Fabian Society at the same time'. His compassion and optimism are apparent in the late designs, 'In the Trail of the German Army' (1914) and 'A Vision of the Future from the Battle Field of the United States of Europe' published in the *Daily Citizen* Calendar of 1915. Mercifully he did not live to know that his younger son, Lancelot, was killed in World War I.

Below left
A Posy for May Day and A Poser for Britannia, 1910, cartoon printed in the May Day number of *Justice*.

Below
Socialism and the Imperialistic Will O' the Wisp, 1907, printed in the May Day number of *Justice*. Crane's enthusiasm for technology is shown here in the electric bulb which replaces the candle that was generally used to signify the guiding light.

A·POSY·FOR·MAY·DAY,·AND·A·POSER·FOR·BRITANNIA

SOCIALISM·&·THE·IMPERIALISTIC·WILL·O·THE·WISP.
SOCIALIST PARTY TO THE BRITISH WORKMAN—"If you follow that lead, my friend, you'll only sink in deeper, especially when you are handicapped like that. Besides, just look at the work waiting to be done at home, on solid ground!"

Two great pictorial banners are carried in Crane's triumphant labour procession of 1891 and it is not surprising, in view of the fact that he was the foremost designer in England to devote his talents to art for the Cause, that John Gorman should also give him credit for having 'shaped the first imagery of socialism among the Unions'.[34] Banners were already a familiar sight at the great reform rallies of the 1860s. Most were produced by George Tutill whose firm was founded in 1837 and which had a virtual monopoly in the business for about fifty years. After the docker's strike of 1889 the trade union force swelled to massive proportions. There was a corresponding boom in banner making and £20,000 worth were said to have been on show at the May Day march in London in 1896 – 'brilliant silken sails of colour up to sixteen by twelve feet in size, painted with emblems and scenes showing the crafts and skills of the trade unionists who carried them'.[35] Crane's first banner commission may not have been for the unions but for the Irish Nationalists, and it was worked in silk by Miss Una Taylor and lent to the Arts and Crafts Exhibition of 1890 by Charles Parnell. Here Shaw criticized its geometrical design as 'being suitable enough if the material were cast steel'.

In the Trail of the German Army, 1914, cover for a special number of the *Daily Chronicle*. By courtesy of Liverpool City Libraries.

The Profits from the Sale of this Publication will be sent to the Funds in aid of the Belgian Refugees.

1/-

ILLUSTRATED WITH 58 SPECIAL PHOTOGRAPHS

IN THE TRAIL OF THE GERMAN ARMY

RHEIMS

LOUVAIN

The Daily Chronicle: Fleet St. London. E.C. 1914.

125

Electrical Trades Union Banner,
designed by Crane in 1898.
Collection John Gorman.

That year Crane helped Henry Holiday decorate the St James's Hall where
Parnell was received at the Home Rule demonstration held on 10 April. He had
previously designed an elaborate allegory of Gladstone's Home Rule policy for
the *Golden Wedding Album* presented to the Liberal leader by the National Liberal
Club in the summer of 1889.[36] The Irish National Banner was more like a flag than
the pictorial trade union banners which were based on Crane's designs. That for
the Electrical Trades Union was specially commissioned in 1898 and it features
the familiar image of the angel of freedom, flanked by flowers and slogans on
one side, and eager workers on the reverse. She was to appear often in such
designs and used to embody the noble aspirations of the union as well as (and
often instead of) a realistic portrayal of the trades they represent, replacing the
more phlegmatic spiritis of Justice, Truth and Friendship so common in earlier
union emblems.[37] Another popular theme was Crane's triumph procession but
most effective were the centralized designs like the 'Garland for May Day'. Rural
Merrie England rather than the bleak industrial reality was preferred by trade
unionists for a suprisingly long time into the twentieth century. Some banner
makers seem to have used *Cartoons for The Cause* as a pattern book. The May Day
'Solidarity of Labour' (1890) and 'Workers' Pay Pole' were adopted, slogans and
all, by the National Union of General Workers for banners dating from between
1910–20. 'Leisure for all', 'employer's liability', 'no starving children in the board
schools' were still unfortunately all too relevant demands. The 'Garland for May
Day' was swathed in ribbon-bearing mottos and these were kept by several trade
union branches some of whom added one from the Communist manifesto

'Workers of the World Unite'.[38]

In his paper 'The Socialist Ideal as an Inspiration in Art' Crane praised the work of the Belgian socialist sculptor Constantin Meunier for its

> Study and realization of the types of heroic labour – the labour that takes its life in its hand in every ordinary day's work – at the furnace mouth or the coal mine.[39]

Likewise he much admired the work of François Millet, Joseph Israels, Max Liebermann and the English painters, George Clausen, La Thangue, Brangwyn, Stanhope Forbes and Ford Madox Brown. His own most ambitious effort in this genre was a series of twelve designs for heroic deeds of the poor, shown at the Arts and Crafts Exhibition of 1890. The scheme derived from an idea of Crane's older friend and fellow socialist G. F. Watts, who wished to commemorate the everyday heroic deeds of rescue from fire and sea which were reported in the newspapers. It was eagerly taken up by Mrs Russell Barrington who agreed to paint a series of mural decorations for Miss Octavia Hill's settlement in Red Cross Street, Southwark, if someone else prepared the designs. Crane complied but the scheme was still incomplete in 1907 when he wrote his memoires and those paintings in place were already damaged by gas fumes. He was involved in the further development of at least three of the twelve subjects. One represented a local nursemaid, Alice Ayres, who died while rescuing three children from a fire in an oil shop. This Crane scaled up to a quarter size pastel cartoon, which Mrs Barrington enlarged on to the panels which were the bases of the murals. Crane finished this and completed the next scene himself – of an accident in which two Paisley railway workers were killed by an oncoming train. The third panel depicted the rescue of a child from a well.[40] He was disappointed in the results of this voluntary venture and let it languish. Although in theory at this stage he liked the idea of decorating public buildings with scenes from heroic moments in ordinary life his efforts were much less successful than those of Brangwyn. Later, when asked to plan the mosaic facade panel for the new Whitechapel Art Gallery (an attempt to bring art to the poor of the East End following the example set by the South London Art Gallery) Crane resorted to symbolic representations of the conventional form used in public art for centuries. In this context it is significant that Whistler's 'impressions' disturbed him despite his admiration for the American painter's decorative art. He peversely insisted on seeing the nocturnes in socialistic terms and criticized them for avoiding the horror and ugliness of industrial London. Fundamentally he believed the modern realistic painter to be a less 'thoughtful and poetic' artist than those who tried to express strong feelings and beliefs through symbol or parable[41] – the means he himself employed so successfully in his socialist designs.

Education

At the end of his life Crane was often still described as the 'Academician of the Nursery'. He resented this deeply, not only because he wanted recognition for more than those achievements which had won him fame forty years previously but also because of his dislike of the term 'Academician' which he associated with an educational system based on absolutes of the kind his own experience led him to reject for more experimental methods. The Black Books reveal the generous and intuitive way in which he could respond to the interests of his own children and attempt to develop their understanding. He also imparted something of this magic in his illustrations to two sets of alphabet readers devized to brighten what was still a gloomy corner of the Victorian school room. The first, Professor J. M. D. Meiklejohn's *Golden Primer Parts I & II* (1884-5) was the finest, being engraved and printed by Evans, and Nellie Dale's *Steps to Reading* of 1898 was followed by a series which ran to many editions.[1] The new Dale system had a pedestrian effectiveness which had great staying power. It was made much more attractive by Crane's colour decorations and many adults today would probably recognize in these remarkably familiar pages the books from which they learned to read.

Crane's specific art educational commitments began around 1885 when he became a socialist and lectured on the function and benefit to be derived from art in a reformed community. These ideas were being put into practice at the same time in his participation in the Art-Workers' Guild whose efforts to improve design took on a more explicit educational function with the opening of the first Arts and Crafts Exhibition in 1888. The work on display provided a practical example complemented by talks in which Crane and his friends explained the fundamentals of design relating to different crafts. It was in his own address on 'Design' that Crane first impressed the audience with his skilful demonstration of blackboard drawing.

The urge to improve design, stimulated by men like Morris, Crane and Mackmurdo, was partly responsible for pricking the national conscience to the point of arousing interest in the problem so effectively spotlighted at the Great Exhibition of 1851, the question of art and industry. In the autumn of 1888 'The National Association for the Advancement of Art and its Application to Industry' held an inaugural meeting at Grosvenor House, chaired by the Duke of Westminster. Three congresses followed, at Liverpool (1888), Edinburgh (1889) and Birmingham (1890), large and lengthy affairs which welcomed notables from the right and left-wing factions of the art world as well as manufacturers, teachers and students. Sir Frederic Leighton presided at Liverpool but this did not restrain the attack of the design lobby, led by Crane as President of the Applied Art Section. 'We must' he declared 'turn our artists into craftsmen and our craftsmen into artists'. The Royal Academy was inevitably criticized for its failure to encourage design while Morris, Crane and their comrades saw to it that the Arts and Crafts Movement 'made way all along the line as the most practical effort to unite Art and Industry'.[2] The text of the paper he gave on this occasion was printed on the front page of the New Year edition of *The Commonweal*. It explored a theme with which English craftsmen and socialists were already familiar: 'Mechanical invention in the interest of trade has dominated us. Mechanical invention has outstripped the invention of the artist. Mechanical smoothness has taken the place of artistic thought and finish. And why? Because, to our great deity of commercial enterprise and successful trade, the amount of the output is more regarded than the artistic quality of the material and work. The very spirit and meaning of the word "artistic" implies something harmonious; something in relation to its surroundings; something arising out of the joy of life etc . . .'[3] Mechanical smoothness was not 'artistic' in Crane's view because it left no trace of individual expression. This aspect of the craft aesthetic – which adhered to the Ruskinian idea that 'you must have some sort of evidence of *pleasure* in the design work on the part of the producer or it will not give pleasure to the beholder'[4] held English designers back from evolving an aesthetic of pure functionalism and happy alliance between art and industry. But their feelings of responsibility for humanity obliged them to help to improve the quality of mass-produced goods. This in turn led to another problem, because if craftsmen aided industry the resulting benefits accruing to the manufacturer were likely to be greater than any felt by the consumer, and artists would thus be helping to feather the nest of commercialism. All acknowledged Morris's awkward position as a man committed to improving the common lot and yet supporting a capitalist regime by acting as an employer, and producing hand-made goods which only the well-to-do could afford. Clearly the answer to cheaper goods lay in the use of machinery. Morris took advantage of this where he considered it expedient and most designers had no alternative but to rely on large manufacturing firms to reproduce their wallpaper and textile patterns. In Metford Warner Crane found an intelligent associate ready to do all he could to reproduce subtle colours as sensitively as machine processes allowed, but he was really giving in to Crane's assumption that machinery should if possible be cajoled into achieving effects alien to it. It was a view which he had to modify in practice in 1894 when Warner had to ask him to limit the number of colours. The lyrical fluency of Crane's style was not something that lent itself to a rigorous machine aesthetic. In this he differed from his more practical colleague W. A. S. Benson or even from the botanist designer Christopher Dresser. Although he welcomed modern inventions he was not emotionally inclined to wax eloquent (as some people did at the Edinburgh Art Congress) on the thrusting, punching power and precision of machinery. His more gentle, romantic response comes out in the description of a launch at Lairds Ship Yard to which the officials of the Liverpool congress were invited, where the christening and immersion are dealt with in fairy-tale terms and the great vessel is finally described as taking the water 'like a swan'.

The paradox of the reforming craftsman's situation was acknowledged in contemporary criticism. Indeed, Morris and Crane were blamed for spoiling the Edinburgh congress by foisting their political views on the assembly. This time it was Morris who was President of the Applied Art section and Crane followed his address with a practical paper on 'Design in Relation to Use and Material'.[5] Both lectured also, before fashionable audiences at meetings arranged by the socialists: Crane on 'The Educational Value of Art'; and Morris on 'The Origins of Ornamental Art'. According to *The Commonweal*'s report of the week's activities most successful of all were the free evening lectures for working folk, which were arranged in association with representatives of the Edinburgh Trades. Morris, Crane, Sanderson and Walker concentrated on their respective specialist skills; Dyeing, The Decorative Illustration of Books, Printing and Bookbinding.[6] W. E. Henley, editor of *The Scots Observer* took a very poor view of all this and attacked 'The Crafty Artsman' who was 'as anxious as ever to save the souls of his neighbours by demoralizing their houses with decoration'. He rated against 'the socialist who ministers to luxury' by preaching 'an illogical creed' and concluded his puritanical tirade by saying that 'the most healthy sign about this present congress is that few of its members, except the Crafty ones, take it very seriously. Were it otherwise we might be sure that we had fallen on an age when artists found it necessary to supplement impotence of hand with liveliness of tongue'.[7]

Such a view was inaccurate because among those who paid serious attention to what was said were the art teachers. In an assessment of how little art had accomplished for industry it was inevitable that the education system (originally reorganized in 1852 with the very aim of improving design) should come under heavy fire. Under Thomas Armstrong, who became Director of Art for the Science and Art Department in 1881, the task of again promoting design teaching in Government schools had begun and among those influenced by this move was Francis Newbery, the young Headmaster of Glasgow School of Art. At the Edinburgh congress he was already able to report an increase in the number of students of decorative art and a reduction of the ranks of 'picture producers'.[8] It was not simply the emphasis on fine art and comparative neglect of design which was wrong with British art schools, however, but their dependence on an atrophied teaching system. Crane attempted to reform both these aspects when he finally agreed to become Director of Design at Manchester School of Art.

In 1883 Crane had refused the post of headmaster of Manchester School of Art because of his commitments as a practising designer. He did so again in December 1892 when a similar offer was made by two Manchester councillors, James Hoy and Charles Rowley. Crane already knew Rowley, a delightful, corpulent character and a socialist who had become friendly with Morris and other left-wing artists and designers through various public-spirited ventures concerning art and education in Manchester. He attended Sunday meetings at Hammersmith and Crane was among many prominent men, including Morris and George Bernard Shaw, whom Rowley and his colleagues on the Ancoats Recreation Committee engaged to speak at Manchester's New Islington Hall. Having already succumbed to the summons from Ancoats, Crane was to find it equally hard to resist Rowley's pleas on behalf of the School of Art. Early in March 1893 he was invited to address an evening gathering there on the study and practice of art. This talk and a subsequent report by him on 'The Aims and Methods of Industrial Art Teaching' were printed and circulated among those concerned with the running of the Art and Technical Schools.[9] Flattered by this deference to his opinion Crane agreed to accept the post of part-time Director of Design at the School of Art, and the appointment was confirmed on 6 September 1893. During the next few years he became very friendly with Rowley and the association lasted long after his resignation from the Directorship in 1896. Liverpool City Libraries own a collection of Crane's witty Rowley memorabilia with records of their visits to Bayreuth in 1894, Italy in 1896 and Egypt in 1897, and designs for Rowley's Round Table, the Ancoats Brotherhood and its cycling magazine.

Rowley's determination to acquire Walter Crane's services was in part the result of advice from his old friend Frederick Shields to 'get a man who has *done* something' but, as Stuart Macdonald has discussed in his detailed study of affairs at Manchester, it was also the result of years of frustration with the established

Suggestion for a monument to be erected in honour of C——s R——y. Eq: J.P.de by admiring friends.

Crane's proposed monument to his friend, the Manchester councellor, Charles Rowley, an indefatigable reformer and follower of William Morris. Reproduced from Rowley's autobiography *Fifty Years of Work without Wages*. Photograph Peter Adamson.

system of education according to which art students wishing to gain certificates in the various stages of the National Course of Instruction submitted laboriously executed drawings, most of them copying exercises involving outline and shading studies from casts and a historical knowledge of ornament. The system was not only stifling for the student but wieldy to administer as all work submitted for examination had to be sent to the National Art Training School at South Kensington. For some years Crane had been an examiner there[10] but he considered his workshop apprenticeship to have been a more valuable kind of training. In *The Claims of Decorative Art* he made his antipathy clear: 'I do not, of course, believe in any cast-iron system of education from any point of view. It must be varied according to the individual. It must be made personal and interesting, or it is of little good; and no system, however good, will manufacture artists in anything, any more than the most brilliant talents will do away with the necessity of passionate devotion to work, careful thought, close observation, and constant practice, which produces that rapid and intimate sympathy of eye and hand, and makes them the responsible and fluent interpreters of that selective and imaginative impulse which results in art'.[11]

Sir Charles Hallé offered Crane the post of Headmaster of Manchester following the retiral of W. J. Muckley in 1883 and when he refused it was accepted by R. H. A. Willis, an able and experienced teacher who, with the help of his deputy John Somerscales, made the School of Art a power to be reckoned with in South Kensington terms. However, prizes and medals did not satisfy Rowley who knew how narrow the teaching system was. Inspired by his contact with Morris and other designers he was anxious to have the School serve the city's needs in as practical a manner as possible. Birmingham, whose School of Art was presided over by Morris led the way in 1890 when the city council set up a new branch school for designers specializing in jewellry and silversmithing under R. Catterson-Smith[12] and in the summer of 1891 Manchester Corporation held an 'Arts and Crafts' exhibition to which students sent designs and samples of printed textiles as well as embroidery, decorative painting and modelling work. Shortly after this the reorganization of the Art and Science institutions in the city resulted in the corporation taking over the running of the Art and Technical Schools. Rowley was elected chairman of the sub-committee responsible for the School of Art. Sensing conflict, or possibly already knowing of his intention to invite Crane as Director over them, Willis and Somerscales resigned. Willis was replaced by Richard Glazier, who was then head of the Art Division of the Technical School, and his position as Headmaster was confirmed when Crane agreed to accept the Directorship on a part-time basis. This entailed his attendance for the first week of every month in term time, during which he gave a lecture to the day students and a repeat performance to evening students.

In these monthly lectures, which were later published as *The Bases of Design* (1898) and *Line and Form* (1900), Crane developed his ideas on art teaching. Before accepting the post he had made a series of *Recommendations and Suggestions* as an alternative or additional scheme of instruction at the School of Art and the Technical School.[13] These had particular reference to the study and practice of design. They were arranged in order of difficulty and devised to develop the student's powers as draughtsman and designer without the customary reference to plaster casts and historical ornament but by encouraging a fluent interpretation of natural form and inventive pattern-making. The first exercise was one Crane considered essential for beginners, experienced students and teachers alike. It involved drawing simple forms in chalk on the blackboard using both hands simultaneously – an exercise in facility and freedom of hand which he had seen used in America and which was a key part of his teaching method; not only as a basic loosening-up exercise but for the teacher whom he expected to demonstrate all his own instructions. The next stage was to memorize the forms used in the previous exercise and combine these into simple designs which were to be executed by modelling or carving and then using brush and water colour. Having been introduced to abstract principles of pattern the student was then directed to study a plant form which he interpreted in terms of silhouette and then of its constructive lines. Here Crane advized the use of herbals, or at least a collection of photographs from them, and of a school conservatory where a variety of flowers and plants would be on hand to satisfy the 'constant necessity of fresh suggestion and resource for the designer'.[14] Meanwhile, on the technical side, the student was being encouraged to adapt his designing to suit different materials, following those crafts in which he showed most aptitude. Life study, 'of the utmost importance to students in all branches of art',[15] came next but instead of being considered in splendid isolation it was to be brought into closer relation with other studies and seen in a colour or an architectural context, or with animal forms from the point of view of comparative anatomy. Most adventurous of all – and in antithesis to the petrified plaster-cast principle – it was to be studied in action by the use of rapid sketches from life and with the help of Eadweard Muybridge's photographs of men and animals in motion. As an aid to colour study he suggested that the school acquire a good costume collection and an aviary. This course taught the student to think of design as a vital, practical, ever-evolving activity and loosened the bonds with which South Kensington had bound it to historical ornament.

Even in his lectures Crane managed to keep the emphasis on positive action rather than passive absorption. Stuart Macdonald has indicated this by a notebook belonging to a student who attended the talks given during the 1894–5 and 1895–6 sessions, which were the foundation of *The Bases of Design* (1898) and *Line and Form* (1900). Crane insisted on students jotting down the diagrams and sketches with which he illustrated these lectures. Emma Bradbury left much of what he actually *said* unrecorded but the meaning of the drawings is clear enough and the very activity of quickly copying Crane's rhythmical patterns must have given her more of the feeling of what it meant to be a professional designer than could ever be experienced in long weeks spent over a carefully stippled drawing from a cast.[16]

The Bases of Design corresponds to the first series of lectures delivered at Manchester and of the two it is the more orthodox teaching manual because it is largely concerned with historical examples. But the approach is different to that of the text-books in general use for design courses of the government programme which relied on Owen Jones's magnificent compendium of styles, the *Grammar of Ornament*, and R. N. Wornum's dry but efficient *Analysis of Ornament*. Instead of presenting design in terms of ornament to be learned for application to objects Crane sought to demonstrate its principles by explaining its origins in different architectural contexts and by an analysis of the influence of material and function. In other words he considered design in its widest context and not in meagre terms of 'applied art' or ornament. While being introduced to ancient decorative styles, the students were also invited to consider work by contemporary designers, and Morris, his daughter May, Cobden Sanderson and L. F. Day also came to lecture on specific subjects. In his discussion of the 'Utility Basis and Influence' as it affected the design of lamps he commended Benson's copper fan-shade lamp as a good solution to a specific problem. Crane had difficulty in sanctioning the design of objects so modified by utilitarian considerations as to be completely

Study of the radiating lines of the pectoral muscle from *Line and Form*, 1900. Photograph Peter Adamson.

·LINES· OF· MOVEMENT

'prosaic' – a knife, for example, with 'no romance' in either blade or handle[17] – thinking that such vulgar assertion of function represented the over-zealous activity of the mechanical side of the utility influence, and one governed by commerce, not art. At the same time he goes surprisingly far in the direction of functionalism with regard to electric lighting when he suggests that 'the naked simplicity of the little pear shaped glasses with their incandescent twist of thread' is preferable to the 'flamboyant excesses' in which many designers mistakenly indulged. 'Decoration, or ornament' he concluded, 'we have been too much accustomed to consider an accidental and unrelated addition to an object not as *an essential expression and organic part of it; not as a beauty which may satisfy us in simple line, form or proportion, combined with fitness to purpose, even without any surface ornament at all'*.[18]

From encouraging an understanding and knowledge of historic and modern design in his first set of lectures, Crane progressed in *Line and Form* to analyze basic elements of picture and pattern-making and give the student some awareness of the expressive potential at his command. These talks were intended to complement the practical course set up according to his previous 'Suggestions'. He begins with line and describes how it may be used to suggest form, texture, surface, to express movement and growth, even moods and emotions. Of paramount importance to the designer, 'line is . . . a language, a most sensitive and vigorous speech of many dialects; which can adapt itself to all purposes'. Form and space are also discussed. In a later chapter he deals with mural painting but quickly moves on to tapestry and wallpaper, and, although he also considers relief and illusions of relief, it is clear that his concern is chiefly with 'design on the flat' and how natural forms may be interpreted for decorative purposes. Using examples like sea-ribbed sand, shells, muscle and wing structure, he illustrates pattern in nature, a subject to which Ruskin had devoted the greater part of Volume IV of *Modern Painters*. Crane's analysis is simplistic in comparison with Ruskin and though not always strictly logical and occasionally repetitive his presentation was effective enough to be of immediate practical use to young students of design. He does not conventionalize nature into the flat-ironed and formalized patterns with which most art teachers were familiar from Sir Richard Redgrave's *Manual of Design* (1876). Instead, following Morris's example of sensitive adaptation of plant form to pattern, he retains a sense of vital growth. Dresser had also laid emphasis on the importance of 'pliant and energetic curvature' and of the 'line of life'[19] in nature and Lewis F. Day's designs show a similar respect for natural form. Crane knew Day's text-books well, including his *Nature in Ornament* (1891) for which he designed a frontispiece. This book stressed the importance of design as a creative process depending on a knowledge of historical forms and close study of nature. Some of Day's designs employ asymmetry as a means to express a kind of organic wilfulness and this feature is further exaggerated by Crane. It distinguishes him from Morris and allies him more closely to Art Nouveau. *Line and Form* contains analyses of various rhythmical principles. The study of a poppy adapted to ornamental design gives a vigorous demonstration of counter-balance and the linear expression of growth and movement.

Line and Form encouraged the development of technical skill by experiment and an analytical approach to nature and design. It may even claim to be a modest precursor of Paul Klee's pedagogical methods. It attempted to arouse the kind of curiosity which was to lead a later generation of artists in the 1950s to study Darcy Wentworth Thompson's *Growth and Form*. *The Bases* and *Line and Form* had an immediate influence on art teaching and soon became standard text-books. They remained in use for almost forty years until British art schools became aware of more progressive design teaching methods emanating from the Bauhaus.

In his *Studio* article of 1895, A. Lys Baldry discussed the effect Crane's teaching was having on work produced at Manchester School of Art.[20] The new course, however, had to be run along with the National Course of Instruction as it was for this that the school was financed by the Government department and not for any prowess displayed under Crane's experiments. Glazier was in an invidious

Below left
Study of a Horned Poppy from Line and Form, 1900. Photograph Peter Adamson.

Below
Study of a Horned Poppy adapted to Design from *Line and Form*, 1900. Photograph Peter Adamson.

STUDY·OF·HORNED·POPPY

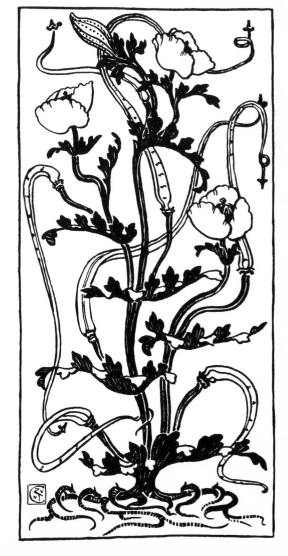

position. He was subordinate to Crane, whose annual salary of £600 as part-time Director exceeded his own as Headmaster. He had no wish to revolutionize South Kensington, and soon he was engaged in preparing an orthodox *Manual of Historic Ornament*. With the students' time and attention divided between two teaching programmes the number of successful passes fell off during this period and Glazier knew these results compared unfavourably with Manchester's successes under Willis. Crane acknowledged that his advice was of most use to practising designers who came to the school for evening classes and that it could jeopardize day-students' chances of gaining their South Kensington certificates. It was decided to run the two types of courses separately. Thus Crane failed to have his ideas incorporated into the rigid structure of the official course but, as he realized when he decided to resign at the end of his third year, he was not just up against two experienced teachers but confronted by a monolithic state system. Glazier and Cadness were not unaffected by his example. They began to illustrate their own lectures with free-drawn designs on the blackboard, a practice to be widely copied in other art schools, and Crane influence is to be seen in Cadness's book, *Decorative Brushwork and Elementary Design* (1902), planned to supplement the Principles of Ornament and Elementary Design sections of the National Course of Instruction.[21] One tangible result of the part-time Directorship was the school museum, whose building was ready in 1898. The idea of a Gallery of Fine and Industrial Arts had been suggested by Sir Henry Cole in 1877 when the new school building was under discussion. On its completion in 1881 the school was given a collection of goods manufactured by Morris's firm and under Willis it obtained a fine collection of casts based on those at South Kensington. But it was Rowley and Crane who promoted the idea of an Arts and Crafts Museum and while Crane was there the school acquired a collection of glass from Powells and metal work from Benson and Company, as well as the loan of Burne-Jones's tapestry 'The Adoration of the Kings'. Many other Art-Workers' Guild members presented items including Crane, Lethaby, Anning Bell and Frampton. The museum was to be the finest of its kind attached to any provincial school of art but unfortunately the policy of stocking a living museum where students could refer to contemporary examples was eventually abandoned and it ultimately came to serve a purely historical function.

After his work at Manchester had ceased with the close of the summer term of 1897 Crane was invited by Professor Mackinder to become Director of the Art Department of a new university college established at Reading. Crane had been instrumental in recommending Morley Fletcher as headmaster there and he took on the Directorship on condition that his duties would be light. These involved a certain amount of promotion of the arts and crafts but many agreeable functions, including that arranged for the Prince of Wales's visit to open the new college. He was given an address illuminated by Crane and a silver enamel casket designed by Nelson Dawson, another member of the Art-Workers' Guild.

Crane's opportunity to build on his experience at Manchester came in July 1898 when he was offered the post of Principal of the Royal College of Art. Before his retirement Thomas Armstrong had expressed a wish that Crane should succeed him as Director of Art at the Science and Art Department at South Kensington. This post was abolished in the reconstitution of the National Art Training School in an attempt to decentralize the national system of art education. The school, renamed the Royal College of Art, was to be run by the Board of Education. Tempted by the honour Crane accepted on the understanding that he would be allowed time for his own work. He found the school 'in rather a chaotic state', having been 'run as a sort of mill in which to prepare art teachers and masters, and supply the finished article to fill such teaching posts or masterships as might fall vacant in any part of the United Kingdom'. The staff were anxious to please, but all except Edouard Lanteri, whose teaching methods he admired[22] had been 'hardened by long service in a system with which I was out of sympathy'. Frustrated by these problems and minor ones like bureaucratic red tape and a bad bout of influenza he soon decided to give up after one year. The post was clearly a full-time affair. Nevertheless, he made a start with his promotion of the arts and crafts by introducing practising designers to the College. The earliest really effective implementation of the aims of the Art-Workers' Guild in a teaching establishment was in Lethaby's Central School founded in 1896. It was sponsored by the London County Council and run specifically for students training in the crafts and not for Fine Art amateurs. Many of Lethaby's staff taught part-time on the principle that they were most useful as teachers if they kept in close touch with practical and commercial realities. Among those whom Crane invited to the Royal College were Alexander Fisher, T. J. Cobden Sanderson, Joseph Pennell and J. S. Sparrow, and on his departure he drafted a report with a scheme for the reorganization of art teaching in which he listed names of those he would like to fill the different posts. This was to be followed closely when Crane was appointed to represent design on the new Board of Education's Council of Advice on Art, on whose recommendations the Royal College was reorganized in 1901 into four schools; Design under Lethaby, Architecture under Beresford Pite, Sculpture under Lanteri and Painting under Gerald Moira. All four men were members of the Art-Workers' Guild as were most of the staff, including the stained glass designer Christopher Whall, the calligrapher Edward Johnston, the printmaker Frank Short, and Henry Wilson who supervised metal work and enamelling. These craft classes were established as a separate part of the five-year course and not merely within Ornamental Design, as had previously been the case. The Royal College was still chiefly concerned with training teachers. Two thirds of its students paid no fees and received County Council grants. Other independent students could afford to train 'for the love of art only' as Crane explained in an interview with Grace Cooke of the *Girls Realm* shortly after taking up his appointment. His socialism extended rather more generously towards the fairer sex than Morris's and he was always sympathetic about their efforts for equality and independence. Grace Cooke's description of his response to her question as to which branch of art he would advise a woman to follow if she had to earn her own living provides insight into the consideration he gave to all details relating to his new position:

Mr Crane hesitated; he drew wonderful geometrical figures in red ink on the blotting-pad in front of him, and it was only when he reached the stage of a design of sunflowers that he answered me, 'The idea of anyone working at art to me is repulsive. I dislike the competition and hack-work which always results. Granted that to make money is necessary to existence; why cannot people be contented with enough? . . . Ambition to succeed in art for art's sake should spur a girl on . . . so many come to me who desire to give up their work through sheer faintheartedness. The best form of art for a girl to succeed in is, I believe, design, decorative work and leather work. Women have always stood high where design is concerned. You see, the work requires great daintiness and nicety of feeling, also that sense of the fitness of things which a woman only seems to possess. A girl is, from her earliest days, trained in decorative schemes. Take her dress, for instance . . . then again . . . black and white work opens out a very large field to the girl artist' . . .[23]

Artistic Dress, illustration for the essay 'The Progress of Taste in Dress in Relation to Art Education' originally written for the Healthy and Artistic Dress Union and published in their journal *Aglaia* in 1894. Photograph Peter Adamson.

It was not surprising, enjoying discussing the minutiae of principles and practice as he did, that Crane was unable to find sufficient time to continue with his own work and he resigned from the Royal College after a year.

His third book of essays *Ideals in Art* was published by George Bell and Sons in 1905. It was illustrated with examples from work produced by students attending Lethaby's design school and Lanteri's modelling school at the Royal College. This volume also contained a reprint of Crane's paper 'The Progress of Taste in Dress in Relation to Art Education', originally written for the Healthy and Artistic Dress Union and published in the journal *Aglaia* in 1894. Having referred to the origins of the movement in the artistic dress of the Pre-Raphaelites Crane went on to criticize the way in which the fashionable world of the 1870s and early 1880s aped 'with more or less grotesque vulgarity what it was fain to think were the fashions of the inner and most refined cult.' If he disliked the excesses of Aestheticism he was equally critical of contemporary conventional dress. Hygiene and reason naturally combine with art in dress. This picturesque ideal was best seen in the habit of the British working man, like the fisherman, ploughman or navvy. The modern gentleman only approached the picturesque when he dressed for action, in cricket flannels or a striped football jersey. The sterile uniform of modern male attire was the result of a life style whose ideal was to look as if he never did any work. In short 'if we lived simple, useful and beautiful lives, we could not help being picturesque in the highest sense'. Both Crane and Henry Holiday, who was on *Aglaia*'s founding committee, continued to promote vaguely Grecian styles for ladies. These, like the smocks which were so suitable for children, could be made more artistic with embroidery.[24] Crane did not join the Anti-Tight-Lacing league and in this was probably influenced by his strong-minded wife who declared that she did not 'altogether disapprove of corsets'.[25]

Crane's involvement with the Board of Education concerned not only the Royal College but the question of art teaching in schools. Previously he had supported the Art for Schools Association which encouraged that classrooms should be brightened up with plants and reproductions of works of art. He illustrated the new *Circular on Primary Drawing* published in 1901, where the more liberal approach developed in the Manchester lectures is adapted and simplified for children. From this point the whole atmosphere surrounding art in school becomes more relaxed. 'Suggestions' were proposed to help the teacher rather than rules being laid down.[26] Children were no longer restricted to using lead pencils but encouraged towards freer expression using a brush. Blackboard drawing enjoyed a certain vogue and colour was eventually given wide approval.

There continued to be a fair amount of copying although children were allowed to choose their own subjects and often asked to study natural form. At an L.C.C. Conference on the Teaching of Drawing in 1908, L. F. Day, Crane's opponent in the 'Friendly Disputes', took a rigid stand against the trend towards imaginative work. 'Don't ask or expect originality from children. Let them begin by copying . . . the present reaction against it has gone far enough, if not too far . . .'[27] Crane, who always hated copying anything, would once again have opposed Day's point of view being more likely to have endorsed that of Henry Wilson, who on the same occasion recommended the complete freedom of expression that is now an accepted part of primary art education: 'Criticism of the work of any child is . . . impossible, suggestion is dangerous, and interference damnable. We can only give the child unlimited pencils and paper and love, and sit at its feet and watch the blossoms of the mind unfold . . .'[28]

Day was a more dogmatic and logical character than Crane, a man criticized by his contemporaries for being rather fonder of preaching than practice. His matter of fact approach to design led him to be an early supporter of the belief that machine made goods could be artistic. Crane was never able to fully acknowledge this. In *Ideals in Art* he appears to have decided to accept that arts and crafts workers play a Fabian role with regard to industry: 'The organized factory and the great machine industries will continue to work for the million, as well as for the millionaire, under the present system of production; but, at any rate, they can be influenced by ideas of design, and it must be said that some manufacturers have shown themselves fully alive to the value of co-operation of artists in this direction'.[29]

At the Central School, Lethaby trained designers in the industrial crafts of textile printing, book production and cabinet making and both he and Ashbee became increasingly disposed to promote co-operation between art and industry. Ashbee criticized the Royal College for teaching only the lighter handcrafts, but there was practical justification for this in that the college trained teachers to carry out similar work in school classrooms. Such criticisms increased when English designers realized that the lead they had given to the arts and crafts was being more effectively developed in Germany – in a wider context outside of a pure craft aesthetic. The Arts and Crafts Exhibition of 1912 was a financial failure in contrast to the great success of the German Werkbund's exhibition in Cologne two years later. These lessons led to the founding of the Design and Industries Association in 1915. Besides promoting principles of sound basic design it acknowledged that 'many machine processes tend to certain qualities of their own'.[30] Though it cannot be said that Walter Crane went as far as Ashbee in accepting the functional aesthetics of the twentieth century, his promotion of design in art education was nonetheless a valuable contribution to the modern movement. By encouraging experiment and spontaneity through his teaching he gave students a real sense of the resilience and adaptability which would be more and more required of designers if they were to respond to the needs of a developing society.

America

At the invitation of the Fine Art Society Crane held his first retrospective in their Bond Street gallery during the summer of 1891. Over one hundred items were shown including sets of book illustrations, designs for wallpapers and decorative schemes, pottery, gesso work and paintings like 'The Bridge of Life' and the ill-fated 'Riddle of the Sphinx'. One critic remarked that 'the difficult thing would be to say what this aesthetic "Admirable Crichton" cannot do. He apparently designs wallpapers with as much facility as he writes poetry; he paints pictures and delivers socialistic lectures with equal readiness; he writes essays and models in gesso with the same dexterity; brass and copper repoussé work and the illustration of books he tackles with similar avidity; a mosaic pavement or a needlework pattern; a frieze or a fresco; a dithyramb or a dado are one and all in his eclectic line. Nay more than this, he adds to his numberless accomplishments quite a pretty capacity for such instrumentation as is involved in the blowing of his own trumpet'.[1] The sting in the tail of this review was provoked by the serious way Crane discussed the stylistic development of his toy books in his catalogue introduction. It was a justifiable indulgence, however, because by this date other critics thought of the early picture books as significant contributions to the English revival of decorative art. Indeed, the importance of this London exhibition lies less in the indication it gives of Crane's popularity at home than in the way it consolidated his reputation abroad. What was not sold that summer formed the nucleus of a touring exhibition which went to the United States and then to Europe. This was a very successful time both from the point of view of recognition[2] and of work accomplished. *Queen Summer* and the first published edition of his poems *Renascence: A Book of Verse* were issued in 1891. Watts honoured Crane by painting his portrait which was hailed as one of that artist's finest works. The year was not without its dark side, however. On 18 March little Myfanwy Crane, who had been born in 1888, died of diphtheria. The family were glad when the opportunity arose to leave London for a while. During the exhibition at the Fine Art Society Henry Blackburn, who had recently returned from a lecture tour of the United States, suggested that Crane should write to the Director of Boston Fine Arts Museum, where he was sure his work would be welcome. General Loring responded with a prompt invitation and offered to defray costs of shipment and customs. The family excepting Lionel who left early to stay with friends in Florida, sailed from Liverpool on 8 October aboard the S.S. Cephalonia. They arrived in Boston on 19 October.

Several friends had already visited the United States. Charles Rowley went there in 1887 and Henry Holiday in 1890,[3] but the best publicized journey was of course that made by Oscar Wilde nearly ten years previously. Wilde had arrived in New York early in January 1882 and stayed in North America for eighteen months. He agreed to the tour in order to promote D'Oyly Carte's production of

Gilbert and Sullivan's comic opera 'Patience' which opened in New York only five months after its London premiere at the Opera Comique on 23 April 1881. His campaign was surrounded by fashionable flurry and amusement at the figure so obviously partly parodied in Bunthorne, the Fleshly Poet of 'Patience'. Americans were also familiar with the *Punch* cartoons by Du Maurier, whose 'Nincompoopiana' series satirizing the Aesthetic Movement had begun in the summer of 1879. The aesthetic artist Maudle and the poet, Postlethwaite, first introduced to Mrs Cimabue Brown early in 1880 shared features variously attributable to Wilde, Swinburne and Whistler, but by July Jellaby Postlethwaite was certainly modelled on Wilde.[4] It was not Wilde's intention to tour as a freak. He had agreed to D'Oyly Carte's sponsorship with a view to informing his transatlantic cousins about new English ideals and aesthetics. Ideas for which Wilde himself was indebted to Ruskin, Morris, Whistler and Pater. These were included in three basic lectures, 'The English Renaissance', 'House Decoration', and 'Art and the Handicraftsman', which were met with varying degrees of success in such diverse centres as Boston, San Francisco, Salt Lake City, Milwaukee and Montreal.

English fashions had already begun to supercede those of France in more sophisticated centres of American life. The taste extended to house decoration. William Morris's wallpapers had been sold in America as early as the 1860s and by the time of the Philadelphia Centennial of 1876, where Jeffrey and Company were among several English firms represented, the work of designers like Crane, Day and Talbert was quite well known. The New York company of Warren and Fuller followed Warner's example and commissioned designs from the American artists Louis Comfort Tiffany and Candace Wheeler.[5] After Wilde's visit trade journals often featured 'English Art Papers', but before his arrival the *American Art Journal* in 1880 illustrated examples of fashionable Japanese styles as well as the full vertical spread of Crane's 'Rush and Iris'.[6] Eastlake furniture had become quite popular since the appearance of the American edition of *Hints on Household Taste* in 1872. It was soon competing with Queen Anne, one of several styles featured in displays at the Centennial. English fabrics were also available in the United States. Later Crane was delighted to discover a curtain of his, 'Luna and Stars' pattern, in a South Pacific Railroad sleeping car.

There can be little doubt that, in America as in Britain, Crane's Toy Books provided many people with an effective introduction to the new art movement. Clarence Chatham Cook's praise of them has already been mentioned. Pirated editions had appeared as early as the 1870s and in 1877 Crane wrote in exasperation to Scribners asking for their co-operation in printing a disclaimer to a bad American edition of *Baby's Opera*.[7] Ironically it was not until the year of his own visit to the United States that he became legally protected against such copyright infringements, by the Chace Act. He told several reporters at this time that it was an American wallpaper with patterns borrowed from his books which had led him to design his own first paper hanging in 1875. The early toy books have a brightness and buoyancy different to the languid aesthetic satirized by Du Maurier and W. S. Gilbert. But the blue and white china, black spindly furniture and tiled interiors of *Buckle My Shoe, Puffy, Little Pig* and *Silverlocks* inevitably identified Crane as an aesthetic practitioner of the arts and crafts. The kind of aestheticism satirized is more pronounced in later books where long proportions and limp hands are increasingly exaggerated and have less of the brisk commonsense associated with the more down-to-earth manifestations of the Arts and Crafts Movement. They were also more 'greenery yallery' in colouring than less sophisticated predecessors like *Little Pig*.[8]

Initially Crane had not been disturbed by being associated with the Aesthetic Movement. When W. S. Gilbert invited him to design a set and costumes for 'Patience' he had felt close enough, as a Grosvenor Gallery exhibitor and acquaintance of Burne-Jones, to fear that he might be helping to guy himself and his friends but he nevertheless did some designs which were never used.[9] Shortly afterwards, during the planning of the Savoy Theatre, Mackmurdo suggested that D'Oyly Carte consult him on its interior design. Crane thought out an elaborate scheme with seating tiered like a Roman amphitheatre but this also came to nothing. In the popular mind Crane was never as closely identified with the movement as were Wilde or Whistler. Whistler had been considered representative enough in the heyday of the 'Patience' era to have given Bunthorne his curly black hair and white forelock but his disdain for Aestheticism grew as his friendship with Wilde cooled. This was all too clear in the Ten O'Clock lecture, given in the Prince's Hall on 20 February 1885: 'If familiarity can breed contempt, certainly Art – or whatever is currently taken for it – has been brought to its lowest stage of intimacy. The people have been harassed with Art in every guise ... Their homes have been invaded, and their walls covered with paper, their very dress taken to task . . . Alas, ladies and gentlemen, Art has been maligned. She has nought in common with such practices. She is a goddess of dainty thought ... purposing in no way to better others. She is, withal, selfishly occupied with her own perfection . . .'[10] Such opinions were diametrically opposed to Crane's own belief, consistent with Ruskinian tradition, that the public had a right to communication from the artist and that beauty was synonymous with virtue and could enhance the quality of life through good design of the humblest items. Generally speaking it was not the ubiquity and everyday character of the Aesthetic Movement which turned Crane against it but the effete and shallow quality that inevitably taints anything fashionable. Crane contributed to two magazines edited by Wilde, *Little Folks* and *Woman's World*.[11] Wilde resigned from the editorship of *Woman's World* in 1889 and this marked the beginning of an increasingly socialist bias in his attitude, explained in 1893 in his essay 'The Soul of Man under Socialism' where he describes his ideal kind of individual anarchism. Crane, understandably, became increasingly sympathetic to Wilde's views as the latter abandoned his belief in Art for Art's sake. Together with Jacomb Hood in 1889 he illustrated the tales for children in which Wilde first revealed his doubts. In the title story, *The Happy Prince*, the idea that Beauty surpasses Use is shown to be fallacious by the prince and the swallow who sacrifice themselves for the poor. Four years later Wilde completed *Dorian Gray* whose theme depends on a *reductio ad absurdum* of the view that Beauty is all that matters in life. In America, however, suspicions surrounding Socialism and English art were yet to be aroused. When he arrived Crane must have seemed eminently aesthetic, having just produced *Flora's Feast* and *Queen Summer*, flower books full of seductively lovely designs of the very emblems which had flourished on Oscar's lapel in former days.

Bostonians prepared for an aesthetic 'Lord High Chancellor of the Nursery'.[12] Newspaper reports of Crane's arrival commented politely upon his versatility noting the humanitarian sentiments which he shared with William Morris. A Chicago paper was to estimate that 'in point of mere popularity' he outranked Morris and Burne-Jones.[13] In Boston Crane was warmly welcomed by General Loring and his staff and liberally plied with cocktails. However, society hostesses had scarcely time to decide whether such a famous master of the lesser arts should be invited to their homes when he offended the city's fashionable society by speaking at a commemoration meeting at the Paine Hall on 15 November in honour of the Chicago Anarchists. Two poems which he had written at the time of their arrest and trial 'On the Suppression of Free Speech at Chicago' and 'Freedom in America' were read and printed next day in the *Evening Transcript*. The newspaper tried to report the issue as delicately as possible, suggesting that his sympathy with the anarchists was 'more for the intellectual and philosophical side, than sympathy with their insane acts' and that his poetic temperament could not but respond to 'all impressions with an intensity unknown to common clay'.[14] Others were less deferential to genius and Crane found a dinner at an exclusive club suddenly 'postponed'. He soon became aware how sensitive many Americans were to any criticism of the handling of the Haymarket Affair.[15] To clear up the misrepresentation of his views he wrote to the *Boston Herald* on 19 November stating he was 'against all violence and coercive methods', and opposed to 'hanging men for their opinions'. Like his English colleagues he did not believe those sentenced had thrown the bomb. Nor did he think he should be expected to change his opinions just because he was not on his home ground. 'As to the meeting I went there at the request of the secretary, who disclaimed expressly any sympathy with dynamite . . . Anarchism simply means a plea for a life of voluntary association, of free individual development – the freedom only bounded by respect for the freedom of others.'

This airing of ideals had its compensations. To make up for the cancelled dinner one friend saw that he had the run of other leading Boston clubs and Crane found himself all the more warmly welcomed by 'the old guard of Freedom of the anti-slavery agitation days' like the German veteran of the '48, L. Prang, who ran a large printing business and commissioned the book *Columbia's Courtship*. He also met Edward Bellamy who was now editor of *The Nationalist* and they discussed the ideas which had led him to write *Looking Backward*. Horace Scudder of the *Atlantic Monthly* asked Crane for an elucidation of the subject of art and Socialism which was published in January 1892 as 'Why Socialism Appeals to Artists'. Winthrope Scudder of Houghton Mifflin and Company commissioned illustrations to Hawthorn's *Wonder Book*. The stir caused the curious to flock to the Art Museum exhibition. Sales were good. 'Pandora' found a home but, as in England, it was chiefly smaller items such as the *Flora's Feast* drawings which were bought.[16]

Crane's notoriety travelled to Chicago, the next city of his itinerary. He was not on an official lecture tour but agreed to give a few talks. Before a large audience at the opening of his exhibition at Chicago's Art Institute on the 5 January he discussed 'Design in Relation to Use and Material',[17] illustrating his meaning with rapid charcoal sketches. About five hundred enthusiastic ladies packed the hall and were so enchanted with the 'chalk talk' that they applauded nearly every stroke. This warm reception scandalized one citizen who wrote to *Inter Ocean* protesting against the welcome given by the foolish women of Chicago to 'Walter Crane, the anarchist', who deserved to be locked up with his brothers at Joliet.[18]

Full descriptions of Walter Crane's impressions of America are recorded in his *Reminiscences*[19] and we need only outline his itinerary and briefly explain the circumstances of commissions. The family left Boston for Chicago on 14 December and arrived after a stop of two nights to see the Niagara Falls. Their host in Chicago was William Pretyman, an English architect at whose Edgewater house they all spent Christmas. Pretyman was on the Committee of the 1893 Columbia Exposition and through him Crane was asked to design a wallpaper and two large panels for the Women's Temperance Building.[20] Early in January they moved to a hotel in town for the opening of the Exhibition at the Art Institute, which ran from 5 January to 1 March. While in Chicago Crane also gave a talk on 'Art and Modern Life' at the Twentieth Century Club. A highlight of their stay was the

The Happy Prince from the book of this title containing stories in which Oscar Wilde proposed socialistic principles in place of his earlier credo of Art for Art's Sake, 1889. By courtesy of the Trustees of the National Library of Scotland.

visit to Henry D. Lloyd's family at Winetka. Lloyd edited the *Chicago Tribune*, had done much for the cause of the Anarchists in 1887 and was currently helping towards the reprieve of those still in prison. Towards the end of January the Cranes went on to St Louis where the Art Institute was also scheduled to take the exhibition. As in Chicago this also housed an art school and Crane addressed the students. From here the family went West, via Kansas City to Los Angeles, Santa Barbara and San Francisco, a city that enchanted Crane with its mixture of exotic elements. They were back in New York early in March and stayed with J. R. Lamb another Englishman with a well established business. He and his son specialized in decorative art work, mostly mosaic, stained glass and church furniture and had carried out the design of the Newark window. Crane contributed a piece to W. D. Howell's monthly *The Cosmopolitan* and took part in a discussion on 'The Effect of Modern and Social Economic Conditions on the Sense of Beauty' at a meeting of the Nineteenth Century Club. This was chaired by Brander Matthews but Crane had not the easy after-dinner manner of Wilde on such occasions and took the whole thing too seriously. He had been wise in his decision not to attempt to lecture much, but rather to finance his trip through his American art commissions. Hamilton Bell, a nephew of Poynter, introduced him to the Players' Club where he dined in the company of another fêted guest, Rudyard Kipling. W. J. Linton came in from New Haven, Connecticut. This was the last time he saw his old master who died in America in 1897 a year after completing his *Memories*. Crane found him looking frail but 'bright and cheery, and as revolutionary in his views as ever . . . with an entire lack of bitterness'. They saw Lionel again in April, at remote Killarney in Florida where a warm quiet interlude provided the opportunity to finish the *Wonder Book* drawings.

From St Louis the exhibition went to Philadelphia's Art Club and after breaking their journey at Washington the Cranes came there at the end of April. This period in the Quaker City was one of the most pleasant of the more official parts of the tour and Crane greatly admired the progressive methods of primary, art and technical teaching encouraged by individuals like Liberty Tadd and Charles Leyland, and seen in practice at the Drexel Institute. He attended his first baseball game, and his sketches and notes from it were printed in the *Philadelphia Press*, along with the inevitable poems from *Renascence*. By 19 May the family were in Brooklyn where the exhibition was to arrive at the Art Institute, but its transfer from Philadelphia was delayed. Disliking Brooklyn itself and having failed to find exhibition facilities in New York, Crane took the family for a holiday in New England. They spent the final week of May at Pride's Crossing, then went on to Eastern Point (where some work on *Columbia's Courtship* was completed) and finally to Nantucket Island where Pretyman gave them the use of his cottage and studio at Wauwinet. The panels for the Chicago Fair were painted here and after six weeks in this beautiful wild spot the Cranes returned to Boston and embarked on the SS Cephalonia for home.

When he set out across the Atlantic, Crane had already a deep respect for the mental background of what Louis Mumford has called America's Brown Decades. From his youth he had admired Ralph Waldo Emerson, whose appreciation of sound workmanship and reverence for nature in so many ways paralleled Ruskin's philosophy. In Boston he was invited out to Concord by Edward Emerson, the son of the philosopher, and was also taken to see Walden Pond. The vital force of the simple life, so fundamental to the writing of Thoreau and Walt Whitman, stirred sympathetic response in the hearts of Englishmen like Morris, Crane and their friends. Whitman's work began to be known in England after 1867 when W. M. Rossetti reviewed *Leaves of Grass*. Swinburne in his ode to the poet had portrayed him as a symbol of democracy and freedom and, as such, he became an inspiration to some English socialists. Within the circle of the arts and crafts his most fervent admirer was C. R. Ashbee who was introduced to Whitman's work by the poet and socialist, Edward Carpenter – a man whom Crane himself described as 'the English Walt Whitman'. Wilde, Carpenter, even Charles Rowley, visited the elderly poet at Camden but he died on 26 March 1892, shortly before Crane arrived in Philadelphia. Among the literary figures Crane did meet were Mrs Julia Ward Howe, James Russell Lowell, Oliver Wendell Holmes and Margaret Deland, for whom he agreed to illustrate a book of poems.

The American Arts and Crafts Movement had not anything like the autonomy its English counterpart enjoyed under the powerful influence of Ruskin and Morris. There were many reasons for this, not least of them being the cultural barriers created by communications problems in such a vast country. A slightly different philosophical basis helped prevent the more wholehearted 'retreat to the

Ordering her United State Coach from *Columbia's Courtship*, 1893. Collection the Beinecke Rare Book and Manuscript Library, Yale University.

First Impressions of Chicago, 1891–92, pen and ink, 8 × 6½ in. (20.3 × 16.7 cm) expressing the alarm experienced by an itinerant Crane at America's elevator buildings. Collection the Houghton Library, Harvard University.

crafts'[21] that took place in Britain. When Crane visited the United States he was struck by the positive way in which Americans embraced the kind of progress Ruskin and Carlyle had been so doubtful about. Electric light and the telephone were taken for granted as part of modern city dwelling while they were still regarded as novelties in London. He told the press that he admired America's new architecture but it is clear that he was also somewhat alarmed at its implications when he put up in Louis Sullivan's recently completed Auditorium Building in Chicago. He was ill at ease in space-saving, skyward-soaring elevator buildings, preferring the leisurely sprawl and intimate scale of life in Concord's woodlands. He warmed to Henry Hobson Richardson's work. Its hewn stone surfaces and rugged picturesque masses appealed to his romantic craftsman's instinct, an appeal reinforced by the attention Richardson paid to the ancillary arts. On his arrival in Boston, Crane stayed at the Brunswick in Copely Square, hard by Trinity Church with its stained glass by the English firm of Clayton Bell and Burne-Jones, and the impressive glowing opalescent glass by La Farge, one of America's leading designers whom he later met at Lamb's studio in New York.

The aims of the Arts and Crafts Movement were very far from reaching down to less privileged ranks of society. 'There must' Oscar Wilde observed in 1882 in a lecture to an audience in Philadelphia, 'be a great mass of handicraft produced before you can hope to effect the masses. And the handicraftsmen must be directed by the artists; and the artists must be inspired with true designs. It is only through those classes we can work'.[23] But America was intoxicated by its industrial progress. Her workers got higher wages than their brothers in Europe. Wilde's vision of the craftsman labouring with love and leisure was entirely utopian in a situation where piecework at machines, mass production and speed were the key to economic success. The Americans thought big and the craft aesthetic must have seemed too tender and delicate a concept to survive in the environment of expanding cities like New York and Chicago. Architects like Sullivan and Frank Lloyd Wright were indebted to the teaching of Ruskin and Morris but their functionalism was uninhibited by fear of technology. Of all the English designers it was Ashbee who eventually acknowledged the truly progressive contribution of American attitudes to design. He was critical at first – much more so than Crane – but after three visits to the United States (in 1896, 1900 and 1908) and the bitter experience of trying to keep his Guild of Handicraft at work in competition with industry, he declared categorically that modern civilization rested on machinery and all teaching of art should take this into account.[24]

Although many of the finest achievements in American design were made within the wide context of architecture, there were aspects of decorative art which may be seen in an arts and crafts context, where there was no replacement for the skilled handicraftsman. English exhibits at the Philadelphia Centennial had aroused much interest among American designers including Candace Wheeler who held them responsible for giving her the idea of founding the Women's Society of Decorative Art in New York early in 1877, which was modelled on the South Kensington School of Art Needlework. Pioneering events in the history of American arts and crafts include the founding of the New York Society of Decorative Art in 1877, and two years later, Louis Comfort Tiffany's Company of Associated Artists was established. In Cincinnati a Woman's Pottery Club was formed in 1879 and the Rookwood Pottery in 1880. The Philadelphian, Charles Leland, who knew Wilde and Crane in England, turned his attention to the crafts with little manuals designed to encourage their practice in villages and schools. The guild idea was copied in the mid 1880s at Providence, R.I. by two painters S. R. Burleigh and C. W. Stetson and an industrialist John G. Aldrich.

Crane was among the English designers best known in America. Indeed, to Candace Wheeler, he stood pre-eminent:

> I had always felt that Walter Crane was the foremost designer of that group of men who brought England into a prominent place in applied art during the last days of the nineteenth century. His designs stood by themselves in certain qualities of grace and appropriateness, and when I found that he was coming to America I was keen to meet him. I think his object in coming was really to *see* what we were doing in America.[25]

Crane was certainly curious to see what American artists and designers were doing. He had already been making a careful study of their graphic work from the journals he could obtain in London. Commercial considerations should not be ruled out either: as long as pirated editions prevented him benefiting from his popularity in the United States he considered extra efforts to promote his work there to be hardly worth while. When the Chace Act was passed in 1891, however, English authors were for the first time able to secure copyright protection in America – though publication had to be simultaneous in both countries and American printings set in type within the United States. Crane also made personal contact with designers and architects in Philadelphia, whom he advised on the founding of an Art-Workers' Guild, and he designed a cover for their magazine.[26] Despite the number of individuals alert to the revival of handicraft and working in their own way towards this end there were yet few organized bodies. It was not until after the Chicago Exposition of 1893 that the movement was really under way and there was anything like a proliferation of 'crafted' furniture and hand thrown pottery.

In Boston Crane was shown Bertram G. Goodhue's medieval-style cover for *The Knight Errant*. Printed by the Elzevir Press and issued first in April 1892 this was significant in the development of the American Arts and Crafts book because it was inspired by the Century Guild's *Hobby Horse*, intended to reflect progressive ideas and to be a 'model of perfect typography and the printer's art'.[27] Crane met Goodhue and the printer Francis Watts Lee and a photogravure reproduction of his 'La Belle Dame Sans Merci' appeared as frontispiece in the next number of the magazine, which also contained an article by Crane called 'Of Aesthetic Pessimisms and the New Hope'.[28] During the month in which Crane had arrived in America a photograph facsimile edition of the first Kelmscott book *The Story of the Glittering Plain* was issued by the Roberts Brothers of Boston. This was soon to prove a 'major catalyst'[29] to the Arts and Crafts book and its influence – every bit as much as that of the *Hobby Horse* and of Crane's decoration – affected the appearance of *The Knight Errant*.

Crane's graphic influence before his visit to the United States may be seen early in the 1880s in the pages of *St Nicholas*, Scribner's illustrated magazine for the young, where a variety of designers began to simplify their styles to purely linear conventions and flattened planes, often with integrated text. By 1887 a sketchier pictorial style began to take over.[30] A bold linear manner is generally characteristic of much work in the 1890s. In the famous *Chapbook* European influences are as much in evidence as specific English influences. Frederick Weinstein has suggested that the Mid-Western illustrator, Frank Hazenplug, is one *Chapbook* contributor particularly indebted to Crane, but he was also ready to fall under Beardsley's spell. In Philadelphia Crane met Howerd Pyle, who was shortly to become director of illustration at the Drexel Institute. He had for some time admired Pyle's work, which until he adopted his later more painterly style, was not unlike

The Button Presser 1891-92, pen and ink, 8 × 6½ in. (20.3 × 16.7 cm). Collection the Houghton Library, Harvard University.

THE BUTTON · PRESSER – FANCY PORTRAIT OF THE MAN OF THE FUTURE.

177

his own. He gave generous praise to the American artist in his book on *Decorative Illustration* where a very Düreresque page from *Otto of the Silver Hand* (Scribner, New York 1888) was reproduced. Crane's influence on younger American designers may be seen in the work of George Wharton Edwards, John Sloan[31] and the English-born Louis Rhead; but these artists, like others such as Edwin Austin Abbey, Lucy Fitch Perkins and Will Denslow, who show even fainter reminiscences of Crane,[32] were open to many other stimulating graphic influences. In this period the American Arts and Crafts book was particularly susceptible to the pervasive effects of Kelmscott publications and the rapid infiltration of spooky elements from Beardsley and the Glasgow School – as can be seen in the work of Will Bradley and the books designed by the artistic community of the Roycrofters run by Elbert Hubbard in East Aurora, New York.

In spite of his notoriety as a left-winger Crane's American tour was a less charismatic affair than that of Wilde. But his presence and the exhibition of his work gave a vital impetus to the revival of handicrafts at a time when American designers were ready to take advantage of his example. His work continued to be featured in journals like the American *Magazine of Art*.[33] In October 1909 an interview with him was published in *The Craftsman* and his importance from the American point of view was generously acknowledged:

> Every American interested in art matters knows the many-sided work of Walter Crane. Both as a member of the famous group of Pre-Raphaelites and as an individual worker he has exerted a strong influence upon the development of modern art in England and abroad, and no nation is more alive to this than we on the western side of the Atlantic.[34]

American socialists used his 'Capitalist Vampire' for their Journal *Comrade* which ran from 1901 to 1905. After his return to Britain he was asked to design book-plates for the bibliophiles Caroline Miller Parker and H. E. Widener; and the mosaic floor of a bank in Cleveland. In two respects he was probably influenced by American art: his 'History of Transport' frieze may well have been suggested by J. Carroll Beckwith's murals of figures representing innovations like 'The Telephone', 'The Arc Light' and the 'Spirit of Electricity' at the Chicago World's Fair[35] and the late glass at Stamford Hill reflects the rich effects of La Farge's work in Trinity Church, Boston.

Commendatore Crane

With the Art Nouveau movement, which flourished during the later 1890s and early 1900s, beauty was often given priority over use. England helped form the new style not only through the example of fluent natural ornamentation set by her designers in the 1880s, but also through the emphasis they put on fine materials and craftsmanship. Ideas linking Morris's movement with folk art and art for the people were influential in certain countries, but many of the more characteristic products of Continental Art Nouveau were sophisticated trinkets for the rich. Crane's part in the promotion of English theory and design abroad was considerable. The sheer quantity, variety and availability of his work made him in several respects a more influential figure than Morris. Warm receptions greeting his touring exhibitions culminated in his triumphant visit to Hungary in 1900 and the award in recognition of his work for the Turin Exhibition of 1902, of the 'Croce di Grande Ufficiale nell' Ordine della Coronia d'Italia'. After this he assumed the title 'Commendatore' and his wife, who had some difficulty persuading her friends to call her 'Dame', came to be known picturesquely enough as 'Mistress Crane'. The Orders of Saints Maurizio and Lazzara were conferred on him in January 1912 by King Victor Emmanuel, which raised him to the rank of Cavaliere.

On their return to London from America the family decided to leave Beaumont Lodge. The house held too many sad memories and was furthermore threatened by the encroaching Central London Railway. Wood Lane had already lost much of its rural character. A big housewarming party was held in December 1892 to welcome their friends to No. 13 Holland Street and Morris distinguished the occasion by turning up in a dress suit. The interior was papered with Crane's own designs, Persian rugs, and a variety of furniture; some pieces designed by himself, old English examples and a Colonial chair brought over from the United States.[1] Mrs Crane kept a chingatoo and doves in the large garden which had fine mulberry trees. Neither she nor her husband were practical in household matters and seem not to have worried overmuch about how their servants behaved. 'The most ridiculous things happened in the grubby picturesque, Bohemian house in Holland Street, Kensington' Ashbee recalled. 'Once a bottle of condy's fluid got mixed up with the claret by mistake and a ghastly terror seized upon the guests as they were standing round the cakes and sandwiches . . .'[2] Crane took a studio fifteen minutes' walk away, in New Road, Campden Hill, and later moved to one at the back of the house.

Like many of his colleagues who helped create the style, Crane disliked Art Nouveau. He called it a 'strange decorative disease'. It seemed to be more self conscious and affected than Aestheticism and, even worse, to promote a 'cult of the ugly' in addition to what he regarded as the natural artistic goal of art – the pursuit of beauty.[3] In England these sinister aspects of the new style were em-

No. 13 Holland Street, Kensington, where the Cranes lived from 1892. Photograph Robin Spencer.

bodied in Aubrey Beardsley's work which was introduced to readers of the new *Studio* magazine by Joseph Pennell in the first number in April 1893. Among the designs printed was a page opening for Malory's *Morte d'Arthur*. These were reproduced from process blocks and, although still of a certain wood-cut character Pennell here praised the 'distinct quality' of Beardsley's pen line. It was this linearism that led to a change of taste in black and white work in the 1890s from styles dependent on the 'velvety fatty quality' of wood engraving to one taking full advantage of the fact that the photographic line block could reproduce the most delicate pen stroke. Like many young graphic artists, Beardsley admired Crane's work.[5] When he became art editor of *The Yellow Book* he sought him out at Holland Street and came away with a photograph of *The Renaissance of Venus* which was published in Volume 2. Beardsley thought it 'a divine Crane (his only really great thing)'.[6] Rossetti, Burne-Jones and Japonism are easily recognisable sources of Beardsley's early style but there were others contributing in a more discreet way to his eclectic, yet highly individual art and Crane may be considered to be among these. The fanciful dress and variety of vegetable forms in the border decorations of the *Morte d'Arthur* drawings could well have been amplified by those from Crane's flower and picture books. The monkey lackeys in Beardsley's frontispiece for *Juvenal*, printed on Volume 4 of *The Yellow Book*, probably derive from a similar theme of Crane's in *Beauty and the Beast*. In *The Yellow Book*'s rival, *The Savoy*, Beardsley's drawings assume an increasingly French eighteenth century character. Studies made in Paris, the styles of Hogarth, Watteau and French engraving all helped towards this development, but Beardsley may well also have referred to the toy books in which Crane so successfully evoked the rich and mannered setting of the Countess d'Aulnoy's fairy tales.

Like any good artist-craftsman, Crane was in favour of designers adapting their approach to suit the capabilities of different techniques but he was less ready than Pennell in acknowledging how appropriate Beardsley's style was to the line block. He criticized his 'general abstract treatment of line and the use of large masses of black and white' which he thought better suited to inlay or enamel than page decoration. These views, discussing recent developments, were published in 1896 in the fourth chapter of *The Decorative Illustration of Books*. Despite his obvious dislike of the 'loathly' and 'corrupt' forms and subjects used by Beardsley, Crane nevertheless gave him his due in the *Reminiscences* as 'a very remarkable designer'. The first of the younger artists discussed in this chapter were Charles Ricketts, the designer and illustrator of most of Wilde's books, and his friend Charles Shannon. Their work depended upon sources dear to Crane, such as Blake and early German and Italian printed books, and showed a craftsmanlike respect for typography and layout. Crane's own example and teaching were also influential for Charles Robinson (three of whose illustrations to *A Child's Garden of Verse* were reproduced by Crane). His brothers William Heath and T. H. Robinson were other young designers who would have acknowledged the importance of Crane's work in the formation of their own different styles. At the 'head of the newer school of decorative illustrators . . . whose taste and feeling for style alone gives him a distinctive place' Crane put Robert Anning Bell, an artist indebted to him not only for features of graphic style but also in the use of coloured gesso relief which Crane did so much to promote. He also mentions Laurence Husman, Fairfax Muckley, Fred Mason, J. D. Batten, Henry Ford, Grandville Fell, Patten Wilson, William Strange and the Scottish designers associated with *Evergreen*, Robert Burns and John Duncan. The most obvious overemphasis in this chapter of *Decorative Illustration* is the attention paid to the Birmingham School, three of whose products C. M. Gere, E. H. New and A.

Gaskin contributed to Kelmscott books.

Crane's selection of examples for discussion and illustration in this chapter reflects much of what was featured in the first few volumes of *The Studio* because it was Gleeson White, the editor,[7] who had persuaded Crane to revise and supplement the Cantor lectures for publication by Bell and Sons. He gave him access to his own collection of modern illustrated books bringing the survey up to date. Throughout the 1890s Crane's work and opinions were featured in this most influential of magazines. Hollyer's photograph of him was given a full page in Volume 2, and he could claim to be *The Studio*'s first pin-up artist. His position with respect to graphic art in England was summed up in 1892: 'Mr Crane . . . is perhaps the best known, as he was among the first, of all those who practise decorative illustration in these days of its wider acceptance . . . he has influenced many at the outset of their career; so many and those so greatly, that a goodly proportion of modern conventional design owes its inspiration to his long-continued example'.[8] The relevance of this may be judged from *The Studio* itself, in its articles on designers like Anning Bell or Grandville Fell who owe an obvious debt to Crane. Even in Arthur Rackham's ghoulish fantasy it is possible to trace the influence of medieval Crane designs like those for Grimm. Among students the effect of his more conventional style can be seen in the submissions to *Studio* competitions, where substantial hellenistic ladies wield banners and hold up palettes with the help of the customary putti. The fluent rhythm of Crane's art and his floral inventions, often so close to Art Nouveau, are not easily isolated as individual influences in the 1890s. As was partly also the case in the United States, its healthy benevolence is less recognisable than the more sinister refinement stemming from Beardsley.

The earliest serious account of Crane's work in France was given by the novelist and champion of Les Indépendents, J. K. Huysmans, who discussed the toy books and those of Greenaway and Caldecott in his Salon Review of 1881. He justified them on the grounds that English picture books, like those of Japan, were the only works of art to be seen in France after the Independents Exhibition had closed.[9] Crane's toy books were issued in France by Librairie Hachette and Huysmans's praise of their wit, vigorous drawing, fine composition, 'archaeological' detail and unique type of female beauty is full of genuine delight. Their matter of fact style of story telling struck him as characteristically English in comparison with Doré's atmospheric and theatrical fantasies. *Little Pig* had a down to earth English feeling about it which left Grandville's ponderous and insipid witticism far behind. *The Fairy Ship* was full of wonderful observation, a feat of draughtsmanship by which quite ordinary and simple forms were transformed into true works of art. Equally deft and expressive drawing could be seen only in the prints of Hokkei and Hokusai.[10] After dealing at rather less length with Greenaway and Caldecott, Huysmans concluded that when these English books became as popular in Paris as they already were at home, artists would favour Crane because he had the most supple and versatile talent. People who liked pretty things would prefer Miss Greenaway's work and the public in general would take Caldecott to their hearts. It is known that Gauguin had a Caldecott book in Brittany and was enthusiastic about the Englishman's economical and spirited drawing of geese, but his opinion of Crane's work is unrecorded although it seems very likely that he and his synthetist friends would have come across the toy books. He may even have seen them while still with his children in 1881 when Huysmans also praised Gauguin.[11] Book illustration was the best known aspect of Crane's work abroad and until the next decade when his current graphic work was exhibited the most familiar examples were probably almost exclusively picture toys.[12]

'The Renaissance of Venus' had been shown at the English Fine Arts section of the 1878 Universal Exhibition in Paris when Burne-Jones's 'Merlin and Nimue' was acclaimed by French critics, but Huysmans in 1881 does not mention Crane's painting.

France was slow to acknowledge Crane in the 1890s. It was Brussels which, thanks chiefly to Octave Maus the founder of the review *L'Art Moderne* (1881) and of the Société des XX (1884), was the centre most sensitive and sympathetic to avant-garde art at the time. Here Crane's work was recognized for qualities it shared with the Post-Impressionists and the Nabis. Paintings by Sickert, Whistler, Wilson Steer and Stott of Oldham had already been shown at Les XX exhibitions. Burne-Jones was invited in 1888 but had refused. Their exhibition of 1891 aroused controversy by showing sculpture and ceramics by Gauguin and a selection of work by Van Gogh as well as many works by younger painters heavily under the influence of Seurat. On this occasion Crane too was invited and he sent water colours of 'Flora' and 'Pegasus'. Sixteen picture books and the book of *The Sirens Three* were lent by the Vingtiste Neo-Impressionist, Georges Lemmen.[13] That year he wrote two articles on Crane for *L'Art Moderne* in which he emphasized the expressive qualities of his line and colour, introducing him as a 'universally known and celebrated name with a reputation earned on the Continent, chiefly through his illustration and children's picture books . . . which were soon popularized in Germany and France.' He admired the invention and delicacy of *Flora's Feast* but, like Huysmans, was fascinated by the toy books and from these he concluded that Crane was 'above all a *decorator*, an artist pre-occupied with shapes, arabesques and lines' whose expressive value he studied in his own illustrated articles on the subject. His compositions were masterly arrangements of violently contrasting brilliant, acid colour.[14] With regard to the Arts and Crafts Movement he remarked that if England were really the only place where it was possible to find objects of artistic quality it was 'thanks to the hard work in aid of beauty undertaken by popular artists like Walter Crane, William Morris and more recently Selwyn Image and others, that people could now admire wallpaper by Jeffrey and Co., furniture by Maple, and Liberty ceramics and fabrics'.[15] Two years later Van de Velde expanded the decorative arts theme in a double article in *L'Art Moderne*. Crane, he said 'held a unique position; his prodigious imaginative ability triumphed wherever he applied himself to the pursuit of beauty in art'.[16] He quoted extensively from Crane's introduction to the catalogue of the 1890 Arts and Crafts Exhibition. Van de Velde's own artistic theories were to be much influenced by Crane's recently published *Claims of Decorative Art*.

In 1893 Holland was introduced to the toy books by A. C. Loffelt[17] and a Dutch edition of *The Claims* was issued with illustrations by G. W. Dijsselhof. Book decoration and illustration in Holland in the 1890s was affected largely by Javanese batik and by English graphics; the latter influence is more obvious in Dijsselhof's work. An illustrator particularly close to Crane for a time was the Dutch artist Van Hoytema.[18] In Holland and Belgium, as in England, avant-gardism was linked to socialism. Toorop was married to an Irish girl and knew Morris and his circle in London and it is significant, as Gillian Naylor has observed, that the title of *The Claims of Decorative Art* was altered to *Art and the Community* when it was published in Dutch.[19] Van de Velde, the most prominent figure to emerge as a practising designer, architect and theorist from the Belgian circle of Les XX, was closely associated with the Belgian Labour Party. Another well known personality in this organization, the lawyer writer Jules Destrée, wrote on 'Art and Socialism' in a pamphlet of 1896 in which his debt to Morris is clear. He cited Crane and Steinlen as artists whose work successfully conveyed a socialist message.[20]

Crane's cartoons were available at the Maison Dietrich in Brussels, where his picture books had been on sale since the time of the 1891 exhibition.

'La Libre Esthétique', the newly named group around Maus in Brussels in 1894, continued to exhibit English work and this often included Crane prints. That year a large exhibition of his graphics and paintings was shown at the Cercle Artistique et Littéraire de Bruxelles and a meeting to discuss it was led by the painter and *Studio* correspondent for 'La Libre Esthétique', Fernand Khnopff. In a review for *L'Art Moderne* he acknowledged that Crane was 'in high fashion . . . his name was always cropping up in drawing room conversations in the same breath as those of a well known tailoress or milliner and everyone was keen to give it the correct English pronunciation as they might that of a jockey'. Although this exhibition enjoyed great public success Khnopff observed that many artists were disillusioned with Crane's painting which they found cold and dry. His graphic work for modern subjects was also surprisingly weak in comparison with the toy books, *Flora's Feast, Queen Summer* or *The Sirens Three*, which he praised for their integration of text and designs. The names of Burne-Jones and Crane were on everybody's lips but it would be better in these days of 'snobisme habillé à L'Anglaise' if these gods remained on their island. Otherwise people would cease to believe in them.[21]

German artists and critics turned their attention to English Arts and Crafts shortly after the movement aroused interest in Belgium, the first studied assessment being made by the Director of Berlin's Museum of Decorative Art, Peter Jessen, in an article in 1892.[22] That same year a picture book of design was published in Stuttgart and among the many English examples Crane's work was especially well represented.[23] His exhibition had been invited to Montreal after Brooklyn and had just arrived back in England when the German critic and collector Fritz Gurlitt proposed that it be sent to Berlin where it was shown at the Museum of Decorative Art during May and June 1893. In his catalogue introduction, Jessen presented Crane as one of the most influential decorative artists in England and a man committed to furthering unity in the arts. Inevitably he was best known as an illustrator but for Crane the most flattering aspect of his reception in Germany, was the approval given to his pictures. He had already shown work at the English section of the Berlin International Exhibition of 1886, when Frederic Leighton first introduced him to F. Gurlitt.[24] Watts and Burne-Jones were also among the painters represented there and this date marked the beginning of increasing appreciation of the work of the Pre-Raphaelites and their followers in Germany.[25] Crane was usually defined as a Pre-Raphaelite follower but the classical aspects of his work were equally acceptable in a country familiar with the fantasies of Max Klinger and the hellenism of Franz von Stuck. Klimt's Vienna Secession graphics later reveal antiquity playing an important part in Austrian Art Nouveau and it is therefore significant that Jessen considered Crane a stylist whose thoughtful invention and restrained charm came near to realizing the true spirit and form of the antique. As far as his illustration was concerned Jessen was as appreciative of *Echoes of Hellas* and the plant study in the borders of *The Book of Wedding Days* as he was of the Düreresque designs for Grimm. Comte Robert de Montesquiou compared Crane's flower maidens to those of 'Parsifal'[26] and this parallel between Wagner and Crane explains why German viewers found a painting like 'The Chariot of the Hours' so inspiring. The surge of 'Neptune's Horses' gave the kind of moral uplift which had been missing from Arnold Böcklin's oceanic romps. In 'The Bridge of Life', where the British public found pedantry, the Teutonic mind was more inclined to read philosophy and idealism. Several of Crane's larger canvases were bought from the Berlin exhibition by Ernst Seeger, who subsequently acquired 'The Bridge of Life'. Other paintings were later purchased in Germany.[27] In 1893 Jessen acquired many small scale designs for the Museum including those for 'Pan Pipes'. The exhibition went on to Government Decorative Art Museums in Leipzig, Munich, Dresden, Frankfurt, Stuttgart, Krefeld, Bremen and Hamburg; to Vienna and Brunn in Austria in 1895; to Prague in Bohemia; and possibly also to Basle in Switzerland before travelling north to Belgium, Holland and Scandinavia. German official recognition came in 1895 when Seeger's 'The Chariot of the Hours' won a gold medal at the Munich Glass Palace Exhibition. Crane was later made an honorary member of the Munich Academy.

During the years following the first tour of his work in Germany Crane's reputation was modified as more publicity was given to other English designers and architects. Hermann Muthesius's first article, published in Germany in 1897, dealt with the London Arts and Crafts Exhibition of 1896 and gave a detailed account of the society and the importance of Morris's influence.[28] For some years in Germany folk art had been promoted as a vital element in the healthy development of architecture and design to counteract the effects of industrialization. The English revival of handicrafts provided an example from which much could be learned. When Crane's *Claims of Decorative Art* was published in German in 1896 the chapter heading 'Art and Social Democracy' was altered to 'Kunst und Volkstum'.[29] A translation of *The Bases of Design* came out the following year.[30] The presentation of these editions reveals how far behind England Germany still was in book design although efforts had already been made to present Morris, Crane and others as examples in this field.[31] The collector Eberhard von Bodenhausen observed that Morris's expensive volumes were hardly suitable as art for the people but nevertheless, in two articles published in *Pan* (1896–7), he praised the English designer for the consistent effort and idealism which, for nearly forty years had inspired a powerful art movement in England.[32] With such an example before them Germany might learn to find her own way. Eckmann, Hoffman, Köpping, and Obrist had already taken the lead. Two important essays on Crane appeared in 1897. In one Wilhelm Schölermann stressed the importance of natural form as an inspiration and praised Crane's architectonic sense of design. He compared his imaginative inventions with those of Böcklin and Klinger and saw sound sense in the idea that the handicraftsman was as important as the painter of easel pictures. Like the Munich writer and designer, Hans von Berlepsch-Valendas, however, he thought Crane's Socialism rather far fetched.[33] In Munich the centre of the early 'floral' Jugendstil of Obrist and Endell, von Berlepsch helped promote English Arts and Crafts. He encouraged Bernard Pankok to turn from painting and illustration to the handicrafts and thus set him in the direction that led to the founding, with Peter Behrens, of the United Workshops in 1897.[34] His study of Crane, published the same year, was the most thorough foreign analysis of his work to date. He began with a quotation from F. G. Stephens introducing Crane as 'the aptest living representative . . . of the all round masters of the fifteenth century in Italy and Germany'[35] which must have struck an appropriately promising note to readers in a country embarking on its own renaissance of design. The next year Crane was invited to prepare a cover for *Jugend* the popular weekly that gave its name to German Art Nouveau.[36] The brooding obsessive quality of Burne-Jones's work and other English followers of Pre-Raphaelitism was appreciated by the Expressionist Movement emerging in the Northern cities of Berlin, Dresden and Munich. These artists were concerned to convey their reaction to the present while English artists preferred to nurse their psychoses in dreamlands of the past.

Scandinavia with its rich heritage of folk art was already alive to English developments by the time Crane's touring exhibition arrived there in the summer of 1896. Three years previously examples of his work had been shown at the Museum of Applied Art in Christiana, which acquired textiles by him for its permanent collection from Berlin's Hohenzoller Kaufhaus in 1894.[37] The next year in Norway there was an exhibition of English printed fabrics at the Vest-landske Art Museum in Bergen and Johan Bogh, the Director, generously praised Crane and his efforts for the 'Reform Movement'.[38] The touring exhibition was shown at the Copenhagen Museum of Decorative Art, and then at the Balanche Konstsalong in Stockholm[39] and finally, in October, at the Christiana Museum of Applied Art.

The Crane exhibition did not visit France, a country which was singularly casual in its acknowledgement of any manifestations of English Arts and Crafts.

Cover for *Jugend*, 1898, Crane's contribution to this popular weekly, which gave German Art Nouveau its name 'Jugendstil', is one of the many indications of the interest his work aroused in Germany at the turn of the century. Photograph Peter Adamson.

Walter Crane and Mary Frances Crane, photograph taken during their visit to Hungary in 1900. Reproduced by courtesy of Mrs A. E. Clark-Kennedy.

The chief article on Crane in the 1890s was one by Gustave Soulier adapted from information given by Gleeson White.[40] French Art Nouveau was to make a fine art out of handicraft. In many ways this reflected the continuing tradition of previous centuries. Octave Uzanne, writing for *Studio* readers in 1894 praised the charm of English interiors in comparison with those in France which were laden with gilded reproductions of Louis XIV and Louis XVI styles. 'The fascinating element of originality in English decoration is as soothing as the first signs of early Spring, and we must admit, however grudgingly, that in decorative art France is barren and unproductive'.[41]

From late in 1895 work by Gallé, Crane and other English, French and Belgian designers, as well as American Tiffany glass was on sale at L'Art Nouveau, Samuel Bing's shop in the Rue de Provence in Paris, christened after its transformation by the architect Louis Bonnier and the painter Frank Brangwyn from a gallery of Oriental *objets d'art* to one embodying what Bing considered representative of the most progressive artistic ideas.[42] English and American art became fashionable. Toulouse Lautrec had his apartment decorated by Bing in the 'Yachting Style' and designed a poster for The Chap Book an Irish American bar in the Rue Royale which had adopted the name of the new Chicago periodical. Somewhere behind the bold colour shapes and strong lines of the Lautrec and Mucha posters which so characterize the spirit of fin-de-siècle Paris lie memories of Crane toy books, but it is in the work of the Symbolists, particularly those associated with the Salon de la Rose + Croix, that English Pre-Raphaelite influence was most strongly felt – Carlos Schwabe, Eugène Grasset and Georges de Feure being particularly indebted to Crane. Grasset, who was only five years younger than Crane, was in several ways his counterpart in France. Trained as an architect he soon turned to painting, then to stained glass, graphics and illustration, becoming known as a teacher through his books *La plante et ses applications ornamentales* (1898–9) and *Méthode de composition ornamental* (1905). He comes closest to Crane in works like the cover for the Christmas number of *L'Illustration* for 1893 and the 'La Belle Jardinière' calendar designs of 1896.[43]

Crane's greatest personal triumph was the exhibition held in Budapest in October 1900. The Hungarian decorative art revival was centred round activity at the Budapest Museum of Applied Arts whose Director, Jeno Radisics, had staged an exhibition of items from South Kensington's National Competition in 1898.[44] The young Hungarian Kalman Rozsnyai[45] stayed with the family in Holland Street for about ten weeks and Crane was easily persuaded to send out what must have been the largest ever exhibition of his work. In Hungary he and his wife were welcomed with speeches, banquets, and great bouquets of flowers. The Minister of Education, M. Wlassics, described him as 'an untiring hero fighting triumphantly . . . for the unity of art' and one who believed in 'the transformation of society by art'. At Pecs they were guests of the son of the famous Hungarian potter Szolnay. Hungary's revered novelist and patriot Maurice Jokai was astonished at Crane's versatility: 'who has got a hundred arms to be able to do the same work? . . . and yet we must follow the example. We must learn how the Hungarian peasant cloaks, flower decorated trunks, dishes, cups, must be transformed into ornaments fit to embellish drawing rooms, palaces, altars; we must learn how to transform into a creating power the aesthetical [sic] sense and artistic inclination of our people . . .'[46] Crane gave his 'Language of Line' lecture at the Casino Club in Budapest and it was translated and printed in a specially designed leaflet.[47] After his visit English Arts and Crafts continued to influence events as can be seen, for example, in the designs and theoretical writing of Aladar Kriesch. An exhibition of British decorative art was put on at the

Museum in 1902 and one of Beardsley's drawings in 1907. Three years later a Hungarian edition of *Line and Form* was issued.[48] Here, as in Scandinavia, the English revival made its appeal in a country rich in folk art and this had strong nationalistic significance in Hungary where the people fretted under Austrian Imperial domination and German influence.

From Budapest the exhibition was invited to Vienna[49] one of the last great European capitals to respond to Art Nouveau. The belated response of Viennese decorating firms to the movement was criticized in *Ver Sacrum* in 1898: 'unlike the decorators in Paris and Berlin they do not stock an entire range of decorative art products designed by such artists as Walter Crane, Gerhard Munthe . . . Köpping, Gallé, Obrist' and prefer to indulge 'their own perfectly absurd orgies of brocade plush and gilt'.[50] Viennese Art Nouveau depended quite heavily on English arts and crafts and the Glasgow School influenced the work of Olbrich and Hoffmann. When Crane's second exhibition was shown in 1901 these developments were well advanced. In a long article at the time M. Dreger compared the childlike innocence and manifold character of his art to that of Raphael. From Vienna the show went on to Darmstadt, Düsseldorf and Frankfurt.[51] Crane then offered it to Turin which was preparing for its 1902 International Exhibition of Modern Art.

Great Britain was represented here in two separate sections: the English Arts and Crafts Exhibition Society, two of whose three rooms were devoted to Crane's display; and a Scottish section represented by Mackintosh and the work of the Glasgow School. Italy was slow to appraise Art Nouveau and her view of its English origins is reflected in the name, Stile Liberty, given to the new style. Her appreciation of Crane was to be generous, if belated.[52] When they were introduced at the Turin Exhibition King Victor Emmanuel remarked that he had known Crane's books for a long time and praised the painting 'The World's Conquerors' which, he said, reminded him of a Carpaccio. Crane was not alone in being honoured by the Crown of Italy. Indeed, Newbery was also made a Knight of the Order of the Crown of Italy although Crane fails to mention this or anything about the Glasgow School in his *Reminiscences*, probably out of pique at Newbery's criticism of the Arts and Crafts Society. Italy continued to acknowledge Crane. In 1911 several of his paintings were shown in Rome and a self portrait was officially requested and received by the Uffizi in 1912.

Honours at home were showered upon him long before the end of his life. He became a full member of the Royal Society of Painters in Water Colours in 1903 and two years later received the Albert Gold Medal of the Society of Arts from the Prince of Wales. Articles on his work had appeared in many journals, from serious art periodicals to women's weeklies and newspapers, and Crane himself wrote the account published in a special *Art Journal* number of 1898. The Konody and Von Schleinitz monographs appeared in 1902 and a few years later Messrs Methuen invited him to write his memoirs. Undaunted by Konody's criticism he had sent a spirited sketch to his friend M. H. Spielmann, editor of the *Magazine of Art* to the effect that despite what biographers of a younger generation might think he was 'covered in leaves but not dead yet'. There were indeed a number of happy productive years ahead. His later lectures and reviews were collected and published in *Ideals in Art* and *William Morris to Whistler*, which included a review of Pennell's *Life of Whistler*. Though not wholly sympathetic to Impressionism Crane's tolerant appraisal of certain Post Impressionist developments indicates the interest with which he continued to regard younger artists' work. It is not known what he thought of Cubism or if he extended his wide sympathies to Vorticism, the English futurist movement given strong support by Konody

Lancelot Crane *Poster* advertising his father's Hungarian exhibition of 1900.

when it emerged in the years before the war. Their aims would probably have seemed too mechanical and harsh in comparison with the more humanitarian revolutionary ideals cherished by the generation of pioneering art workers to which Crane belonged.

His family life was for the most part a very happy one. His gifted children were all interested in the arts. Beatrice was a young woman of very modern and independent views and married twice. Lionel became an architect and by his marriage to Frederick Sandys' youngest daughter, Gertrude, in 1913, linked two memorable Victorian artistic families.[54] After her death in 1920 he married her eldest sister, Winifred. Lancelot followed his father more closely as a designer and a painter of considerable sensitivity. It was he who intended to write his father's biography and redress the harm done by Konody.[55] Walter Crane planned a quiet retirement in the country at Knob Hill Farm, Warnham in Sussex but he was caused great anxiety by his wife's failing health. Her death in January 1915 left him stricken and 'only half alive' as he said in a letter to a friend. He survived her by a few months and died after a three week illness at Horsham Cottage Hospital on 14 March.

Of the many obituaries Ashbee's unpublished appreciation remains among the most poignant. It vividly evokes the warmth and wit, eccentricity and earnest optimism of this Victorian polymath:

Crane is dead. His death marks the end of a period. It was a great period for it was always young and heart-whole. But 'tis well that he should die for now in the last eight months we have all grown old, and there has been a passing of joy. He was not a strong man but he was lovable . . . He had a sort of linear memory. He had no need to think, he could just pour out forms from the pen point. Morris once said of Crane he was a Gothic soul with a Renaissance training; it was the Gothic soul in him that made him so lovable. He fitted too, in many ways into the early Renaissance. The Socialism of the nineteenth century had that naiveté . . . He couldn't think things out or see deeply, but he had 'empfindung' and a power of expression . . . Even the most childlike of his little weaknesses was of the fairy story type. He called himself 'Commendatore Crane' because the king of Italy had once given him a title for arranging the Arts and Crafts exhibition:

'I had a little nut tree nothing would it bear
But a silver nutmeg and a golden pear
The King of Spain's daughter came to visit me
And all for the sake of my little nut tree.'

He loved that remote title, but the nut tree was the real thing and he never valued that enough. I suppose many others of the Society would have got that title too, had they gone out and smiled at Royalty – but they wouldn't have put it on their visiting cards . . . He just loved being an 'official', but he was so fundamentally 'unofficial' that nobody minded . . . nobody could possibly hurt Crane.

I don't think he got over his wife's death . . . She too came out of a fairy story, it was all very natural when you knew the Cranes, it was their life – but 'commonsensible people' always said 'as how she was a bit odd', a kind, motherly, plump, fantastic creature who called herself 'Mistress Crane', no one exactly knew why, but it somehow fitted the 'Commendatore'. I remember her in various moods – always picturesque, and always the unconscious model of her husband's florid, childlike fancy. She would be driving a pair of coloured ponies in a kind of ringing Norwegian barouche –

I don't know if it was a barouche or Norwegian, or if it rang, or what the colour of the ponies, but that's the sort of vision one recalls. She would ride in the Park in a gown of red velvet, for what does the nursery rhyme say? 'She had rings on her fingers', and we who knew her were certain that if the velvet gown were wind-lifted it would reveal the bells on her toes too. She kept a chingatoo with a prehensile tail in her back garden, and once at a great party of seven hundred guests she received us dressed as a sort of sunflower. We went home and laughed but we enjoyed ourselves. It is those generous unselfconscious souls – such as Crane and his wife, that make the world go easy . . .

Tadema once said to me: 'The dream of Crane's life is to think himself a painter'. To which one could retort: 'The dream of Tadema's life is to imagine himself an artist'. Crane had a greater gift, and his little nut tree was worth miles of those emply classic canvases of Tadema's . . . His perception and his humour were of finer stuff. For him:

> 'There were raisins in the cabin and almonds in the hold
> The sails they were of satin and the mast it was of gold'[56]

Notes

Introduction

1 Anthony Crane, 'My Grandfather, Walter Crane' *Yale University Library Gazette,* XXXI (Jan. 1957). Based on a lecture with the same title given on 3 Oct. 1956, on the occasion of the opening of an exhibition of the work of Walter Crane selected from the collection given to Yale University by Mrs George L. Patterson, and the publication of Crane's *Mr Michael Mouse Unfolds his Tale* from the MS in the Patterson Collection, Beinecke Rare Book and Manuscript Library, Yale University.

2 W. Rothenstein *Men and Memories* London 1931, pp. 292–3.

Childhood

1 Unless otherwise noted all facts relating to Walter Crane's life and work and illustrations of work not reproduced in this volume are to be found in his autobiography *An Artist's Reminiscences* (Methuen 1907) [C.R.] Republished by the Singing Tree Press, Detroit, USA, 1969.

2 As Crane points out (C.R. p. 41), Beck Common was to be the site of the 'aesthetic suburb', Bedford Park.

3 These were mostly scenes of combat and included the fight between Morton and Balfour of Burleigh in *Old Mortality* (C.R. 33 and 45).

4 R. McLean *Victorian Book Design* (2nd ed., London 1972) Ch. 9. Several of these were based on early illustrated MSS; indeed one of the earliest *The Illustrated Calendar* (Longman 1845) copied *The Hours of Anne of Brittany*. Others explored variations on this theme, like the voluptuous black and white border designs by Noel Humphreys for *The Poet's Pleasuance* (Longman, 1847).

Apprenticeship

1 Full details of the process of drawing on wood for engraving are described by Linton in *Wood Engraving. A Manual of Instruction.* (London, 1884) Chapter V.

2 C.R. p. 46.

3 W. J. Linton *Memories*, (London, 1895), F. B. Smith *Radical Artisan, William James Linton 1812–97.* (Manchester, University Press 1973.)

4 The chief publications on black and white work of this period are: Gleeson White *English Illustration, The Sixties, 1855–70.* (Constable 1897, reissued 1970); Forrest Reid *Illustrators of the Sixties* (Faber 1928); G. Dalziel *The Brothers Dalziel: A record* (Methuen 1901).

5 *A Memoir of Thomas Bewick Written by Himself* (London, The Cresset Press 1961) Edited by Montague Weekley; S. Roscoe *Thomas Bewick A Bibliography Raisonnée* (London, 1953).

6 C.R. p. 49.

7 J. Jackson *Treatise on Wood Engraving* includes a list of painters who occasionally drew on wood, e.g. Ansdell, Holman Hunt, Millais.

8 W. J. Linton *Specimens of a New Process of Engraving for Surface Printing* (London 1861). The terms 'on-surface' and 'off-surface' printing derive from the fact that in wood cuts or wood engraving it is the surface of the block untouched by the cutting tool which prints. Hence the design remains 'on-surface'. In metal engraving the line bitten into the surface by either needle, graver or acid, becomes the printed line: after inking, the plate is wiped clean and the ink remains in the incised lines, to be squeezed out on to the paper under pressure during printing. Ruskin was among those intrigued by Linton's pamphlet and paid a visit to Hatton Garden to inquire about it. This was Walter's first personal encounter with Ruskin.

9 Linton cut the following Pre-Raphaelite illustrations for the Moxon *Tennyson:* 'Mariana in the South' p. 82 and 'Sir Galahad' p. 305 by Rossetti; and 'A Dream of Fair Women' p. 149 and 'Day Dream' p. 317 by Millais.

10 Anthony Crane 'My Grandfather, Walter Crane', p. 99.

Black-and-white Illustration: The Sixties

1 In the *Reminiscences* Crane refers to two publishers of religious tracts. This could mean Wertheim and Co. and William Macintosh, both of Paternoster Row, but these firms must have worked together or amalgamated because some booklets have the imprint Wertheim, Macintosh and Hunt.

2 Published by Longmans Green, Longman and Roberts in 1862. All fifty-one illustrations were engraved on wood by Linton with the exception of six plates from a French folio of Gaimard's expedition.

3 *The Imprint* (1913) *Notes on my own books for children* by W. Crane, p. 81. Reprinted in *The Junior Bookshelf* Vol. 5, No. 1, Oct. 1940.

4 See *The Bookseller* 1 December 1862. There was a later Artist's Edition of *The New Forest* with additional twelve etchings by Heywood Sumner. All the original New Forest drawings were kept by the publisher after Crane had transferred them to the blocks for engraving.

5 For discussion of the *Once a Week School* see Gleeson White op.cit, Chapter Two pp. 16–17. Also Forrest Reid op.cit. Chapter Two.

6 Volume IV pp. 48–61, and later published in *The London Home Monthly* July 1895.

7 The *Art Union* of 1851 published a series entitled 'Examples of German Artists' including engravings after biblical pictures by the Nazarene, Julius Schnorr von Carolsfeld (1794–1872) and his pupil, G. Jäger (1808–71), and two

articles on Albrecht Dürer. These must have been among the numbers so carefully studied by young Walter Crane in his father's studio in Torquay when, as he relates in the *Reminiscences,* he first encountered reproductions of 'The Great Horse', 'Melencolia', and 'Knight, Death and The Devil'. The first two were reproduced on pp. 143 and 144, although 'The Knight' does not appear in this Volume.

8 P. Muir *Victorian Illustrated Books* (London 1970) p. 93, F. B. Smith *Radical Artisan* Note (3) Chapter II p. 151.

9 *Walter Crane Hazelford Sketchbook* Cambridge, John Barnard Associates, Massachussetts, p. 15. Rossetti published only ten black and white cuts: one for Allingham's *Music Master;* five in the Moxon *Tennyson;* two to Christina Rossetti's *Goblin Market* (1862); and two to his sister's *Prince's Progress and Other Poems* (1866).

10 C.R. p. 60 'The Legend of the Portent' was first published in *The Cornhill* Volume 1 (First Series) May 1860, p. 615.

11 *The Bookseller* 12 December 1865, p. 1021 Warne Advertisement, states that he was contributing black and white illustrations to their *One Shilling Books* along with J. D. Watson, Henley, Absolon and others.

12 See Appendix A.

13 Some of those from the large collection of Crane sketches in the Houghton Library, Harvard University, were published in the *Walter Crane Hazelford Sketchbook* op.cit.

14 A. Crane 'My Grandfather, Walter Crane' 1957 p. 102.

15 For his contributions see Appendix A.

16 See Appendix A.

Colour Work for Edmund Evans:
Yellow Backs & Toy Books 1863–75

1 M. Sadlier *Collecting 'Yellow Backs' – Victorian Railway Fiction,* Aspects of Book Collecting (1938); M. Sadlier *Nineteenth Century Fiction* (1953); R. McLean *Victorian Book Design* (London, 2nd Ed. 1972).

2 R. McLean, *The Reminiscences of Edmund Evans* Oxford, 1967, p. 19.

3 *The Moors and the Fens* cover is reproduced as a frontispiece in the original five shilling edition of F. C. Trafford's book. *Nursery Songs* cover design appears also as a frontispiece in the 1866 volume published by Ward Lock and Company. Evans's own account of his colour printing of yellow backs is relevant to the *Moors and The Fens* proof. From the engraving of the original drawing which must have been supplied by Crane on the block, two 'transfers' were taken. These impressions, while still wet, were 'laid down on plain blocks, then used one for Red printing, the other for Blue printing, the red being engraved in gradation to get the light tints, such as faces, hands, etc. The blue block . . . to get the best results of texture, pattern or sky, crossing the blue over the red to get good effects of light and shade.' McLean op.cit. pp. 26–28.

4 *The Home Treasury* was produced by Joseph Cundall and the printer Charles Whittingham at the Chiswick Press. Among the first Home Treasury titles published in 1843 were *Jack the Giant Killer; Little Red Riding Hood; Beauty and The Beast;* and *Bible Events* (this last with illustrations after Holbein). For a full list see M. F. Thwaite *From Primer to Pleasure* (London 1963) p. 100. For further details of Cole's printing venture see McLean op.cit. (1972) pp. 41–42, and F. J. H. Darton *Children's Books in England* C.U.P. 1932.

5 Before and at the beginning of Victoria's reign, tales like *Valentine and Orson; Dick Whittington; Jack the Giant Killer; The Children in the Wood;* and *Little Red Riding Hood* were more likely to be found in chap books than the publications of Harris. Thomas Darton issued early prints of *Bluebeard* and

Valentine and Orson. See A. W. Tuer *Forgotten Children's Books* (1898) p. 211, and *1000 Quaint Cuts from Books of Other Days* (1886) for an idea of the range of subjects in chap books; from cooking recipes, religious tracts, ABCs, nursery rhymes to shortened versions of historical tales and literary classics like *Robinson Crusoe.*

6 *Histoire du Conte du Temps Passé; avec des Moralitez* (Paris 1698). The moralising endings were mostly dropped in popular versions of these 'contes'. For unexpurgated versions see *The Fairy Tales of Charles Perrault* translated by Norman Denny (Bodley Head, 1951). For further details on the contributions of Perrault and the Countess d'Aulnoy (Marie Catherine la Mothe) see M. E. Storer *La Mode Des Contes De Fées* (Paris Champions 1928). P. H. Muir *English Children's Books 1600–1900,* London, 1954 and Darton op.cit. In 1871 Perrault's *Diamonds and Toads* was issued in Warne's Aunt Louisa London Toy Series, with illustrations by Kate Greenaway, who about the same time produced designs for *Mme d'Aulnoy's Fairy Tales,* published by Gall and Inglis of Edinburgh.

7 Peter and Iona Opie *The Oxford Dictionary of Nursery Rhymes* (Oxford 1951).

8 The first translation of the *Arabian Nights* was made for Europeans by Galland (1704–17) and was popular throughout the eighteenth century, especially *Aladdin and Sinbad.* The Lane edition which Crane knew was the first in English and the one most often adapted for children in the Victorian period. *Goody Two Shoes* dates from the late eighteenth century. Possibly written by Oliver Goldsmith it was first published by Newbery, probably in 1765. *My Mother* was written by Ann Taylor early in the nineteenth century.

9 *The Bookseller,* 29 Nov., 1858.

10 W. Crane *The Decorative Illustration of Books* George Bell and Sons, 1896, p. 128.

11 In a letter to Thomas Jones, 19 January 1898 (the Beinecke Library, Yale University) Crane stated that he designed a set of illustrations for a *History of Jenny Wren* for Ward Lock and Company about 1865. He thought this was his first toy book – *The House That Jack Built* and *Dame Trot and Her Comical Cat* appeared shortly afterwards published by the same firm. It was included in a Ward Lock advertisement in the Christmas number of *The Bookseller,* 1865, among a set of six titles, described as 'embellished with large spirited engravings printed in colour by Edmund Evans. Post quarto fancy wrappers' (1) *The House That Jack Built;* (2) *Death and Burial of Cock Robin;* (3) *The Comical Cat;* (4) *The Affecting Story of Jenny Wren;* (5) *Mamma's New Picture Alphabet;* (6) *Nursery Rhymes and Rigmaroles.* See Appendix B.

12 *The Bookseller* 12 Dec. 1865. In one of the earliest reviews of picture books (p. 846) Ward Lock's *Comical Cat* and Routledge's *Cats Tea Party* were highly praised. No special mention was made of the two Routledge Sixpenny Toys just produced by Crane and Evans, although the Aunt Mavor Series was described as 'moderately good'.

13 Costing 6d (1/- on linen), the titles of which were listed as (1) *London Alphabet;* (2) *Country Alphabet;* (3) *Alphabet of Games and Sports,* and described as having 'entirely new illustrations by Crane, Phiz. Printed in colours with handsome covers'. *The Bookseller* 12 Dec. 1865.

14 Possibly as early as 1855. Thwaite op.cit. Chapter 4.

15 Anthony Crane *My Grandfather, Walter Crane,* p. 102.

16 Anthony Crane op.cit. p. 101.

17 Illustrated by M. Hiswell, Victoria and Albert Museum Library.

18 Railway ABCs were still quite a novelty, R. McLean *Pictorial Alphabets* (London 1969) p. 37. In preparing this book Crane referred to Z. Coburn's *Locomotive Engineering and the Mechanisation of Railways* (1864). Noted in a sketchbook of 1865, now in the Houghton Library, Harvard.

19 C.R. p. 76 and 'Notes on my own Books for Children', by Walter Crane, *The Imprint* 1913 p. 81. The earliest evidence of oriental influence in Crane's work is in the first of his illustrations to Anne Hereford, *The Argosy*, December 1867, where there is a Japanese folding screen. He was given the prints on a visit to family friends, the Wilbrahams, at Rhode Hall in Cheshire, probably in late summer of that year.

20 W. Crane *Decorative Illustration* op.cit. p. 128.

21 Crane's design for the *Ridiculous Rhymes* cover is in the Birket Foster Sketchbook in Manchester City Art Gallery. Stylistically it is closely related to the cover soon introduced as standard for Crane's Sixpenny Toy Books.

22 *Silverlocks and the Three Bears*.

23 In the Houghton Library, Harvard University.

24 See below, Chapter 11.

25 *The Work of Walter Crane With Notes by the Artist* Art Journal Easter Art Annual for 1898, p. 3.

26 W. Crane *The Imprint* op.cit. pp. 85 and 86.

Painting 1860–80

1 In 1859 he finished a copy in oils of Wilkie's 'Blind Fiddler' C.R. p. 52.

2 Some evidence of this survives in fragmentary studies in the Houghton Library, Harvard; notes in a sketchbook of 1863; and the water colour study of Madeleine praying reproduced in C.R. p. 64, a more demure rendering than Millais's version exhibited at the R.A. in 1863.

3 Sketchbook of 1863 in the Beinecke Library, Yale University.

4 These notes on landscape are in a sketchbook dated 25 March 1865, Houghton Library, Harvard University.

5 C.R. p. 84.

6 In the collection of the Ein Harod Kibbutz, Israel. See Lionel Lambourne 'A Simeon Solomon Sketchbook' *Apollo* Jan. 1967 p. 59.

7 A. McLaren Young *James McNeill Whistler*, catalogue to the exhibition held in The Arts Council Galleries, London, and in the Knoedler Galleries, New York in 1960, p. 18; R. A. Spencer *The Aesthetic Movement* (London 1972) Ch. I.

8 Walter Pater 'Aesthetic Poetry', first published as part of 'Poems by William Morris' in the *Westminster Review* 1868.

9 See No. 13 of the catalogue to the Piccadilly Gallery exhibition *Symbolists 1860–1925* London, June, 1970.

10 A. C. Swinburne *William Blake: A Critical Essay* (John Camden Hotten, 1868) c.f. the coloured woodcut of Blake's 'Milton' design reproduced opposite p. 258.

11 Catalogue to the exhibition *George Howard and His Circle 1843–1911* City Art Galleries Carlisle 1968. Crane visited George Howard's Cumberland home, Naworth, in 1871 and 1877.

12 Reviewed in *The Art Journal* 1870 p. 211.

13 This little water colour with its carefully arranged composition of a parkland view from a colonnaded terrace containing peacocks, a chaffinch, a blue and white plate and jar, was first painted on a visit to Rhode Hall in 1869. Crane was asked to paint two copies, one dated 1871 was sold by the Fine Art Society in 1968. This setting was also used for 'Bluebeard and Gloriana' (Dudley Gallery 1871).

14 C.R. p. 122.

15 Illustrated in P. G. Konody *The Art of Walter Crane* p. 128. Burne-Jones did not begin 'Leus Veneris' for William Graham until 1873 but Crane may have known the original sketch for the picture which dates from 1861, or perhaps the design for the tapestry scene of 'The Passing of Venus' which he completed for titles to be executed by Morris and Co. that year. *Sir Edward Burne-Jones' Laus Veneris* by William Waters issued by Laing Art Gallery, Newcastle upon Tyne, 1973.

16 The sketch is reproduced in colour as a frontispiece for the *Art Journal Easter Art Annual* of 1898. The final version is in Birmingham City Art Gallery.

17 Illustrated C.R. p. 139.

18 On one occasion when Graham Robertson visited the studio he sensed that Crane resented too much being made of Burne-Jones's part in the frieze, W. G. Robertson *Time Was* (1931) p. 45. Crane was certainly still at work on the project in 1878 C.R. p. 188. Further information on the decoration is contained in Charles Henry Roberts *The Radical Countess* (Carlisle 1962); 'The Cupid and Psyche Frieze by Sir Edward Burne-Jones' *The Studio* XV No. 67 October 1898; A. L. Baldry *Modern Mural Decoration* (London 1902). A concise analysis of Burne-Jones material relating to 'The Earthly Paradise' designs is to be found in Birmingham City Art Gallery Catalogue of Permanent Collections of Drawings (1939).

19 C.R. p. 174.

20 W. Hamilton *The Aesthetic Movement in England* (London 1882) p. 27. This painting was in the collection of Karlsruhe Museum until 1923, but its present whereabouts are unknown.

Illustration up to 1890

1 C.R. p. 179.

2 C.R. p. 179. This letter from Herkomer to Crane is dated 8 December 1876.

3 Crane did add, in fairness to Kate Greenaway's powers of observation, that these fashions for the young were to be seen 'in the actual life of the day', M. H. Spielmann and G. S. Layard *Kate Greenaway* (London 1905) p. 71.

4 This letter 'Out of the Mouth of Babes' was published on 22 March and was Crane's response to one by Ruskin of 16 March in which he stated that he knew nothing about what had been taught the youth of his time 'except that their fathers were apes, and their mothers winkles; that the world began in accident and will end in darkness' etc. Ruskin responded to Crane's reply on 25 March with a letter 'By Ear or Eye' in which he made several complimentary remarks about *Baby's Opera* but squashed the notion that the eye was the primary source of knowledge by stating that 'well-bred children learn through every bit of their bodies' etc. E. T. Cook and A. Wedderburn *The Works of John Ruskin* Volume 34 (1908) pp. 590–591.

5 C.R. p. 159–160. Thomas Crane probably became Art Director of the firm in the late 1870s and may well have been responsible for the fine series of picture books issued at that time including *The Picture Library of Animals* and *The Parables of Our Lord*.

6 The water colour designs for 'Time's Garland' are in Liverpool City Art Gallery, and one for the Marcus Ward set on buff paper is in the Whitworth Art Gallery, Manchester University. A coloured supplement in *The Graphic* of 28 Nov., 1874, included six seasonal greeting designs by Crane: two are in an earlier style and feature a Christmas pudding, and a turkey leapfrogging a clown; the others have the captions 'A Christmas Figure', 'A Christmas Stocking for You', 'Everyman's Candidate' and 'Fortuna'. The card 'Open Wet or Dry' of the same format was probably issued at the same time as part of a *Daily Graphic* advertising feature. In Feb. 1875, a full-page coloured Valentine design by Crane appeared in *The Graphic*. The A. P. Tankard gift in Liverpool City Libraries contains two versions of large cards advertising 'Cinderella', the Crystal Palace Grand Christmas Pantomime, 1875, and a printer's proof of one for 'Jack in Wonderland' (n.d.). Crane greeting cards are to be found in the Victoria and Albert Museum, London, the John Johnson Collection in

the Bodleian Library, Oxford, and in Liverpool City Libraries.

7 R. McLean *Victorian Book Design* London 1972, p. 222 and R. McLean *Victorian Publishers' Book Bindings* London 1974.

8 For a list of these see Appendix D. Crane is not acknowledged as the illustrator of his first Molesworth book *Tell Me a Story* and Mrs Molesworth used her maiden name, Ennis Graham, up to and including *The Cuckoo Clock*. The series was issued in globe octavo and sold at 4/–. (*Herr Baby* was in globe quarto and cost 6/–.) M. Laski *Mrs Ewing, Mrs Molesworth and Mrs Hodgson Burnett* (1950).

9 The large scale edition of *The First of May* cost £12 10s the other cost 6 guineas. Boston, Osgood and Company issued an autographed edition in 1881 which cost £10.

10 R. Schmutzler 'The English Origins of Art Nouveau' *Architectural Review* Vol. CXVII 1955 p. 109.

11 The influence of Blake is not obvious in Crane's work until two years later, but this illustration suggests that he may already have been taking lessons from the wood engravings of Edward Calvert, six examples of which Crane later used to illustrate his Cantor lectures when they were published in *Decorative Illustration* in 1896, pp. 115–116. 'The Brook' contains most parallels with 'The Goose Girl'.

12 He had already designed a frontispiece to *The Library* by Andrew Lang. This contained a chapter on modern English illustrated books by Austin Dobson (Macmillan 1881).

13 These three lectures were given during May and were published in *The Journal of the Society of Arts* on 13, 20 and 27 October 1882. Comyns Carr left the editorship of the *English Illustrated* in 1886, Mrs Comyns Carr *Reminiscences* (Macmillan 1883) pp. 66 and 73.

14 C.R. p. 50. His work may be seen in S. C. Hall (Editor) *The Book of British Ballads* Volume I, (London 1842). Linton was among the engravers.

15 R. Schmutzler, 'Blake and Art Nouveau', *The Architectural Review* Vol. CXVIII, 1955, pp. 90–97.

16 N. Pevsner *Studies in Art Architecture and Design* (Volume II 1968) Chapter VII 'Arthur H. Mackmurdo' p. 132.

17 *Journal of the Society of Arts* 1 Nov. 1889 p. 889.

18 From the preface to *Legends for Lionel*.

19 Printer's proofs of these two leaves survive in Liverpool City Libraries Crane collection, but it has not been ascertained where these were published.

20 Crane op.cit. *The Imprint* (1913) p. 84.

21 Gleeson White 'Children's Books and their Illustrators' *Studio* Special Winter Number 1897–98. First of the quartos (which cost 5/– or 6/–) was *Afternoon Tea* (Warne 1880) designed by J. C. Sowerby, followed by *At Home* (1881) also illustrated by Sowerby but with decoration by Thomas Crane. *Abroad* (1882) and *London Town* (1883) both had illustrations by Ellen Houghton and decoration by T. Crane. All these were published by Marcus Ward and from the character and tasteful care of the decoration it is clear that Thomas Crane played a considerable part in giving these little volumes their peculiar aesthetic charm.

22 Henry Holiday and G. F. Watts were among the artists designing sets and costumes for this production. Poynter had been involved with Warr and Sir Charles Newton in preparing the scenery for the first performance of 'The Tale of Troy', C.R. pp. 284–286 and the introduction to *Echoes of Hellas*. Further information about these aesthetic theatricals is to be found in Ian Fletcher's essay 'Bedford Park: Aesthete's Elysium?' published in *Romantic Mythologies* (1967) p. 169 and R. A. Spencer *The Aesthetic Movement* (1972) pp. 104 and 110.

23 A similar idea attracted Crane in 1866 when he listed a 'Dial of Flowers' given by the botanist designer, Christopher Dresser, including their names and the times of day at which their petals opened. The sketch book is in the Houghton Library, Harvard University.

24 *Journal of the Society of Arts* 23 October 1889, p. 882. See also Crane's later recommendations on art teaching for Manchester School of Art discussed in Chapter 10 below. Several tailpieces in *Household Stories* suggest that Crane may have been using herbals as sources for design motifs as early as 1882. W. Blunt *The Art of Botanical Illustration* (London, 1950) Chapters 5 and 6.

Decorative Art

1 Lionel Lambourne, *The Arts and Crafts Movement Artists, Craftsmen and Designers 1890–1930*, catalogue for the Fine Art Society Exhibition October 1973.

2 Gillian Naylor *The Arts and Crafts Movement*, London 1971. Also includes further bibliographical references. The official history of the Art-Workers' Guild (AWG) is by H. J. L. J. Massé *The Art-Workers' Guild*, Shakespeare Head for the AWG, 1935.

3 W. Crane 'The English Revival of Decorative Art' *Fortnightly Review*, Volume 52 December 1892, p. 312. The Fifteen derived its name from a popular puzzle game although the group never numbered this many. C.R. p. 223–4. Crane lists the original members but not all of these appear on the engraved card in a collection of early Crane material, mounted in a volume by Zaehnsdorf (d. 16 Jan. 1885) in Liverpool City Libraries. J. D. Sedding and Henry Page are described as early members and yet do not appear, whereas two figures, one with the initials M.H. and an architect called Lonsdale are among those depicted. Crane knew Day from earlier in the 1870s when both were associated with The Quibblers, a sketching club who joined up with a group of architects called The Picts. They met at each others houses where the host of the evening suggested a subject to be sketched by his guests. Crane was on the committee. C.R. p. 156.

4 C.R. p. 286–88. W. Crane *Fortnightly Review* op.cit. p. 819 and *The Artist* 1 Sept. 1886, p. 301.

5 W. Crane *Fortnightly Review* op.cit. p. 817.

6 Ibid. p. 810–11. See also Alistair Grieve 'Rossetti's Applied Art Designs' *Burl. Mag*: 1. 'Picture Frames' Jan. 1973, p. 16. 2. 'Book-Bindings' Feb. 1973, p. 79.

7 W. Crane *Fortnightly Review* op.cit. p. 811–12.

8 The firm Morris, Marshall, Faulkner and Co. was formed in April 1861. Crane was only seventeen at the time of the 1862 Exhibition, but he was involved in it as the designer of a stall belonging to the patentee and manufacturer of a new lead pencil. C.R. p. 72. A note and little sketch referring to this are contained in a sketchbook of April 1861 in the Houghton Library, Harvard University.

9 In his *Fortnightly Review* article of 1892 (op.cit.) Crane quoted Eastlake's unsigned essay in *The Cornhill* March 1864, Volume IX No. 51 'The Fashion of Furniture': 'Lost in the contemplation of palaces we have forgotten to look about us for a chair,' p. 344. The subject was expanded in a series of articles in *The Queen*, the first published 24 June 1865, called 'Hints on Household Taste'. It was continued until late in 1866. Eastlake used the pseudonym Jack Easel. Revisions of these and others from the *London Review* were published with illustrations by Longmans Green and Company in 1868 as *Hints on Household Taste*. See John Gloag's introduction to the Dover edition of 1969.

10 C.R. p. 156. Through Tarver, Crane later designed a series of frieze panels of Aesop's Fables in raised gesso for the house of Mr Lea of Worcester (of the firm Lea and Perrins). Other early design work included three painted panels with scenes from *A Winter's Tale* for an old oak chimney piece at Boarzell, a manor house at Hurst Green in Sussex owned by a former M.P. George Gregory. Nothing remains there now. In 1876 he designed a scheme for the billiard room of Lord Wharn-

cliffe's home, Wortley Hall, but this never came off. C.R. p. 173.

11 'Some Victorian Designers' paper to be read at the Design Club 24 November 1909 at the request of L. F. Day in Metford Warner notebooks, Victoria and Albert Museum Library. A. V. Sugden and Edmondson *A History of English Wallpaper 1509–1914* (1925) Jeffrey and Company Mill Records reproduced pp. 204–212.

12 'A Designer of Paper Hangings. An Interview with Mr Walter Crane'. *The Studio* Volume 4 1894 pp. 76–83.

13 Interview with W. Crane on the death of Morris *The Daily News* 20 October 1896.

14 Lucy Crane op.cit. Chapter III, p. 126.

15 W. Crane *The Studio* (1894) op.cit. p. 79.

16 W. Crane *Arts and Crafts Exhibition* (*A. and C.*) *Catalogue* 1888 'Of Wallpapers'.

17 S. T. Madsen *Sources of Art Nouveau* (Oslo 1956) pp. 148–150, 172–3.

18 Barbara Morris *Victorian Embroidery* (1962) Chapter 7.

19 B. Morris op.cit. p. 136 and 179 (ill.).

20 C.R. p. 199. A water colour design for this is in the Victoria and Albert Museum Print Room.

21 See B. Morris op.cit. p. 133 fig. 15 and W. G. Paulson Townsend *Embroidery or the Craft of the Needle* (1899) which had a preface by Crane and illustrations of his designs, pls. 23, 24 and 26.

22 A. Crane, 'My Grandfather, Walter Crane', p. 105.

23 A. Crane op.cit. p. 105. The cabinet is in the possession of Anthony Crane and was last exhibited in 1952, in the Exhibition of Victorian and Edwardian Decorative Arts at the Victoria and Albert Museum (VEDA M29).

24 The contract is mentioned in a letter to J. Wilson 25 Feb. 1891 in the Houghton Library, Harvard University. The William Morris Art Gallery has a set of coloured examples. For illustrations see *The Studio* 1894 Volume 2 p. 28 and the *Art Journal* Easter Annual on 'The Work of Walter Crane' (1898) [EAA], pp. 15 and 25 and VEDA M48. The Victoria and Albert Museum has a sketch for another damask design incorporating peacocks and pomegranates. See *The Studio* A and C catalogue 1896 p. 56.

25 'Pax' is reproduced in colour; J. S. Boggs 'European Drawings from the National Gallery of Canada' *Apollo* Aug. 1969 p. 152 p. IV. The text implies that this is a wallpaper design but, according to the A and C catalogue of 1903 it was for a printed hanging.

26 Designs for these two textiles are in the Victoria and Albert Museum, which also has a sample of printed 'Golden Pheasant' (VEDA M46).

27 VEDA M49 M50. Samples of these carpets are now in the Victoria and Albert Museum which has a design for 'Daffodil and Bluebell' and one for a Wilton or Axminster carpet (d. 1900) with a formalised flower pattern. Crane was invited by Lady Pembroke to Wilton in 1880 and asked to design a carpet incorporating the Pembroke Arms but the commission did not materialise C.R. p. 216–217.

28 W. Gaunt and M. D. E. Clayton-Stamm *William de Morgan* (London 1971) E. Aslin *The Aesthetic Movement* (London 1969) Chapter 7.

29 C.R. p. 93. All the Crane correspondence has been removed from Wedgwood's letter books, which suggests that he may have left under a cloud.

30 EAA p. 20. Hugh Wakefield *Victorian Pottery* (London 1962) p. 184.

31 Aslin op.cit. p. 130. These American manufactures are discussed by Lucile Henzke *American Art Pottery* (N.Y. 1970) pp. 304–314.

32 T. Affleck Greeves 'London's First Garden Suburb Bedford Park, Chiswick' Parts I and II *Country Life*, 7 and 14 Dec. 1967. Ian Fletcher 'Bedford Park: Aesthete's Elysium?' in *Romantic*

Mythologies ed. by I. Fletcher p. 109.

33 EAA pp. 22 and 31 (ill.) VEDA M53–56. All were designed in 1889 and exhibited at The A. and C. 1890 although they continued in production after this date. These seven designs are most conveniently differentiated as the 'Swan', 'Greek Women', 'Seated Warriors', 'Kneeling Warrior', 'Mermaid' and 'Musician' vases, and the 'Ship' jug.

34 'Death in the Workshop – And Death to Art'; a letter by Crane to the Editor of the *Daily Chronicle* 24 Nov. 1892.

35 Abraham Lomax *Royal Lancastrian Pottery 1900–1938* (1957). I am indebted to Mr Anthony J. Cross for the following list of Crane designs for Pilkingtons. These are discussed in his book *Pilkington's Royal Lancastrian Pottery and Tiles* (1975): 'Sea Maiden' vase, 'Lion' bowl, 'Bon Accord' Vase, 'Figures Ogee' vase, 'Figures Striped' vase, 'Three Graces' vase, and the 'Manchester' flask.

36 By February 1880 Crane had received £700 from Spottiswood for his work on the saloon.

37 Combe Bank is now a convent school. The saloon (now the library) was restored in 1965. John Newman *West Kent and the Weald* (1969) p. 532 and p. 92. The ceiling design appears in *R.I.B.A. Transactions* Vol. VII NS, 1891 where Crane's lecture 'Decorative Plaster Work' was published pp. 72–84. EAA pp. 15–18 and p. 27. The fibrous plaster panels were supplied by Jackson and Sons of Rathbone Place, London, who also made casts of repeating sections from Crane's models.

38 C.R. p. 218. Crane's participation probably dates from 1881. Notes on the dining-room decoration are in a sketch book of this year in the Houghton Library, Harvard University. *Building News* 21 Dec. 1883 p. 999; 21 Mar. 1884 pp. 4, 88, 442. Gleeson White, 'An Epoch-Making House', *The Studio*, Vol. 12, 1898, pp. 102–112.

39 Christie's Sale *Catalogue of Modern Pictures and Drawings* 15 Mar. 1902. Appendix 3 'Budby Water', 'Sherwood Forest'. Goupil Gal. Exh. Catalogue April 1893 Appendix 4, 'Two Landscapes'. 1926 Homewood Dispersal Christie's Catalogue Appendix 6 'Landscape' costing £80.

40 *Building News* 2 May 1884. Fireplace no longer *in situ*.

41 As usual Crane modelled the clay or gesso relief which was then cast in fibrous plaster by Weeks and by Flavell (see A and C catalogue). Crane's first designs were for a frieze of pattern symbolising the arts for the picture gallery. He then completed relief decorations for the drawing room and library. The house has been destroyed. EAA p. 17.

42 'Europa' and 'The Sea Maiden' are illustrated by Von Schleinitz *Walter Crane* (Leipzig 1902). A sketch of 'The Divers' shield appeared in *The Builder* 14 Oct. 1893. Crane also helped design reliefs for a silver cup. C.R. p. 187.

43 Made like the mosaics for the Arab Hall by the Murano Company of Venice. The South Audley Street decorations included four small panels of Elements, and two arched panels in recesses of Stags Drinking, and a Fawn and Satyr.

44 *The Studio* Vol. 11, 1897, p. 131 (ill.).

45 C.R. p. 241. EAA p. 18. Von Schleinitz op.cit. pp. 116–7 (ill.). The cartoon for 'Sphaera Imaginationis' is in the William Morris Gallery, Walthamstow.

46 Von Schleinitz op.cit. p. 118 (ill.).

47 Reviewed in *The Builder* 31 Oct. 1896 p. 354, also by L. F. Day 'The Windows of a New Church' *Art Journal* 1896. The Houghton Library, Harvard University, have the designs for this glass. Von Schleinitz op.cit. pp. 119–122 (ills).

48 EAA p. 20.

49 Review of 'The A and C' *The Studio* 1896 pp. 57 and 61. Von Schleinitz op.cit. p. 123.

50 C.R. pp. 323, 377. Von Schleinitz op.cit. pp. 84, 85 (ill.). The floor for South London Art Gallery is discussed C.R. p. 358; also in the *Daily Graphic* 7 Jan. 1898. This survives although another covering has been laid on top to protect the surface.

51 C.R. Ashbee *Memoirs* unpublished typescript in the Victoria and Albert Museum Vol. VII Part III Ch. 13 p. 271.

52 When describing what he felt was lacking in Frank Lloyd Wright's buildings, C. R. Ashbee wrote that he would not wish 'to alter their structure in plan or form, or carcass, but to clothe them with a more living and tender detail'. Naylor op.cit. p. 175.

Late Work

1 Robertson *Time Was* p. 37.

2 A small part of the frieze above the windows is now missing. This work is illustrated in Von Schleinitz op.cit. pp. 32–39.

3 *Truth* 25 June 1891 'Art Notes'. *Connoisseur* May 1969 (col. ill).

4 Von Schleinitz *Walter Crane* p. 45 (ills).

5 F. G. Stephens *The Portfolio* 1890, Vol. XXI p. 44 (ill.).

6 A sketch for this is illustrated by Von Schleinitz p. 99 and the finished work is reproduced in 'The Art of the Age' The Work of Walter Crane *Pearson's Magazine* June 1906 No. 126 p. 576.

7 Von Schleinitz pp. 100–101, (ills). A drawing from 'The Crest of a Wave' is reproduced in the New Gallery Catalogue (1903), No. 40.

8 Konody *The Art of Walter Crane* p. 18 (ill.).

9 Konody p. 102 (ill.). This work is now in the collection of Luigi Squarzina, Milan.

10 *Beauty's Awakening A Masque of Winter and of Spring* Studio Special No, 1899. The watercolour of 'The Dance of the Five Senses' is now in the Squarzina collection, Milan.

11 *Beauty's Awakening* op.cit. p. 28. See also the *Daily Chronicle* publication *New London, Her Parliament and Its Work*, illustrated with cartoons by Crane, Burne-Jones and Sambourne, 1895.

12 Crane's MS of this book is in New York public library.

13 Chapter VIII p. 217 *Line and Form*. Crane explained that: 'The inner vision hangs the mind's house with a mysterious tapestry of figurative thoughts, a rich and fantastic imagery, a world where the elements are personified, where every tree has its dryad, and where the wings of the wind actually brush the cheek.'

14 'L'Absinthe' sold for £180 at Christies in 1893.

15 W. Crane *William Morris to Whistler* (London 1911) p. 234.

16 The edition consisted of 250 on paper at £5 and 7 on vellum at £20. H. Halliday Sparling *The Kelmscott Press and William Morris Master Craftsman* (London & New York 1924) p. 156.

17 W. Crane EAA p. 10.

18 A revised small octavo edition was issued in 1897.

19 G. Wakeman *Victorian Book Illustration The Technical Revolution* (1973) p. 136, discusses this process. *The Merry Wives* was issued by George Allen. Unlike the previous sets of designs, the pages were bound and not in a presentation box.

20 C.R. 456. The designs were exhibited at Van Hoytema's Gallery in Bond Street afterwards. Crane is surprisingly casual in his references to this large folio bible in view of the vast amount of work it entailed for him. In addition to 5 illustrations he completed designs for headings, tailpieces, page decorations and historiated initials. The Victoria and Albert Museum has a volume containing most of the material completed in a binding designed by Crane. See Appendix.

21 A. Crane 'My Grandfather, Walter Crane', p. 449.

22 Egerton Castle *English Book-Plates: An Illustrated Handbook for Students of Ex-Libris*, Bell & Sons, 1892; enlarged ed. 1893, Norma Labouchere *Ladies' Book-Plates* (London 1895).

23 Much of this material may be consulted in Liverpool City Libraries.

24 W. Crane *On The Practice and Study of Art* Manchester 1893, p. 8.

25 M. H. Spielmann, 'Posters and Poster Designing in England', *Scribners' Magazine*, Vol. XVIII, 1895, p. 36.

26 W. Crane *William Morris to Whistler* op.cit. p. 252.

Socialism

1 These verses, from Crane's poem 'The New Era' were first published in *The New Party* (1895) ed. Andrew Reid p. 27.

2 C.R. p. 410 p. 287 (ill.).

3 C.R. p. 254.

4 Ibid. p. 255. This lecture was given first at the Leicester Secular Society on 23 January 1884 and published as a pamphlet at Leek, 1884. May Morris *The Collected Works of William Morris*, XXIII pp. 192–214.

5 On Engels' advice this began as a monthly, Henderson *The Letters of William Morris to his Family and Friends* (London 1950), letter of 11 March 1885. It was issued weekly from May 1886.

6 Paul Thompson *The Work of William Morris* (London 1967), p. 204.

7 Margaret Cole *The Story of Fabian Socialism* (1961) p. 7 and W. B. Yeats *The Trembling of the Veil* (1922).

8 Edward P. Thompson, *William Morris, Romantic to Revolutionary* (London 1955) p. 385.

9 That Crane was not a Fabian Member when he agreed to lecture on 16 October is clear from his letters to Frederick Keddell in Nuffield College, Oxford. In one dated 15 October 1885 he states . . . 'I cannot as yet claim to be a Fabian'. In November the society was planning to publish a paper by him and he may have been a member by this time. Minutes in Nuffield College, Oxford survive only from 23 December 1885. The first mention of Crane here is at an executive meeting of 24 June 1886 when it was resolved to invite him to chair the meeting for Morris's lecture on 2 July. M. Cole op.cit. p. 25 Note 3. Crane never sat on the executive of the Fabian Society but in 1887 he was asked along with seven others, to join a committee with the executive to discuss a revision of the Basis. E. R. Pease *The History of the Fabian Society* (3rd. edn. 1963) p. 71.

10 G. B. Shaw's appreciation of Crane in the *New Statesman* 20 March 1915. The strain lecturing put on him is clear from Crane's letters. In one to the Fabian Society dated 6 March 1891, he wrote: 'I have been obliged to give up lecturing to a great extent as I find it impossible to give the time and energy necessary to it, as well as to my ordinary work, and lecturing, at all, brings many applications which it is impossible to satisfy. If I did not find it exhausting and felt I could do more effective work for the cause of Socialism in that way than in others, I might give up more for it . . .'. On 17 July 1891 he wrote again asking to have his name removed from the lecture list 'for the present'. (Nuffield College, Oxford, Fabian Letters.). By permission of the Fabian Society.

11 J. Bruce Glasier *William Morris and the Early Days of the Socialist Movement*, 1921, p. 92.

12 W. Crane *Claims* p. 12. From the lecture 'The Architecture of Art' which had a subtitle 'Art and Commercialism'. It was first read at a meeting of the Architectural Association on 18 February 1887 and published in *The Builder* 26 February 1887 p. 313. The expression 'cheap and nasty' derived from Carlyle and was used by Morris in his memorable first lecture on 'The Lesser Arts' in December 1877. E. P. Thompson op.cit. p. 284.

13 W. Crane *Claims* pp. 14–15. The anti-academic implications of this passage were developed by Crane in a review of the Royal Academy printed in *Justice* 13 June 1885 p. 4.

14 W. Crane *Claims* p. 28.

15 Ibid. From the lecture 'Art and Labour' p. 56.

16 Ibid. p. 155.

17 Crane's first design in memory of the Paris Commune was published in *The Commonweal* in 1887 and the second in *Black and White* 4 April 1891, p. 285 accompanied by a poem written in March that year, the last verse of which began:
'Maligned, betrayed, short-lived to act and teach,
Her blood lies still upon the hand that slew.
E'en now when Labour knocks upon the gate
That shuts on Priviledge, he thinks of you,
And what men dared and suffered . . .'
Both designs appeared in *Cartoons for the Cause*.

18 W. Crane *Claims* pp. 80–81.

19 'Bernard Shaw's Appreciation' of Walter Crane, *The Co-Operator's Annual* 1937 p. 13.

20 M. Cole op.cit. p. 29 quotation from Webb in *Fabian Essays*.

21 E. P. Thompson op.cit. pp. 694–5 Manifesto of English Socialists of May 1893. cf. Pease op.cit. p. 697.

22 D. D. Egbert *Social Radicalism and the Arts, Western Europe; A Cultural History from the French Revolution to 1968.* (N.Y. 1970) p. 442.

23 C.R. pp. 439–40.

24 C.R. p. 264. Crane's original idea was to call her Madam Bourgeois. Morris advised Mrs Grundy 'as a foreign language will not be understood by all our customers'. J. L. Joynes's poem explaining the cartoon 'Mrs Grundy's mishap' appeared in the same number of *The Commonweal* p. 37.

25 These so-called 'Anarchists' were arrested in Chicago after a bomb exploded in the midst of a body of police at an eight-hour day demonstration. Four were executed on 11 November 1886, the others imprisoned. E. P. Thompson op.cit. pp. 572–85. These 'judicial murders' became the occasion for annual demonstration by English socialists. Immediately after the incident, which took place in June 1886, Crane wrote his poem: 'On the Suppression of Free Speech at Chicago' and he continued to express his disgust at what he considered this travesty of American justice in October 1887 in a poem 'Freedom in America'. Both were published in *Renascence A Book of Verse* 1891 pp. 156, 157.

26 C.R. p. 267.

27 *The Clarion* first came out on 12 December 1890, edited by Robert Blatchford. Merrie England is also the keynote of an advertisement that year for the first Socialist Carnival to be held under the auspices of the I.L.P. in Holburn Town Hall, Von Schleinitz op.cit. p. 93 (ill.).

28 Pease op.cit. p. 57.

29 *Justice* 18 March 1915 p. 5. See also *Labour Leader* May Day Supplement 29 April 1910 'The Banner of Art' by W. Crane.

30 In 'Art and Social Democracy' Crane suggested that artists make use of Ruskin's parallel between the feudal Crag Baron and his modern counterpart the Bag Baron 'the baron of modern commercialism, with his own appropriate scenery behind him – his castles, gaunt factories, and instead of the forest of lances, a forest of chimneys.' *Claims* p. 152.

31 Pease op.cit. pp. 129–133. Crane gave a detailed account of his reasons for opposing the Fabian standpoint on this matter in a letter to the Society, dated 11 Feb. 1900. (Nuffield College, Oxford.)

32 The dated newspaper cutting is in the Liverpool City Libraries but it is not known where this was published. Crane's frontispiece to Robert Williams *Patriotism False and True* (London 1900) is another expression of his disillusion at the war.

33 Letter in the University of Birmingham Library.

34 John Gorman *Banner Bright* (1973) p. 15.

35 Ibid. p. 21.

36 Shaw's review of the A. and C. Exhibition of 1890 was published under the pseudonym Corno di Bassetto (Victoria and Albert Museum Library Crane newspaper cuttings). For details of his decorations for the Home Rule demonstration and work for Gladstone's 'Album see C.R. p. 329–331, 195 (ill.).

37 R. A. Leeson *United We Stand* an illustrated account of Trade Union Emblems (London 1971) refers to a Crane design for the United Pattern Makers Association (sketched by Crane and finished by a Woolwich member) produced by Blades, East and Blades p. 68.

38 For illustrations and references to these and other Crane designs see Gorman op.cit.

39 This paper was first written for the *International Review* and was published again in *From William Morris to Whistler*.

40 Mrs Russell Barrington 'The Red Cross Hall' *English Illustrated Magazine* Vol. X, June 1893, pp. 610–618. Other reports are to be found in 'Deeds of Daring', the *Pall Mall Budget* 9 October, 1890 p. 1304, and in 'A Chat with Mr Walter Crane' *The Sketch*, 19 July, 1893, pp. 642–3.

41 W. Crane *Claims* p. 50.

Education

1 Nellie Dale *On the Teaching of Reading* (1898) is a commentary on her *Walter Crane Readers*, those published by J. M. Dent and Company include a *First* and *Second Primer* and *The Walter Crane Infant Reader* issued in 1899, followed in 1902 and 1907 by *The Dale Readers Book I and II*, published by George Philip and Son.

2 C.R. p. 325. 'The British Ass. for British Art', as the Art Association was nicknamed, was founded to compliment the British Association for the Advancement of Science. The Transactions of the Liverpool and the Edinburgh Congresses were published in London in 1888 and 1890.

3 C.R. p. 325.

4 From Crane's 'Friendly Dispute' with Day on 'Poetic Ornament' *The Art Journal* 1902 p. 270. These conversations were published together in 1903 under the heading *Moot Points, Friendly Disputes on Art and Industry between W. Crane and L. F. Day.*

5 Published in the *Transactions* of the Edinburgh Congress op.cit. and in Crane's *Claims* p. 90.

6 *The Commonweal* 16 Nov. 1889, 'The Art Congress'. For summaries of the evening talks to working folk see the *Transactions* op.cit.

7 *The Scots Observer* 2 Nov. 1889 p. 652–3.

8 I. Spencer 'Francis Newbery and the Glasgow Style' *Apollo* Oct. 1973 p. 286–293.

9 Crane's address 'On the Study and Practice of Art' was given to the art students of the Municipal School of Art and the Technical School on 4 March and published by the Manchester Guardian Printing Works. See the report of the Proceedings of the Technical Instruction Committee (Manchester) 1890–93 (pp. 12–16) and Stuart Macdonald's unpublished thesis *The Art-Workers' Guild and Schools of Arts and Crafts 1894–1914* (Manchester College of Education Library Ph.D. 1971).

10 Crane's official connection with South Kensington dated from 1879 C.R. p. 206.

11 W. Crane *Claims* p. 89 from the lecture 'On Teaching Art'.

12 S. Macdonald *The History and Philosophy of Art Education* Manchester, 1970.

13 An MS version of Crane's *Suggestions for the Municipal School of Art: Manchester* d. 1893 is in the Victoria and Albert Museum Library. The expanded *Recommendations and Suggestions for Adoption either as distinct from, or addition to the Present System of Instruction in Art in the Manchester School of Art and Technical School, especially with reference to the Study and Practice of Design* was printed in Manchester in March 1893.

14 W. Crane *Recommendations and Suggestions* op.cit. p. 2 Section VI.

15 Ibid. p. 3 Section XII.
16 Macdonald op.cit. 1971, Chapter 4 and Appendix C.
17 W. Crane *The Bases* Chapter 2 'Of the Utility Basis and Influence' p. 47.
18 Ibid. p. 86.
19 S. Tschudi Madsen *Art Nouveau* (1967) p. 49 'The Cult of Line'. The most useful modern analysis of Christopher Dresser's work yet published is the catalogue by Stuart Durant to the Fine Art Society exhibition London, 1972.
20 'The Manchester School of Art' by A. Lys Baldry *Studio* Vol. 15 1895 p. 104–109.
21 Macdonald op.cit. 1971 Chapter 4.
22 These methods depended on demonstration see 'Sculpture Demonstrations by M. Lanteri at Glasgow', by F. H. Newbery *The Scottish Art Review* Vol. 1 (1859) p. 340–341.
23 *Girls Realm Annual* 1899 p. 573.
24 Stella Mary Newton *Health, Art and Reason* (London 1974). For Henry Holiday's account of the founding of the *Aglaia* see his biography *Reminiscences of My Life* (London 1914) Ch. XXIX.
25 A. Crane 'My Grandfather, Walter Crane' p. 106.
26 Gordon Sutton *Artisan or Artist? A History of the Teaching of Art and Crafts in English Schools* (London and New York 1967) p. 199.
27 Ibid. p. 215.
28 Ibid.
29 W. Crane *Ideals in Art* p. 31.
30 Naylor *The Arts and Crafts Movement* p. 184.

America

1 *Truth* 25 June 1891.
2 F. G. Stephens wrote two very favourable articles, 'The Designs of Walter Crane' and 'The Later Designs of Walter Crane'; *The Portfolio* 1890, Volume XXI pp. 12 and 45.
3 C. Rowley *A Workshop Paradise and other Papers* 1905 and H. Holiday *Reminiscences of My Life* London 1914.
4 Du Maurier's cartoons were appropriated by newspapers like the New York *Daily Graphic*. Lloyd Lewis and Henry Justin Smith *Oscar Wilde Discovers America 1882* New York 1936 p. 19.
5 Donald G. Mitchell 'Industrial and Architectural Designs' *Reports and Awards of The International Exhibition* Vol. VII Group 27 Washington D.C. 1888, pp. 642–51, 653–69. Catherine Lynne Frangiamore 'Wallpapers in Nineteenth Century America' *Antiques* December 1972 pp. 1042–1051.
6 The American *Art Journal* Volume VI 1880 p. 8.
7 In this letter, d. 25 May 1877 and published in *Scribner's*, Crane protested that the New York firm of McLoughlin had issued a pirated edition which 'grossly misrepresents my drawings both in style and colouring'. The editor replied sympathetically, adding: 'We join our earnest appeal to his quiet and modest one, that the American public will respect his work, will refuse to put into their children's hands, just because it is a little cheaper, a shabby travesty of a beautiful original.' *Scribner's Monthly* XIV, 1877, pp. 721–2. Routledge's Toy Books were pirated by the Worthington Co. of New York (advertised in 1875), who in 1890 brought out a version of Crane's *Household Stories* by the Brothers Grimm – a book also pirated by Thomas T. Crowell of New York. The Macmillan edition of Mrs Molesworth's *Grandmother Dear* was rearranged and published by M. A. Donahue of Chicago in 1878. F. D. Weinstein *Walter Crane and the American Book Arts* Columbia University Ph.D. 1970 Library Science, pp. 129–133. For details of how designs were altered in pirated versions see also A. Crane 'My Grandfather, Walter Crane', pp. 98–99.

8 The 'greenery-yallery Grosvenor Gallery' artists were satirised in the libretto of 'Patience'.
9 Gilbert consulted Crane on the costumes and setting and he planned a garden scene. When he saw 'Patience' Crane thought that some of his ideas had influenced the final effect. A costume drawing by him, of a figure in classical draperies with cymbals, is in Carlisle City Art Gallery. It was probably intended for the end of Act 1 where Bunthorne enters, accompanied by a procession of maidens who 'are dancing classically, and playing on cymbals double pipes and other archaic instruments'. *Albert Moore Exhibition Catalogue*, Laing Art Gallery 1972 p. 33.
10 J. M. Whistler *The Gentle Art of Making Enemies* London 1892 p. 136.
11 Crane's work for *Little Folks* includes 'Lancelot's Levities' published in 1888, Vol. XXVII, pp. 5–7, pp. 104–6, pp. 200–2, pp. 264–6, 320–1, pp. 407–9; an illustration in Vol. XXVIII to Beatrice Crane's poem 'The Flock of Sheep' on p. 25 and to her story 'The Oyster and the Pearl' on p. 169. In each monthly issue of 1889 he contributed an illustration of a personification of the month accompanying poems by Beatrice, Vols. XXXIX and XXX. In Vol. XXXI, p. 890, he illustrated her story called 'The Hot Cross Bun'. To *Woman's World*, edited by Wilde during 1888 and 1889, Crane contributed a design for the 'Ministering Children's League' p. 78 and one for Beatrice Crane's 'Legend of the Blush Roses' p. 177 in Vol. I, 1888. Examples of his gesso work were reproduced in 'Suggestions for Decoration in Gesso' by Ellen T. Masters Vol. III, 1890, pp. 593–7.
12 *Boston Evening Transcript* 16 November 1891.
13 *Inter Ocean* 3 January 1892 p. 12.
14 *Evening Transcript* 16 November 1891.
15 Henry David *The History of the Haymarket Affair* New York, 1958 (2nd Ed.) p. 426. By this time attempts were being made to obtain pardons for the three men still in prison at Joliet, although these were not to be granted until 26 June 1893.
16 The Puss in Boots set was bought by Mrs John Gardner, and is now in Boston Fine Art Museum.
17 This talk was given on two previous occasions in America, C.R. p. 372–3.
18 *Inter Ocean* 7 Jan. 1892 p. 4.
19 W. Crane 'Some Impressions of America' was also published with sketches in *Scribner's Magazine* Vol. X No. 57, 189, pp. 150–163. David H. Dickason *The Daring Young Men; The Story of the American Pre-Raphaelites*, Bloomington, Indiana University Press 1953, has a chapter on Crane in America.
20 Crane had provided a set of illustrations to Mrs Burton Harrison's *Folk and Fairy Tales* Ward and Downey, 1885, (originally published by Scribner's as *Bric a Brac Stories*). In America he was commissioned to prepare drawings for *The Vision of Dante, A Story for Little Children and a talk to their Mothers* by Miss Elizabeth Harrison of Chicago, U.S.A.: The Chicago Kindergarten College, 1894.
21 Naylor *The Arts and Crafts Movement* p. 24.
22 David A. Hanks 'The Arts and Crafts Movement in America 1876–1916' *Apollo* Feb. 1973 p. 182–188, and R. Judson Clark Catalogue of the exhibition *The Arts and Crafts Movement in America 1876–1916* (Princeton University 1972).
23 Lewis and Smith op.cit. p. 64. O. Wilde *Art and Decoration* (1920) and the chapter 'Art and the Handicraftsman' which is a revised version of the Philadelphia speech of 1882.
24 C. R. Ashbee *Should We Stop Teaching Art?* (1911) Naylor op.cit. p. 172.
25 C. Wheeler *Yesterdays in a Busy Life* New York, 1918, pp. 210–12 and p. 241.
26 'Art Magazines in America' *Studio* Volume I No. I p. 147. Crane knew Blomfield Bare in Liverpool. He was an architect and became honorary secretary of the Philadelphia Guild.
27 Ralph Adams Cram *My Life in Architecture* Boston 1936;

Judson Clark op.cit. p. 97.

28 *The Knight Errant* Vol. I July 1892 pp. 40–3.

29 Susan Otis Thompson 'The Arts and Crafts Book', Judson Clark op.cit. p. 94.

30 Weinstein op.cit. pp. 160–3.

31 Helen Farr Sloan *American art nouveau: the poster period of John Sloan* published privately, Lock Harvey, U.S.A. 1967.

32 Weinstein op.cit. pp. 179–184; p. 164

33 References to Crane in *The Magazine of Art*, New York include No 19 1896; No 22 1897; No 24 1898; No 25 1900; No 26 1902; 'An Afternoon with Walter Crane' May 1903. 'Crane and Morris' *Art Annual* U.S.A. 1899; *Great Masters – Crane* U.S.A. 1900; *Brush and Pencil Magazine* U.S.A. Vol. 10 1902; *Chautauquan* Dec. 1902; *Architectural Record* New York 12 Dec. 1902; *Current Literature* New York 43 Dec. 1907; *Dial* Chicago Dec. 1907; *Good Housekeeping Magazine* New York 51, Nov. 1910; *Outlook* New York March 1915.

34 M. Irwin MacDonald 'An Afternoon with Walter Crane. His views on the Artistic, Social and Industrial Conditions prevailing in England' *The Craftsman* XVII October 1909, p. 33. *The Craftsman* was published in Syracuse, New York, edited by the designer Gustav Stickley. It ran from 1901 to 1916 and thus spans the most active period of American Arts and Crafts.

35 Pauline King *American Mural Painting* (New York 1902) p. 74.

Commendatore Crane

1 'English Interiors, William Morris and his Influence, A Chat with Mr Walter Crane' *Daily News* Tuesday October 1896 p. 6. The painted settle Crane designed for his dining room is discussed here. See the photograph in Konody *The Art of Walter Crane* p. 8; also John Bell 'Mr Walter Crane at Home' *Universal and Ludgate Magazine* 1901, pp. 360–365.

2 C. R. Ashbee *Memoirs* Victoria and Albert Museum Library Typescript Volume VII Ch. 13 Part III p. 273.

3 W. Crane *William Morris to Whistler* p. 232.

4 J. Pennell 'A New Illustrator: Aubrey Beardsley' *The Studio* Vol. I, No. 1 p. 17.

5 In a letter to G. F. Scotson-Clarke of 9 Aug. 1891 he expressed his annoyance at having missed Crane's Fine Art Society Exhibition. J. Maas, J. L. Duncan and W. G. Good *The Letters of Aubrey Beardsley* London 1971 p. 24.

6 Letter of 27 June 1894 to F. H. Evans Ibid. p. 72.

7 Crane had already collaborated with Gleeson White on the latter's work *Ballads and Rondeaus* London, 1887, which included two Rondeaux by Crane on p. 136. See also Gleeson White *Letters to Living Artists* London 189x, pp. 54–64.

8 Charles G. Harper *English Pen Artists of Today* London, 1892 p. 75.

9 J. K. Huymans *L'Art Moderne* Paris 1883 pp. 211–12.

10 Ibid. p. 219–220.

11 A. S. Hartrick, in his autobiography *A Painter's Pilgramage Through Fifty Years* Cambridge, 1938, p. 33, remembers Gauguin showing him one of Caldecott's picture books in Brittany and enthusiastically praising the English Artist's drawing of geese. The book was probably *John Gilpin*. See H. R. Rookmaaker *Synthetist Art Theories* Amsterdam, 1959, pp. 64, 126 and *Notes in Letters pertaining to Synthetist Art Theories* p. 15 note f.

12 Librairie Hachette also issued Mrs Molesworth books with Crane illustrations, for example *Les Aventures de M Baby*, 1882.

13 Bruce Laughton 'The British American Contribution to Les XX 1884–93' *Apollo* Nov. 1967 p. 273.

14 G. Lemmen 'Walter Crane' *L'Art Moderne* 1 March 1891 p. 68.

15 G. Lemmen 'Walter Crane' *L'Art Moderne* 15 March 1891 p. 86.

16 H. Van de Velde 'Artistic Wallpapers' *L'Art Moderne* 18 June 1893 pp. 193–195 and 25 June pp. 202–204.

17 A. C. Loffelt *Beschrijvende Catalogus van Englische Prentkunst voor Groote en Kleine Kinderen*. Walter Crane, Kate Greenaway, Randolph Caldecott and others. Cover design by Crane. Mouton and Company, Gravenhaage 1893.

18 See his 'Ugly Duckling' illustrations *Studio* Vol. IV pp. 133 and p. XXXI.

19 Translated by Jan Veth *Kunst en samenleving* Amsterdam 1894.

20 D. D. Egbert *Social Radicalism and the arts; Western Europe*, London 1970, p. 609.

21 P. Khnopff 'Exposition de Walter Crane au Cercle Artistique' *L'Art Moderne* 16 Dec. 1894 p. 39.

22 P. Jessen 'Der Kunstgewerbleiche Geschmak in England' *Kunstgewerbeblatt* 1892–3; Stefan Muthesius *Das englische Vorbild* (A study of English influence on the reforms in architecture and design in late Germany nineteenth-century Germany) Munich 1974, Ch. 7.

23 Julius Hoffmann *Bilderschatz für das Kunstgewerbe* Stuttgart 1892.

24 S. Muthesius loc.cit.

25 Ibid. p. 125 Gurlitt's brother, Cornelius, published a monograph on Burne-Jones in 1893.

26 Konody *The Art of Walter Crane* p. 31.

27 Crane's 'Mower' was bought by Hans Thoma in Karslruhe and 'The Rape of Persephone' by Karlsruhe Museum from a later Crane exhibition there in 1902. 'The Harvest in Utopia' was purchased in Austria by the Vienna K.K. Ministerium für Cultus und Unterricht in 1895–6.

28 H. Muthesius was technical attaché to the German Embassy in London from 1896–1903. *Centralblatt der Bauerwaltung* 3–5, 29–31, 39–41.

29 W. Crane *Die Forderung Der Dekorative Kunst* Berlin 1896. S. Muthesius loc.cit.

30 W. Crane *Die Grundlagen der Zeichnung* Leipzig 1897–1901.

31 G. Doepler 'Schrift und Zeichnungen in Auchgewerbe' *Zeitschrift fur Bildende Kunst* 1894 Vol. 2.

32 E. Von Bodenhausen 'English Kunst im Hause' pp. 329–36, and 'Das Englische Buch', pp. 337–344, *Pan* 1896–97.

33 W. Schölermann 'Walter Crane' *Zeitschrift fur Bildende Kunst* 1897 Vol. 8, pp. 81–92; S. Muthesius loc.cit.

34 Berlepsch knew Morris and Crane personally, C.R. p. 488, E. Canziani *Round About Three Palace Green* London, 1939, p. 205.

35 F. G. Stephen's *The Portfolio*, 1890; Von Berlepsch 'Walter Crane Eine Studie' *Die Graphischen Kunste XX*, 1897, pp. 61–96.

36 In 1898 an article on Crane by C. Gurlitt was published in *Die Kunst* Vol. 9.

37 The Norwegian authorities asked Crane for this exhibition which was held in October and attracted great attention, *Annual Report* Oslo Museum of Applied Art 1893.

38 Vestlandske Kunst-industrimuseum i Bergen, *Beretring om Museets Virksomhed i Aaret* 1895, pp. 23–27.

39 A warm welcome to the exhibition in the Blanche Konstsalong was given by the art critic of the newspaper *Dagens Nyheter*, Edward Alkman, in a long review of 15 August. Another measure of Swedish respect for Crane may be gauged from the visit made to him in London by Crown Prince Oscar. C.R. p. 443.

40 G. Soulier 'Walter Crane' *Art et Decoration* IV 1898 pp. 165–176; Soulier also discusses Crane's work in the review 'L'Exposition des "Arts and Crafts"' *Art et Decoration* XIII 1903 p. 87–97. In 1896 William Ritter discussed Crane's work in an essay 'Un Poète pour petits et grands'. Parts of this are quoted by Konody but the original has not been examined.

41 O. Uzanne 'Eugène Grasset and Decorative Art in France' *Studio* Vol. IV No 20 p. 37.

42 R. Koch 'Art Nouveau' *Gazette des Beaux-Arts* 1959 Ser. 6,53 pp. 179–190; S. Bing *Artistic America, Tiffany Glass and Art Nouveau*. Introduction by R. Koch, Cambridge Mass; London, 1970.

43 O. Uzanne *The Studio* op.cit. and the Catalogue of the Art's Council Exhibition of 1972 of *French Symbolist Painters* p. 57–59.

44 Judith Koos 'Walter Crane and Hungary' *Ars Decorativa I* Budapest 1973 pp. 153–167. Other accounts of the Hungarian visit are given in C.R. p. 467–479 and by L. F. Day 'Walter Crane – A Hungarian Appreciation' *Art Journal* 1901 p. 79–82.

45 Rozsnyai, who used the pen-name Van der Hoske displeased Crane, probably chiefly over the matter of a special number of the *Arts and Crafts Journal of Budapest Museum* for which Crane designed a cover in the belief that it was to be devoted to his work alone.

46 C.R. p. 472.

47 Koos op.cit. p. 164.

48 Ibid. pp. 155 and 165.

49 It was shown at the K.K. Osterr. Mus. fur Kunst und Industrie in 1901.

50 R. Schmutzler *Art Nouveau* New York 1962 p. 244.

51 M. Dreger 'Zur Walter Crane Ausstellung im Osterreichischen Museum' *Kunst und Kunsthandwerk,* Vienna 1901 p. 93 ff. A list of the purchases made by Prince Leiningen is given in C.R. p. 486.

52 F. Newbery 'The International Exhibition of Modern Decorative Art at Turin. The English Section' *Studio* Vol. 26 No. 114 p. 251 ff. Crane reviewed the Turin Exhibition for the *Art Journal*, where he made brief mention of the Scottish exhibit but was generally at pains to let English readers know that neither British exhibit was officially government sponsored and had therefore much smaller resources to call on than was the case with the expensive schemes of other countries. A special cover designed by him for *Deutsche Kunst und Dekoration* Feb. 1903, was published in an issue containing Newbery's account of 'Morris, Walter Crane, Ashbee, Voysey und die Englische Abteilung in Turin 1902' p. 209 ff.

53 A. Agresti 'Artisti e Decorati' a study of Crane and Morris appeared in *Nuova Anthologia* Vol. 32 Ser. V-16, 1907.

54 A. Crane 'The Pater' Catalogue to the *Frederick Sandys* Exhibition held in Brighton Museum and Art Gallery, 1974, p. 13.

55 Examples of Lionel's architectural work are to be seen in *Ideals in Art* pp. 116, 148–151, and of Lancelot's painting on p. 37 as well as in Von Schleinitz op.cit. p. 141. Lancelot leapt to the defence of his father in a letter to the *Burlington Magazine* 12 July 1915, responding to the criticisms contained in Robert Ross's obituary printed in the April number of the same journal and correcting Ross's view that *The Renaissance of Venus* could not survive long because it was in mixed medium. *Burl. Mag.* 1915 pp. 44, 196, 197.

56 Ashbee *Memoirs*, Vol. VII Ch. 13, p. 271, Victoria and Albert Museum Library.

Appendix

Appendixes A and B are intended to supplement the *Bibliography of First Editions of Books Illustrated by Walter Crane* by G. C. E. Massé (1923) which does not cover the early works in detail, nor include a complete list of Toy Books. A list of principal publications after 1874 is given in Appendix E.

A. Books designed between 1860 and 1874

List of work, excepting toy books, designed by Crane and published between 1860 and 1874. Unless otherwise noted the drawings are in black and white and signed by Crane either with his initials or a monogram.

1861 W. J. Linton *Specimens of a New Process of Engraving for Surface-Printing* London. One ill. p. 5 prepared by Linton and Hancock.

Entertaining Things Vol. I; No. 5, May pp. 136 and 144; No. 7, Jul. p. 223; No. 9, Sept. pp. 329 and 378; No. II, Nov. p. 329; No. 12, Dec. p. 378.

The Illustrated News of the World has unsigned ills. in the following Nos. of the Vol: 12 Oct. p. 232; 16 Nov. p. 309; 30 Nov. p. 345; 21 Dec. p. 391 and in the 1862 Vol: 22 Feb. p. 113. The cut on p. 377 of the 14 Dec. 1861 issue and the unsigned cut on p. 284 of that of 1 Nov. 1862 may also have been drawn by Crane.

1862 *London Society* Vol. II 'The London Carnival' p. 79; 'Fashionable Promenades' p. 172; 'Which is the Fairest?' p. 244; Vol. IV 1863, 'Dickens's Dogs' pp. 48–61; 'Fashionable Promenades: Richmond Hill', p. 164 accompanying a poem by Lucy Crane. All were cut by Linton.

A. J. Symington *Pen and Pencil Sketches of Faröe and Iceland* London: Longmans, Green, Longman and Roberts, 51 ills by the author 'finished' by Crane and cut by Linton.

The Rev. H. A. Stern *Wanderings among the Falashas in Abyssinia* London: Wertheim, Macintosh and Hunt. Ills on pp. 98, 110, 148, 275 and 293 cut by W. D. Willis.

The Rev. P. B. Power *The Eye Doctor* London: Wertheim and Co. Cover by Crane cut by Willis.

Ellen's Trials or The Young Nursery Maid London: Wertheim, Macintosh and Hunt, frontispiece cut by Willis.

The Rev. P. B. Power *The Talking Fire-Irons* London: Wm Macintosh. 2 ills cut by Willis.

The Rev. P. B. Power *Stamp-on-it John* London: Wm Macintosh not signed but attributable to Crane on stylistic grounds.

Another in this series (not examined). An advertisement for Wm Macintosh publications in *The Bookseller* 10 Dec. 1863 p. 864 reproduces a Crane ill., cut by Willis.

C. Hadley *Stories of Old: or Bible Narratives* London: Smith and Elder. Two Series: Old Testament and New Testament, each with 7 ills cut by Swain.

W. Collins *After Dark* London: Smith Elder and Co. Pictorial title page cut by Dalziel.

Fun Vol. III 8 Nov. p. 79, 'A Clerical Mudie'; 31 Jan. 1863, p. 197, 'On Change' and possibly also 14 Feb. 1863, p. 217, 'The Weather' which is unsigned.

1863 Mrs Agnes de Havilland *Stories from Memel for the Young* London: Wm Hunt and Co. 6 ills cut by Willis.

J. R. Wise *The New Forest: its History and its Scenery* London: Smith, Elder and Co. 63 ills cut by Linton.

Good Words p. 796, 'Treasure Trove' cut by Dalziel.

Once A Week Vol. IX, 19 Dec. p. 713, 'The Castle of Mont Orgeuil' cut by Swain. Vol. XIII, 30 Dec. 1865, p. 763, 'Have you seen Galignani?'

C. Hadley *Children's Sayings or Early Life at Home* London: Smith, Elder and Co. 4 ills cut by Dalziel.

H. Lee *The True Pathetic History of Poor Match* London: F. Warne and Co. 4 ills cut by Evans.

F. C. Trafford *The Moors and the Fens* London: Smith, Elder and Co. 4 ills and a pictorial title page cut by Evans.

1864 T. Miller *Goody Platts and Her Two Cats* London: Sampson Low, Son and Marston. Frontispiece cut by Evans, handcoloured.

S. Warner *Maggie's Christmas, or The Rose in the Desert* London: Routledge, Warne and Routledge. Frontispiece cut and printed in colour by Evans.

Gertrude and Lily, or Good Resolutions London: Routledge, Warne and Routledge. Frontispiece cut and printed in colour by Evans.

Mrs Henry (Ellen) Wood *Verner's Pride* London (not examined but proofs of the frontispiece and title page designs are in Liverpool City Libraries) cut by Swain.

The Month Vol. I, one full page ill. in each monthly issue from Aug. to Dec. pp. 123, 177, 310, 369, 463 all (except the last) signed and engraved by Linton. Vol. II 1865, as above from Jan. to June on pp. 1, 97, 249, 295, 554 cut by Linton. The ills in Vols I and II include designs to the serial 'Constance Sherwood' among other designs.

1865 N. Hawthorne *Transformation: or, The Romance of Monte Beni* London: Smith Elder and Co. 4 ills and a pictorial title page cut by Linton.

The Perils of Greatness: or, The Story of Alexander Menschikoff Edinburgh: Wm Nimmo frontispiece printed in colour.

G. Meredith *Farina: A Legend of Cologne* London: Smith, and Co. Standard Authors No. 28. Cover and frontispiece (same design) cut by Linton.

A. J. Barrowcliffe *Normanton* London: Smith, Elder and Co. Standard Authors No. 29. Cover and frontispiece (same design) cut by Linton.

Routledge's Every Boy's Annual colour frontispiece 'Football' printed by Evans. *Routledge's Every Boy's Magazine* for 1866 colour frontispiece of 'Skating' printed by Evans.

Routledge's Magazine for Boys Oct. 1867 (incorporating *Every Boy's Magazine*) contents page and ills to Mrs Henry Wood's serial 'The Orville College Boys'. Also reproduced in *Routledge's Every Boy's Annual* for 1868 including a coloured frontispiece and title page with designs for 'Work' and 'Play' respectively and a black and white version of 'Skating' facing p. 21, all cut by Evans. *Every Boy's Annual* for 1872 reproduces the 'Work' and 'Play' designs again. In 1879 Crane produced a new colour design for the title page of *Routledge's Every Boy's Annual*, which continued in use until 1889.

Favorite [sic] Nursery Rhymes c. London: Ward, Lock and Co. colour proof of cover in John Johnson Collection, Bodleian Library, Oxford, cut by Evans.

1866 *Heiress of the Blackburnfoot: A Tale of Rural Scottish Life* London: Smith, Elder and Co. Standard Authors No. 43. Cover and frontispiece (same design) cut by Linton.

Nursery Rhymes New and Old London: Ward, Lock and Tyler cover and frontispiece (same design) printed in colours by Evans, title page. The cover carries the title 'Nursery Songs'.

M. Lemon *Wait for the End* London: Bradbury, Evans and Co. frontispiece and title page.

Warne's Picture Book London. 4 ills under the heading 'Pictures of Master Charlie' p. 55, and 4 ills under 'Pictures of Little Fanny' p. 74, cut by Dalziel. Originally intended for Warne editions, planned in 1865, of *Sandford and Merton* by Thos. Day, and *Evenings at Home* by Dr Aitken and Mrs Barbauld (not examined).

Punch Vol. 51, 21 July, p. 33 'Great Show of Chignons. A Hint for the Hairdresser's Society'.

Pictures of Society London: Sampson Low, Son and Marston. 2 ills from *London Society* on pp. 21 and 124.

A. Trollope *Miss MacKenzie* listed by Forrest Reid *English Illustration* 'The Sixties', p. 277 (not examined).

1867 *Routledge's Christmas Annual* frontispiece.

Routledge's Sunday Album for Children London. ill. 'The Maiden and the Roses' p. 43.

The Bird's Nest A Series of Story Books for the Little Ones London: T. Nelson and Sons. A colour proof of Crane's cover for this series, with the title 'Bird's Nest Stories', is in Liverpool City Libraries, printed by Evans.

Edmund Yates *Broken to Harness* London: John Maxwell and Co. Frontispiece and vignette on title page.

The Argosy Cover for the new series in 1868. From Vol. V, 1 Dec. 1867 to Vol. VI, 2 Nov. 1868, Crane provided a monthly ill. to Mrs Henry Wood's 'Anne Hereford', cut by Dalziel. Another ill. opposite the poem 'Margaret' by Lucy Crane is on p. 280 in the number for 2 Mar. 1868, cut by W. Cheshire.

1868 *People's Magazine* Vol. II, Jan. 'The Dwarf and Tuflongbo' p. 27; 1 Feb. 'The Walrus' p. 80; ills to 'Parables of Animals' (part III) 2 Mar. p. 145, (part V) 1 May p. 281, all cut by H. Orrin Smith. In Vol. II on 1 Aug. he began to contribute a monthly design for 'Esther: A story of Cologne' which continued into Vol. III up to 1 Mar. 1869 p. 129, all cut by Orrin Smith. In Vol. IV 1869 are 3 ills to 'Hubert and Ida' 1 Jul. p. 1, 2 Aug. p. 65, 1 Sept. p. 129, the last two signed by Orrin Smith.

J. S. Roberts *Legendary Ballads of England and Scotland* London: F. Warne and Co. 3 ills cut by Evans.

J. Cundall *Poetry of Nature* listed by Gleeson White *English Illustration, The Sixties* p. 136 (not examined).

1869 *The Churchman's Shilling Magazine* Vol. V, 2 ills to 'A Lonely Life' by G. S. Arnold opp. pp. 267 and 441 and a third in Vol. VI 1869-70 opp. p. 221. Another Crane design appears in Vol. V opp. p. 332 to 'The Trials of Margaret Brandreth' by S. R. Townshend Mayer. The design opp. p. 267 was cut by Linton, the others by Jenkins.

J. Sheridan Le Fanu *Guy Deverell* London: Chapman and Hall's Select Library. Cover colour-printed by Evans.

The Brothers H. and A. Mayhew *The Magic of Kindness: or, The Wondrous Story of the Good Huan* London: Cassell, Petter and Galpin. 8 ills cut by D. J. Anderson.

W. Marshall (Heraclitus Grey) *King Gab and His Story Bag* London: Cassell, Petter and Galpin. 8 ills, cut by J. Anderson.

J. D. Wyss or J. Lovell (ed.) *The Swiss Family Robinson* colour proof for frontispiece in Liverpool City Libraries, book not examined.

1870 H. Zschokke *Labour Stands on Golden Feet* London: Cassell, Petter and Galpin, 2 ills.

M. Jones *Stories of Olden Time from De Joinville and Froissart* London: Cassell, Petter and Galpin, 2 ills.

The Queen of the Tournament London: Cassell, Petter and Galpin. Listed by Gleeson White op.cit. (not examined).

Tales for Tiny Tots Fennimore Cooper *The Red Indian* dated designs for both these books are in the Houghton Library, Harvard University, but the books have not been examined.

1871 *Sunny Days, or A Month at the Great Stowe* London: Griffith and Farran, 4 ills.

M.E.G. *The Merrie Heart* London: Cassell, Petter and Galpin, 8 colour ills.

1872 Mother Carey *Our Old Uncle's Home, and What the Boys did There* London: Griffith and Farran, 4 ills.

Mrs Henry Wood *Lord Oakburn's Daughters* London: Richard Bentley and Son frontispiece and vignette on title page cut by Swain.

1873 *Hood's Wit and Humour* London: E. Moxon, Son and Co. Beeton's Humorous Books. Cover printed in colour by Evans.

1874 *Hood's Oddities* London: E. Moxon, Son and Co. Beeton's Humorous Books. Cover printed in colour by Evans.

Hood's Whims London: E. Moxon, Son and Co. Beeton's Humorous Books. Cover (probably by Crane) printed in colour by Evans.

Mark Twain (S. L. Clemens) *The Jumping Frog* London:

The Percy Anecdotes, Hood's Whims and Oddities, Dr Antonio designs and proofs for these three titles dating probably from 1874-5 are included among others for Beeton's Humorous Books in the Birket Foster Sketchbook, containing Crane material, in Manchester City Art Gallery. The publisher may have been Ward, Lock and Co.

Brett Harte *Sensation Novels* London: Ward, Lock and Co., cover printed in colour by Evans.

B. Toy books

The following chronological list of picture books has been drafted wherever possible using advertisements announcing new titles in *The Bookseller* (Bksllr). Other sources of information are Crane's *Reminiscences* (C.R.), Edmund Evans's *Autobiographical Notes* (EE), the list compiled by P. Muir in *Victorian Illustrated Books* (PM) and accession dates of examples in Cambridge University Library (CUL).

Single titles:

1865 *The House That Jack Built* Bksllr. Christmas Number. The first of six titles in Post 4to listed for Ward, Lock and Tyler's New Shilling Series with engravings printed by Evans. Three of these were by Crane.

The Comical Cat Bksllr. The third title in the above mentioned list.

The *Affecting Story of Jenny Wren* Bksllr. The fourth title in the above mentioned list.
1866 *Cock Robin* One of Aunt Friendly's threepenny coloured Picture Books (sixpence on linen), in imperial 16mo. Published by Fredk. Warne and Co.

In 1865 Crane began to design for the Aunt Mavor Series of Toy Books for Routledge later known as the Sixpenny Toy Series. These picture books were in 4to and most of them were also available on linen at one shilling. All were printed by Evans. Numbering follows that used by the publishers.

1865 No. 37 *The Railroad Alphabet* (Aunt Mavor Toy) (EE)
     No. 40 *The Farmyard Alphabet* (Sixpenny Toy) (EE)
1866 No. 60 *Sing a Song of Sixpence* (CUL)
     No. 61 *A Gaping-Wide-Mouth Waddling Frog* (CUL)
1867 No. 62 *The Old Courtier* (Bksllr)
     No. 63 *Multiplication Table in Verse* (Bksllr)
     No. 64 *Chattering Jack* (Bksllr)
1868 No. 69 *How Jessie was Lost* (Bksllr)
     No. 70 *Grammar in Rhyme* (Bksllr)
1869 No. 77 *Annie and Jack in London* (Bksllr)
     No. 78 *One, Two, Buckle my Shoe* (Bksllr)
1870 No. 95 *The Fairy Ship*
     No. 96 *The Adventures of Puffy*
     No. 97 *This Little Pig Went to Market*
     No. 98 *King Luckieboy's Party*
     Fairy Ship and *Little Pig* were designed in 1869 (CR p. 107) but probably published with Nos 96 and 98 in 1870. *King Luckieboy* was designed in 1870. The titles of these 4 are listed together on *Luckieboy's* back cover.
1872 No. 100 *Noah's Ark Alphabet* (CUL)
1873 No. 103 *My Mother* (Bksllr)
     No. 104 *Ali Baba and the Forty Thieves* (Bksllr)
     No. 105 *The Three Bears* (Bksllr)
     No. 106 *Cinderella* (Bksllr, all Walter Crane Sixpenny Toy Books)
1874 No. 107 *Valentine and Orson* (CUL)
     No. 108 *Puss in Boots* (CUL)
     No. 109 *Old Mother Hubbard* (CUL)
     No. 110 *The Absurd ABC* (CUL)
1875 No. 111 *Little Red Riding Hood*
     No. 112 *Jack and the Beanstalk* (PM)
     No. 113 *Bluebeard* The Victoria and Albert Museum Library's copy of The Bluebeard is dated 1875
     No. 114 *Baby's Own Alphabet*
1876 No. 116 *The Sleeping Beauty in the Wood* (PM)

Crane's contributions to the Shilling Series overlapped with the Sixpennies. All were in demy quarto and available on linen at two shillings. Numbering follows that of this already long established series.

1874 No. 70 *The Frog Prince*
     No. 71 *Goody Two Shoes*
     No. 72 *Beauty and the Beast*
     No. 73 *The Alphabet of Old Friends*
1875 No. 76 *The Yellow Dwarf*
     No. 77 *Aladdin*
     No. 78 *The Hind in the Wood*
     No. 79 *Princess Belle Etoile*

Volumes containing several titles:
Routledge and Sons (London): *Routledge's Coloured Picture Books* comprising a series of eight volumes in super royal 8vo with illustrations by Crane, Charles Bennet etc., printed by Evans and Leighton Bros. at 2/6 each, were issued early in 1871. Of those designed by Crane No. 3 contained the sixpenny toys Nos 61 and 60; No. 4, Nos 64 and 63; No. 5, Nos 69 and 70; No. 6, No. 77;

No. 7, No. 78; No. 8, Nos 95 and 96.
1871 *King Luckieboy's Picture Book* containing the sixpenny toys Nos 98, 97 and 62 and illustrations to *Horses* by another artist. (CUL)
     Routledge's Book of Alphabets containing the sixpenny toys Nos 37 and 40 and three alphabet sequences by others. (Listed on the back of *King Luckieboy's Picture Book*.)
1873 *Walter Crane's New Toy Book* containing the sixpenny toys Nos 78, 96, 97, 100, 103, 104, 105 and 106. (Bksllr)
1874 *Walter Crane's Picture Book* containing the sixpenny toys Nos 62, 63, 64, 69, 70, 77, 95 and 98.

John Lane (London), Stone and Kimball (Chicago): *Walter Crane's Picture Books* issued in four volumes with the original designs printed from Evans's blocks and new title pages, endpapers and covers by Crane.
1895 Vol. 1 *This Little Pig his Picture Book* containing the original colour designs from the sixpenny toys Nos 97, 95 and 98.
1897 Vol. 2 *Mother Hubbard her Picture Book* containing the sixpenny toys Nos 109, 105 and 110.
     Vol. 3 *Cinderella's Picture Book* containing sixpenny toys Nos 106, 108 and 107.
1898 Vol. 4 *Red Riding Hood's Picture Book* containing sixpenny toys Nos 111, 112 and 104.

John Lane (London and New York): *Walter Crane's Picture Books – Large Series.*
1901 Vol. 1 *Beauty and the Beast Picture Book* containing the shilling toy book Nos 72, 70 and 78.
     Vol. 2 *Goody Two Shoes Picture Book* containing the shilling toy Nos 71, 76 and 77.
1909 Vol. 3 *The Song of Sixpence Picture Book* containing the sixpenny toy No. 60 and the shilling toys Nos 79 and 73.
1910 Vol. 4 *The Buckle My Shoe Picture Book* containing the sixpenny toy Nos 78, 61 and 103.

John Lane (London), John Lane & Co. (New York), Bell and Cockburn (Toronto).
1914 *Puss in Boots and the Forty Thieves* the 'miniature' 16° edition in one volume of two toy books.
     The Sleeping Beauty and Bluebeard as above.
     The Three Bears and Mother Hubbard as above.

C. Picture Books for Beatrice, Lionel and Lancelot

Most of these remain unpublished. They are now in the Crane collections in the Beinecke Rare Book and Manuscript Library, Yale University (Y) and in the Houghton Library, Harvard University (H). Earliest of all these are sketches, in both collections, for a book called *His Majesty's Servants* which may have evolved from ideas planned to amuse Beatrice after the arrival of her baby brother Lionel in May 1876. Its format, however, follows that used for *Baby's Opera* and the cover design with 'Walter Crane's New Series of Sixpenny Toy-Books' indicates that Crane was thinking of publication. Several pages are worked up to a high degree of finish. This is not the case with the books listed below which are drawn in a spontaneous free style quite different to that of the toy books he had recently completed for Routledge. In its turn this freedom was conveyed to the Marcus Ward Picture Books of 1885 and 1886, *Slateandpencilvania*, *Little Queen Anne* and *Pothooks and Perseverance* which depend on the private picture books for many of their images.

1879 *Beatrice in Fairyland* (H)
     Nov. *Lionel His Primer and Copy Book* (Y)

1880 April *An Animal Book for Lionel* (Y)
June *Beatrice's Chronicles Book* (H)
A Book for Beatrice (Y)
1880–1 *Lionel's New Picture Book* (H)
Lionel Takes the First Steps to Knowledge (H)
1881 Jan. *Lionel's Own Book* (H)
April *Beatrice's Drawing and Painting Book* (H)
The Adventures of Beatrice (H)
The Signs of the Zodiac (Y)
1882 *Original Water Colour Drawings in a Notebook for Beatrice* (H)
1883 *Beatrice's Bearings* (H)
1884 Feb. to July *Lionel's Looking Glass* (H)
Oct. *Lancelot's Levities* (Y). Published in *Little Folks* Vol.
XXVII, 1888.
1885 July *Lancelot's Levity Book*. On the American art market in
1973. Catalogue of Childrens Books, Drawings and
Juvenilia 5 June 1973, No. 68 Sotheby, Parke Bernet Inc.
1885 *Legends for Lionel* (H). Published by Cassell & Co. in 1887.
Children's Book of Sept. 1885 (H).
1886 March *Beatrice Her Books of Beauties* (H)
These designs were worked up together into two pages
called Leaves from Beatrice's Book of Beauties. Printed
proofs survive in Liverpool City Libraries but their
place and date of publication has yet to be discovered.
1887 *Mr Michael Mouse Unfolds his Tale and the History of Bronwen
the Brown* (Y)
An edition of 300 copies of *Mr Michael Mouse* was published by Yale University Press in 1956 with an introduction by Mrs Catherine Tinker Patterson. It was
reproduced in facsimile by collotype with stencilled
colours by Maria Bittner.
March *Larks for Lionel* (H)
1888 Feb. *Lancelot's Looking Glass* (H)
1888–9 *Lancelot's Levities* (H)
1890 *The House That Art Built* (Y)

Five books are undated. Of these:
A Boy's Book of Alphabet (Y)
A Book for Lionel (Y)
Sixty Four Drawings for Children including an Alphabet for Lionel (H)
probably date from before 1883 when Crane began to use ink
and water colour instead of the pencil and water colour used here.
The other two are in ink and water colour and therefore later,
which is also borne out by the drawing style:
Lionel Crane His Book (H)
Times Show (Y)

D. Books by Mary Molesworth, illustrated by Crane

The series was published by Macmillan and Co. and Crane
designed seven black and white plates and a title page for each
book, which was in octavo with a red cloth cover and a design in
black and gold also by Crane. Exceptions are noted.

1875 *Tell Me a Story*
1876 *Carrots*
1877 *The Cuckoo Clock*
1878 *Grandmother Dear*
1879 *The Tapestry Room*
1880 *A Christmas Child*
1881 *The Adventures of Herr Baby* (with 12 illustrations, globe 4to
with pink cloth cover).
1882 *Rosy*
1883 *Two Little Waifs*

1884 *Christmas-Tree Land*
1885 *Us*
1886 *Four Winds Farm*
1887 *Little Miss Peggy*
1888 *A Christmas Posy*
1889 *The Rectory Children*
1890 *The Children of the Castle*
1893 *Studies and Stories*. Not part of the Macmillan series but
published in London by A. D. Innes and containing only
a frontispiece design by Crane.

E. List of Crane publications from 1875

1875 *Mrs Mundi at Home, The Terrestrial Ball, Lines and Outlines*
by Walter Crane. London: Marcus Ward and Co.
1876 *The Quiver of Love, A Collection of Valentines Ancient and
Modern* containing four designs by Crane and four by
Kate Greenaway, London: Marcus Ward and Co.
1877 *The Baby's Opera, A Book of Old Rhymes with New Dresses*,
by Walter Crane printed in colours by Edmund Evans.
London and New York: George Routledge and Sons.
1878 *The Baby's Bouquet, A Fresh Bunch of Old Rhymes and Tunes* a
Companion to *The Baby's Opera*. The tunes collected and
arranged by Lucy Crane. Arranged and decorated (in
colours) by Walter Crane. Printed by Evans. London and
New York: George Routledge and Sons.
1880 *The Necklace of Princess Fiorimonde and Other Stories* by Mary
de Morgan, illustrated by Crane. London: Macmillan
and Co.
1882 *The First of May, A Fairy Masque* by John R. Wise with
designs by Crane. London: Henry Southeran and Co.
Household Stories from the Collection of the Brothers Grimm.
Translations by Lucy Crane. Illustrated by W. Crane.
London: Macmillan and Co.
Art and the Formation of Taste, Six Lectures by Lucy Crane.
With illustrations drawn by Thomas and Walter Crane.
London: Macmillan and Co.
1883 *Pan Pipes, A Book of Old Songs*. Newly arranged with
accompaniments by Theo Marzials. Designs by Crane.
Printed in colours by Evans. London: George Routledge
and Sons.
The Golden Primer by Professor J. M. D. Meiklejohn Parts I
and II. Illustrated by Crane. Edinburgh: William
Blackwood and Sons. 1884–5.
1885 *Folk and Fairy Tales* by Mrs Burton Harrison. Illustrated by
W. Crane. London: Ward and Downey.
1886 *The Sirens Three, A Poem* written and illustrated by Crane.
London: Macmillan and Co.
A Romance of the Three Rs. Penned and pictured by Walter
Crane. London: Marcus Ward and Co. Comprising
Slateandpencilvania (first published in 1885), *Little Queen
Anne* and *Pothooks and Perseverance* (published separately
in 1886).
1887 *Legends for Lionel, In Pen and Pencil*, by Walter Crane.
London: Cassell and Co.
The Baby's Own Aesop. Being the Fables condensed in Rhyme.
With portable morals pictorially pointed by Walter
Crane. Printed in colour by Evans. London: George
Routledge and Sons.
*Echoes of Hellas. The Tale of Troy and the Story of Orestes from
Homer and Aeschylus*. With introductory Essay and Sonnets
by Professor George C. Warr. Presented in 82 designs
by Walter Crane. London: Marcus Ward and Co. 1887–8.
1888 *The Happy Prince And Other Tales* by Oscar Wilde. Illustrated
by Crane and Jacomb Hood. London: David Nutt.

1889 *The Book of Wedding Days*. Quotations for Every Day in the Year. Compiled and arranged by K. E. J. Reid, May Moss and Mabel Bamfield. With devices and decorations for each page by Walter Crane. London: Longmans, Green and Co.

Flora's Feast, A Masque of Flowers. Penned and pictured by Walter Crane. London, Paris, New York and Melbourne: Cassell and Co.

1891 *Society for the Encouragement of Arts Manufacture and Commerce*. Cantor Lectures on the Decoration and Illustration of Books delivered before the Society on 4, 11 and 18 March, 1899. By Walter Crane. London: W. Trounce.

Queen Summer or The Tourney of the Lily and the Rose by Walter Crane. London, Paris and Melbourne: Cassell and Co.

Renascence, A Book of Verse by Walter Crane. London: Elkin Matthews.

1892 *Catalogue of a Collection of Designs* by Walter Crane, including original drawings for Books, Decorations and Pictorial Work; with prefatory notes by the artist. Leek: Nicholson Institute. The same collection as that listed in the Fine Art Society Catalogue No. 89, 1891.

The Claims of Decorative Art by W. Crane. London: Lawrence and Bullen.

A Wonder Book for Girls and Boys by Nathaniel Hawthorne. Boston: Houghton, Mifflin and Co., London: Osgood, McIlvaine and Co. Illustrations by Crane.

1893 *Columbia's Courtship* by Walter Crane. Boston USA: Prang and Co.

The Old Garden, and other Verses by Margaret Deland. Decorated throughout in colours by Walter Crane. Boston: Houghton, Mifflin and Co., London: Osgood, McIlvaine and Co.

Arts and Crafts Essays by members of the Arts and Crafts Exhibition Society, including an Introduction by W. Crane and his essay 'Of Decorative Painting and Design'. London: Longmans Green and Co.

The Tempest by William Shakespeare. Illustrations by W. Crane. London: J. M. Dent and Co.

1894 *The History of Reynard the Fox*. A free rendering into verse by F. S. Ellis, with devices by Walter Crane. London: David Nutt.

The Story of the Glittering Plain. Written by William Morris. Ornamented with 23 pictures by Walter Crane. Hammersmith: Kelmscott Press.

The Merry Wives of Windsor by William Shakespeare. Illustrations by W. Crane. London: George Allen.

Two Gentlemen of Verona by William Shakespeare. Illustrations by W. Crane. London: J. M. Dent and Co.

The Faerie Queene by Edmund Spencer edited by T. J. Wise with illustrations by W. Crane. Issued in 19 parts. London: George Allen 1894–7.

1896 *Cartoons for the Cause, A Souvenir of the International Socialist Workers and Trade Union Congress 1886–96*. Illustrations by W. Crane. London: Twentieth Century Press.

Of The Decorative Illustration of Books Old and New by W. Crane. London: George Bell and Co.

1898 *The Work of Walter Crane with Notes by the Artist*. The Art Journal Easter Art Annual. London: Virtue and Co.

A Floral Fantasy in an Old English Garden. Set forth in verses and coloured designs by Walter Crane. London: Harper and Brother.

The Shepheard's Calendar by Edmund Spenser. Newly adorned with 12 pictures and other devices by Walter Crane. London and New York: Harper and Brothers.

The Bases of Design by W. Crane. London: Bell and Co.

1899 *Beauty's Awakening: A Masque of Winter and of Spring presented by Members of the Art-Workers' Guild*. The Studio Summer Number.

Triplets: Comprising The Baby's Opera, The Baby's Bouquet and The Baby's Own Aesop. With the original designs by Walter Crane, printed in colour by Evans. London: George Routledge and Sons Ltd.

The Holy Bible containing the Old and New Testaments according to the Authorized Version. Illustrated by modern artists, autotypes engraved and printed by Lemercier and Co., Paris. Intended for publication in two volumes by the Illustrated Bible Society, London, New York, Paris, Berlin, Amsterdam. Probably only issued in America in a series of twenty parts, with the number of illustrations for the New Testament much reduced. 1899–1900.

1900 *Don Quixote of La Mancha*. English abridgement by Judge Parry. Illustrated by W. Crane. London: Blackie and Son Ltd., and Manchester: Sheratt and Hughes.

Line and Form by W. Crane. London: George Bell and Sons.

1901 *A Masque of Days, From the Last Essays of Elia*. Newly dressed and decorated by Walter Crane. London: Cassell and Co.

1902 *The Art of Walter Crane* by P. G. Konody. London: George Bell and Co.

Walter Crane by Otto von Schleinitz. Bielefeld and Leipzig.

Catalogue to the Doré Gallery Exhibition of 1902, London.

1903 *Moot Points, Friendly Disputes on Art and Industry between W. Crane and L. F. Day*. London: Batsford.

1904 *The Financial News*, 23 January 1904. Illustrations by Crane for the Twentieth Anniversary Number.

1905 *Ideals in Art*. Papers theoretical, practical, critical, by W. Crane. London: George Bell and Sons.

A Flower Wedding, Described by Two Wallflowers. Decorated by Walter Crane. London: Cassell and Co.

1906 *Flowers from Shakespeare's Garden: a Posy from the Plays*. Pictured by Walter Crane. London: Cassell and Co. Ltd.

1907 *Catalogue to the Exhibition of Watercolours of India and Ceylon held in the Dowdswell Galleries*, London.

India Impressions by W. Crane. London: Methuen and Co.

An Artist's Reminiscences by W. Crane. London: Methuen and Co.

1909 *The Rosebud and other Tales* by Arthur Kelly. Illustrations by W. Crane. London: Fisher and Unwin.

1911 *King Arthur's Knights* by H. Gilbert. Illustrations by W. Crane. Edinburgh and London: T. C. and E. C. Jack.

William Morris to Whistler by W. Crane. London: George Bell and Sons.

Rumbo Rhymes or The Great Combine by A. Calmour. Illustrations by W. Crane. London: Harper and Bros.

1912 *Catalogue of Watercolours* from an Exhibition held in the Leicester Galleries.

Robin Hood and the Men of the Greenwood by H. Gilbert. Illustrations by W. Crane. London and Edinburgh: T. C. and E. C. Jack.

1913 *The Story of Greece* by M. MacGregor. Illustrations by W. Crane. London and Edinburgh: T. C. and E. C. Jack.

1914 *Illustration et Décoration du Livre* by Walter Crane from the catalogue to the British Arts and Crafts Exhibition held in the Louvre, Paris, in 1914.

1923 *A Bibliography of First Editions of Books Illustrated by Walter Crane* by G. C. E. Massé. London.

1937 *Walter Crane, Hazelford Sketchbook*. Cambridge, Mass. USA: John Barnard Associates.

1956 *Michael Mouse Unfolds His Tale* by Walter Crane. Yale University Press, USA.

1957 'My Grandfather, Walter Crane' by Anthony Crane. The Yale University Library Gazette, January, 1957, Vol. 31 No. 3.

1975 *Walter Crane as a Book Illustrator* by R. K. Engen. London: Academy Editions. New York: St Martin's Press.

F. Wallpapers designed by Crane and printed by Jeffrey and Company

Except for the nursery papers these were block printed. Illustrations are to be found in Konody *The Art of Walter Crane*; The Art Journal Easter Art Annual for 1898 of *The Work of Walter Crane* by A. V. Sugden and Edmondson *A History of English Wallpapers* and the article 'Walter Crane's Paper-Hangings' *The Studio* Vol. 4 1894. The list has been compiled from these sources, reference to the Art and Crafts Exhibition catalogues and reviews in contemporary journals, and from the collections of Crane wallpapers in the Victoria and Albert Museum, London, and the Whitworth Art Gallery and the City Art Gallery of Manchester. The name of the filling design is given first followed by accompanying patterns for ceiling, dado and frieze.

1875 'The Queen of Hearts' (Machine printed)
1876 'Humpty Dumpty' (Machine printed)
   'La Margarete' Sold with the 'Dove' ceiling, 'Lily and Dove' dado and alternative 'Alcestis' or 'Dove and Daisy' frieze.
1877 'Froggy Would A 'Wooing Go' (Machine printed)
   'Iris and Kingfisher' Sold with the 'Swan, Rush and Iris' dado and frieze designs of alternating 'Boat and Iris' pattern.
1878 'Peacocks and Amorini' Sold with a dado of a 'Fish in a Roundel' pattern, and friezes of frontal 'Peacocks' or 'Peacocks and Amorini holding Sickles'.
   'Almond Blossom and Wallflower' Sold with 'Almond Blossom and Swallow' frieze.
1879 'Sleeping Beauty' (Machine printed)
   'Billow' Available with or without fish. Sold with 'Scallop Shell' ceiling and 'Mermaid' frieze.
1880 'Awakening Day' (For a staircase)
   'Briar Rose' sold with 'Rose and Cupid' dado and a frieze of 'Hearts and Arrows', frieze of 'Girls Skipping'.
1886 'The House That Jack Built' (Machine printed)
   'Woodnotes' Sold with a frieze of running 'Deer and Rabbits'.
1887 'Golden Age'
1889 'Peacock Garden' Sold with a frieze of 'White Peacock'.
1890 'Corona Vitae' Sold with the 'Four Winds' ceiling paper and 'Corona Vitae' frieze.
   'Fairy Garden' (Machine printed)
1891 'Cockatoo' Sold with a frieze of 'Iris and Pomegranate' and 'Hammersmith' ceiling.

(In 1892 Crane designed a scheme for the Chicago Exhibition of the following year of allegorical figures and ships representing the four quarters of the world. It was printed by an American firm. See EAA pp. 80 and 81.)

1893 'Trio' Sold with the 'Pilaster Decoration' dado and 'Plumes' frieze designed for Jeffrey & Co. for the Chicago Exhibition.
   'Summer Chintz'
   'Seed and Flower' And the 'Juno' ceiling paper.
1894 'Lily and Rose' With the 'Lily and Rose' frieze.
   'Pomegranate and Teazle'
1895 'Fig and Peacock'
   'Artichoke'
1896 'Meadow Flowers' With 'May Tree' frieze.
1897 'National'
1898 'Day Lily'
1899 'Cockatoo and Pomegranate' With 'Cockatoo and Pomegranate' frieze.
1900 'Rose Bush' With 'Lion' frieze.
1901 'Dunbar'
   'Lily'
1902 'Olive Stripe'
   'Dawn'
   'Pax'
   'Orange Tree' With 'Fruit' frieze.
1903 'Mistress Mary' (Machine printed). Possibly of a slightly earlier date.
1904 'Oak' Incorporating frieze and border decoration.
   'Myrtle Wreath'
   'Dulce Domum'
   'The Formal Garden'
1908 'Rosamund' With 'Rosamund' frieze.
   'Macaw'
1909 'Saxon'
1910 'Scallop Diaper' With frieze.
   'Marathon' With frieze.
   'Classic' With frieze.
1911 'Laurel'
1912 'Vineyard'

Other ceiling papers include 'Vine' and 'Sunflower' (both dating from before 1900). The Victoria and Albert Museum has a fragment of a 'Lizard and Cockatoo' frieze and a filling of 'Pine' pattern. Both are undated.

Index

Numbers in italics refer to illustrations